THE SEA AND THE JUNGLE

H. M. TOMLINSON

THE SEA
AND THE JUNGLE

PREFACE BY EVAN S. CONNELL

TᴹP

The Marlboro Press/Northwestern
Evanston, Illinois

The Marlboro Press/Northwestern
Evanston, Illinois 60208-4210

The Sea and the Jungle first published in 1912. This edition published by
The Marlboro Press. Preface copyright © 1989 by Evan S. Connell.
The Marlboro Press/Northwestern edition published 1996.
All rights reserved.

Second printing 1999

Printed in the United States of America

ISBN 0-8101-6011-0

Library of Congress Cataloging-in-Publication Data

Tomlinson, H. M. (Henry Major), 1873–1958.
  The sea and the jungle / H.M. Tomlinson ; preface by Evan S.
Connell.
      p.   cm.
  Originally published in 1912.
  ISBN 0-8101-6011-0 (pbk. : alk. paper)
  1. Amazon River—Description and travel. 2. Madeira River (Brazil
and Bolivia)—Description and travel. 3. Capella (Ship). 4.Tomlinson,
H. M. (Henry Major), 1873–1958—Journeys—Brazil. I. Title.
F2546.T662 1996
828'.91203—dc20
[B]   96-3476
                                                                   CIP

The paper used in this publication meets the minimum requirements of
the American National Standard for Information Sciences—Permanence of
Paper for Printed Library Materials, ANSI Z39.48-1984.

THE SEA AND THE JUNGLE

Being the narrative of the voyage of the tramp steamer *Capella* from Swansea to Para in the Brazils, and thence 2000 miles along the forests of the Amazon and Madeira Rivers to the San Antonio Falls; afterwards returning to Barbados for orders, and going by way of Jamaica to Tampa in Florida, where she loaded for home. Done in the years 1909 and 1910.

DEDICATED TO THOSE WHO DID NOT GO

PREFACE

Accorning to that redoubtable traveler and storyteller Mr. Somerset Maugham, during the early part of the nineteenth century there were fewer amusements than there now are, one result being that readers did not mind if their fiction moved at a deliberate pace; they would accept with no reluctance "a dilatory exposition and a sauntering digressiveness." These days, however, in an age of multiple amusements, alarums and distractions, we have little patience with leisurely authors.

The Sea and the Jungle was written during the early part of our own century, and it is not fiction—excepting perhaps some infrequent embellishment—but it is decidedly dilatory and sauntering, which might explain why it is seldom read. Indeed, when I asked an erudite friend if he had read it, he replied: "Never heard of it." I myself have known the title and the author's name for at least thirty years, but somehow never quite got around to the reading. It was just one of those books. *Clarissa Harlowe. Typee. Erewhon. Quentin Durward. The Wings of the Dove. O Pioneers!* I could make a list of fifty such books, which would have nothing in common except that I know the titles and authors and have not quite got around to reading them.

Year after year, decade upon decade, I have felt uneasy about this. I do plan to read *Typee*, of course, and expect to hack a more visible trail through Henry James' foliage— possibly next month. In any case, *The Sea and the Jungle* would qualify for that humiliating list. Now it can be scratched, which leaves me not just nominally gratified but surprised. The reason is best explained indirectly.

One cold, drizzly, October afternoon I visited the Rijksmuseum in Amsterdam. It was stuffed with tourists, most of them shuffling like pilgrims toward Rembrandt's *Night-*

watch. Well, this is a nice painting which I had seen before and wanted to see again, but not with so much company, so I descended to ground level where less exalted works find a home, and stopped to look at some Japanese ceramics—subdued, serene artifacts conceived on a modest scale. Among them was a sixteenth-century tea bowl by the potter Chojiro, fashioned under the guidance of his patron, a famous tea master named Sen-no-Rikyu. This bowl had been broken once upon a time and subsequently repaired. Now, ordinarily when we tinker with a damaged piece of goods we try to conceal or at least to minimize the damage, because that seems logical; but that is not how this bowl had been handled. Whoever undertook the restoration had a particular idea. Chojiro's bowl was not patched with clay, but with gold.

I stood for half an hour gazing at this commonplace masterpiece, impressed by such audacity, marveling at the glorious effect. Here was a treasure I had not anticipated. So it is with Tomlinson's book.

Another reason I am glad to have read *The Sea and the Jungle*—a grubby reason quite lacking spirituality—is that now I feel no obligation to explore the Amazon. Fifteen years ago I spent several days in Manaus and quickly understood that Brazilian fungus of one sort or another would gobble up anybody not born to the place. I left Manaus with distinct relief, but ever since have wondered if perhaps I left too soon. I kept thinking I should go back, give the Amazon a second chance. No longer do I think so. Tomlinson's book compelled me to remember a humid settlement beside a languid tawny river, the aerial circus of mosquitoes, preternatural crawling specimens, suffocating heat, lethargic days, identical nights—tomorrow and tomorrow and tomorrow.

H. L. Tomlinson has been compared in certain ways to Joseph Conrad, we are told by *The Reader's Encyclopedia*, and with this book he established himself as a writer of "real literature." Mr. V. S. Pritchett, reflecting upon an earlier edition of *The Sea and the Jungle*, says things just as true. Yet something more should be said. The book is hilarious. Oh, Pritchett does find him "an amusing traveler" who "saw the humor of his situation." True enough. Quite right. Hear hear. But let me tell you, friends, *The Sea and the Jungle* is a madhouse.

Tomlinson stuck to the back of an insane mule galloping into the forest toward an unknown destination. The river pilot Jim—"his eyes dreamy through barley juice"—who dynamited the Amazon, bringing up a dazed and furious alligator. A wild female peccary, trotting across the deck of the good ship *Capella* gnashing her tusks while every man on board scrambled up a ladder or vanished into a closet. Mack the monstrous parrot, "a disrupted and angry rainbow," which so horrified the ship's terrier that the dog fell over backward . . .

The book is packed with such business. Why Mr. Pritchett and the encyclopedia editors consider it no more than faintly diverting is a bit of a puzzle.

Tomlinson does not fumble for effects. Invariably he displays the crisp hand of a professional. On a rainy night in Swansea just before the *Capella* sailed he was accosted near the wharf by a drunken old salt: "His oilskins gathered the reflected street shine, so that he looked phosphorescent, an old man risen wet and shining from the ocean. He was looking for Buenos Aires, he explained, and hadn't got any matches."

Casually but expertly, Tomlinson will sketch a place you have no trouble recognizing, whether you have been there or not. Here is what he noted in the engine room, an incandescent dungeon crammed with riotous steel: "The massive metal waves of the shaft were walloping and plunging in their pits with an astonishing bird-like alacrity; about fifteen tons of polished steel were moving with swift and somewhat awful desperation. The big room shook and hummed . . ." Each word has been thoughtfully selected, the rhythm deliberately orchestrated.

With apparent negligence he will evoke a startling figure. He met one gaunt, grizzled, dangerous individual named O'Brien, wearing a battered pith helmet and high boots laced to the knee, who had crossed the Peruvian Andes alone: "Prospecting for his illusion . . . he broke an arm in a fall on the mountains, set it himself, and continued. On the Rio Japurá an Indian shot an arrow through his leg, and O'Brien dropped in the long grass, breaking the arrow short each side of the limb, and in an ensuing long and watchful duel presently shot the Indian through the throat. And then, coming out on the Amazon, his canoe overturned, and the pickle jar full of gold dust was lost."

There is page after page of that, and a bucket more, the singular creation of an obscure journalist who chucked his job at the London *Morning Leader* for the sake of this trip, and after a most extraordinary adventure went back to work in the same slot. How is it possible?

We are told that he wrote several novels, one of which earned a prize, and he wrote other travel books, but this remained his magnum opus.

Pritchett met him twice, first in 1922: a stumpy man with a sallow face and a bulbous nose, who smoked a pipe. His ears stuck out, says Pritchett. The man's ears were large, he was deaf, and he wore a bowler. The second time they met was at the newspaper office in 1958. Tomlinson had not much changed. He still wore his bowler and he looked like a retired foreman who had come back to visit the shop. It is hard to match that proletarian figure with this felicitous book, but as somebody once remarked, behind the forehead of every man lies a world of streaming shadows.

There may be no more perceptive critique of *The Sea and the Jungle* than that offered by Tomlinson himself when alluding to *South Atlantic Sailing Directions*, his favorite reading matter in the *Capella's* chart-room: "I do not think this noble volume is included in the best hundred books, but I know it can release the mind from the body."

——EVAN S. CONNELL

THE SEA AND THE JUNGLE

I

THOUGH it is easier, and perhaps far better, not to begin at all, yet if a beginning is made it is there that most care is needed. Everything is inherent in the genesis. So I have to record the simple genesis of this affair as a winter morning after rain. There was more rain to come. The sky was waterlogged and the grey ceiling, overstrained, had sagged and dropped to the level of the chimneys. If one of them had pierced it! The danger was imminent.

That day was but a thin solution of night. You know those November mornings with a low, corpse-white east where the sunrise should be, as though the day were still-born. Looking to the dayspring, there is what we have waited for, there the end of our hope, prone and shrouded. This morning of mine was such a morning. The world was very quiet, as though it were exhausted after tears. Beneath a broken gutterspout the rain (all the night had I listened to its monody) had discovered a nest of pebbles in the path of my garden in a London suburb. It occurs to you at once that a London garden, especially in winter, should have no place in a narrative which tells of the sea and the jungle. But it has much to do with it. It is part of the heredity of this book. It is the essence of this adventure of mine that it began on the kind of day which so commonly occurs for both of us in the year's assortment of days. My garden, on such a morning, is a necessary feature of the narrative, and much as I should like to skip it and get to sea, yet things must be taken in the proper order, and the garden comes first. There it was: the blackened dahlias, the last to fall, prone in the field where death had got all things under his feet. My pleasaunce was a dark area of soddened relics; the battalions of June were slain, and their bodies in the mud. That was the prospect in life I had. How was I to know the Skipper had returned from the tropics? Standing in the central mud, which also was black, surveying that forlorn end to devoted human effort, what was there to tell me the Skipper had brought back his tramp steamer from the lands under the sun? I knew of nothing to look forward to but December, with January to follow. What should you and I expect after November, but the next month of winter? Should the cultivators of London backs look for adventures, even though they have read old Hakluyt? What are the Americas to us, the Amazon and the Orinoco, Barbadoes and Panama, and Port Royal, but tales that are told? We have never been nearer to them, and now know we shall never be nearer to them, than that hill in our neighbourhood which gives us a broad prospect of the sunset. There is as near as we can approach. Thither we go and ascend of an evening, like Moses, except for our pipe. It is all the escape vouchsafed us. Did we ever know the chain to give? The chain has a certain length—we know it to a link—to that ultimate link, the possibilities of which we never strain. The mean range of our chain, the office and the polling booth. What a radius! Yet it cannot prevent us ascending that hill which looks, with uplifted and shining brow, to the far vague country whence comes the last of the light, at dayfall.

It is necessary for you to learn that on my way to catch the 8.35 that morning—it is always the 8.35—there came to me no premonition of change. No portent was in the sky but the grey wrack. I saw the hale and dominant gentleman, as usual, who arrives at the station in a brougham drawn by two grey horses. He looked as proud and arrogant as ever, for his face is as a bull's. He had the usual bunch of scarlet geraniums in his coat, and the stationmaster assisted him into an apartment, and his footman handed him a rug; a routine as stable as the hills, this. If only the solemn footman would, one morning, as solemnly as ever, hurl that rug at his master, with the umbrella to crash after it! One could begin to hope then. There was the pale girl in black who never, between our suburb and the city, lifts her shy brown eyes, benedictory as they are at such a time, from the soiled book of the local public library, and whose umbrella has lost half its handle, a china nob. (I think I will write this book for her.) And there were all the others who catch that train, except the young fellow with the cough. Now and then he does miss it, using for the purpose, I have no doubt, that only form of rebellion against its accursed tyranny which we have yet learned, physical inability to catch it. Where that morning train starts from is a mystery; but it never fails to come for us, and it never takes us beyond the city, I well know.

I have a clear memory of the newspapers as they were that morning. I had a sheaf of them, for it is my melancholy business to know what each is saying. I learned there were dark and portentous matters, not actually with us, but looming, each already rather larger than a man's hand. If certain things happened, said one half the papers, ruin stared us in the face. If those things did not happen, said the other half, ruin stared us in the face. No way appeared out of it. You paid your halfpenny and were damned either way. If you paid a penny you got more for your money. Boding gloom, full-orbed, could be had for that. There was your extra value for you. I looked round at my fellow passengers, all reading the same papers, and all, it could be reasonably presumed, with foreknowledge of catastrophe. They were indifferent, every one of them. I suppose we have learned, with some bitterness, that nothing ever happens but private failure and tragedy, unregarded by our fellows except with pity. The blare of the political megaphones, and the sustained panic of the party tom-toms, have a message for us, we may suppose. We may be sure the noise means something. So does the butcher's boy when the sheep want to go up a side turning. He makes a noise. He means something, with his warning cries. The driving uproar has a purpose. But we have found out (not they who would break up side turnings, but the people in the second class carriages of the morning train) that now, though our first instinct is to start in a panic, when we hear another sudden warning shout, there is no need to do so. And perhaps, having attained to that more callous mind which allows us to stare dully from the carriage window though with that urgent din in our ears, a reasonable explanation of the increasing excitement and flushed anxiety of the great Statesmen and their fuglemen may occur to us, in a generation or two. Give us time! But how they wish they were out of it, they who need no more time, but understand.

I put down the papers with their calls to social righteousness pitched in the upper register of the tea-tray, their bright and instructive interviews with flat earthers, and with the veteran who is topically interesting because, having served one master fifty years, and reared thirteen children on fifteen shillings a week, he has just begun to draw his old age pension. (There's industry, thrift, and success, my little dears!) One paper had a column account of the youngest child actress in London, her toys and her philosophy, initialed by one of our younger brilliant journalists. All had a society divorce case, with sanitary elisions. Another contained an amusing account of a man working his way round the world with a barrel on his head. Again, the young prince, we were credibly informed in all the papers of that morning, did stop to look in at a toy-shop window in Regent Street the previous afternoon. So like a boy, you know, and yet he is a prince of course. The matter could not be doubted. The report was carefully illustrated. The prince stood on his feet outside the toy shop, and looked in.

To think of the future as a modestly long series of such prone mornings, dawns unlit by heaven's light, new days to which we should be awakened always by these clamant cockcrows bringing to our notice what the busy-ness of our fellows had accomplished in nests of intelligent and fruitful china eggs, was enough to make one stand up in the carriage, horrified, and pull the communication cord. So I put down the papers and turned to the landscape. Had I known the Skipper was back from below the horizon—but I did not know. So I must go on to explain that that morning train did stop, with its unfailing regularity, and not the least hint of reprieve, at the place appointed in the Schedule. Soon I was at work, showing, I hope, the right eager and concentrated eye, dutifully and busily climbing the revolving wheel like the squirrel; except, unluckier than that wild thing so far as

I know, I was clearly conscious, whatever the speed, the wheel remained forever in the same place. Looking up to sigh through the bars after a long spin there was the Skipper smiling at me.

I saw an open door. I got out. It was as though the world had been suddenly lighted, and I could see a great distance.

We stood in Fleet Street later, interrupting the tide. The noise of the traffic came to me from afar, for the sailor was telling me he was sailing soon, and that he was taking his vessel an experimental voyage through the tropical forests of the Amazon. He was going to Para, and thence up the main stream as far as Manaos, and would then attempt to reach a point on the Madeira river near Bolivia, 800 miles above its junction with the greater river. It would be a noble journey. They would see Obydos and Santarem, and the foliage would brush their rigging at times, so narrow would be the way, and where they anchored at night the jaguars would come to drink. This to me, and I have read Humboldt, and Bates, and Spruce, and Wallace. As I listened my pipe went out.

It was when we were parting that the sailor, who is used to far horizons and habitually deals with affairs in a large way because his standards in his own business are the skyline and the meridian, put to me the most searching question I have had to answer since the city first caught and caged me. He put it casually when he was striking a match for a cigar, so little did he himself think of it.

"Then why," said he, "don't you chuck it?"

What, escape? I had never thought of that. It is the last solution which would have occurred to me concerning the problem of captivity. It is a credit to you and to me that we do not think of our chains so disrespectfully as to regard them as anything but necessary and indispensable, though sometimes, sore and irritated, we may bite at them. As if servitude fell to our portion like squints, parents poor in spirit, green fly, reverence for our social superiors, and the other consignments from the stars. How should we live if not in bonds? I have never tried. I do not remember, in all the even and respectable history of my family, that it has ever been tried. The habit of obedience, like our family habit of noses, is bred in the bone. The most we have ever done is to shake our fists at destiny; and I have done most of that.

"Give it up," said the Skipper, "and come with me."

With a sad smile I lifted my foot heavily and showed him what had me round the ankle. "Poo," he said. "You could berth with the second mate. There's room there. I could sign you on as purser. You come."

I stared at him. The fellow meant it. I laughed at him.

"What," I asked conclusively, "shall I do about all this?" I waved my arm round Fleet Street, source of all the light I know, giver of my gift of income tax, limit of my perspective. How should I live when withdrawn from the smell of its ink, the urge of its machinery?

"*That*," he said. "Oh, damn that!"

It was his light tone which staggered me and not what he said. The sailor's manner was that of one who would be annoyed if I treated him like a practical man, arranging miles of petty considerations and exceptions before him, arguing for hours along rows of trifles, and hoping the harvest of difficulties of no consequence at the end of the argument would convince him. Indeed I know he is always impatient for the next step in any business, and not, like most of us, for more careful consideration. "Look there," said the sailor, pointing to Ludgate Circus, "see the Putney 'bus? If it takes up two more passengers before it passes this spot then you've got to come."

That made the difficulty much clearer. I agreed. The 'bus struggled off, and a man with a bag ran at it and boarded it. One! Then it had a clear run—it almost reached us—in another two seconds!—I began to breathe more easily; the danger of liberty was almost gone. Then the sailor jumped for the 'bus before it was quite level, and as he mounted the steps, turned, and held up two fingers with a grin.

Thus was a voyage of great moment and adventure settled for me.

When I got home that night I referred to the authorities for the way to begin an enterprise on the deep. What said Hakluyt? According to him it is as easy as this: "Master John Hawkins, with the Jesus of Lubeck, a ship of 700 tunnes, and the Solomon, a ship of seven score, the Tiger, a barke of 50, and the Swalow of 30 tunnes, being all well furnished with men to the number of one hundred three-score and ten; as also with ordinance and vituall requisite for such a voyage, departed out of Plinmouth the 18 day of October in the yeere of our Lord 1564, with a prosperous wind."

But we all know such things were done far better in that century. Yet Master John Hawkins, who seems to have handled a fleet with greater facility than I do this pen now I am so anxious to scratch it across preliminaries and get it to sea, did not come to a decision by the number of passengers on a Putney 'bus. So I turned to a modern authority. Yet Bates, I found, is worse than old John Hawkins, Bates actually arrives at his destination in the first sentence. He steps across in thirty-eight words from England to the Amazon. "I embarked at Liverpool with Mr Wallace, in a small trading vessel, on the 26th day of April 1848; and, after a swift passage from the Irish Channel to the equator arrived on the 26th of May off Salinas."

Well, I did not. I say it is a gross deception. Voyaging does not get accomplished in that offhand fashion. It is a mockery to captives like ourselves to pretend bondage is puffed away in that airy manner. It is not so easily persuaded to disencumber us. Indeed, with this and that, I found the initial step in the pursuit of the sunset red a heavy weight, and hardly suited to the constitution of men who have worked into a deep run; but that high resolution and a faith equal to belief in the liquefaction of St Januarius' blood are needed to drop the protective routine of years, to sheer off the dear and warm entanglements of home and friendships; to shut the front door one bleak winter evening when the house smells comfortable and secure, and the light on the hearth, under such circumstances, is ironic in its bright revelation of years of ease and stability till then not fully appraised; and so depart in the dusk for an unknown Welsh coaling port, there

to board a tramp steamer for a voyage that has some serious
doubts about it, though its landfall shall be near the line, and
have palms in it. The door slammed, I noticed, in a chill and
penetrating minor, an incident of travel I have never seen
recorded.

Now do I come at last, O Liberty, my loved and secret
divinity! Your passionate pilgrim is here, late, though still
young and eager eyed; yet with his coat collar up-turned for
the present. Allons! the Open Road is before him. But how
the broad and empty prospects of his freedom shudder with
the dire sounds and cries of the milk churns on Paddington
Station!

And next I remember black night—it was, I think, about
three a.m.—and a calamitous rain, and a Welsh railway
station where I had alighted, faint with a famine, a kit bag
soon to increase in weight and drag, and a pair of numbed
feet. There was a porter who bore himself as though it were
the last day and he knew the worst, a dying station light, the
wind and rain, and me. Outside was the dark, and one of the
greatest coaling ports in the world. As I could not see the
coal in great bulk I could not admire it. The railway man
turned out the light, conducted me politely into a puddle,
set my course for the docks in uncharted night with a dexter
having no convictions, and left me. I began to hate the land
of the wild bard in which I found myself for the first time,
and felt a savage satisfaction in being nearly a pure blooded
London Saxon; and as I surveyed my prospects in that
country, not even the fact that I had a grandparent named
Hughes would have prevented me striking Wales with my
umbrella, for it is only a cheap one; but I had left it in the
train.

It had never occurred to me (any more than it did to you
when you got this book to learn about the tropic sea and the
jungle) that the Open Road, where the chains fall from us,
would include Swansea High Street four hours before sunrise
in a steady winter downpour. But there I discovered that
trade wind seas by moonlight, flying fish, Indians, and
forests and palms, cannot be compelled. They come in their
turn. They are mixed with litter and dead stuff, like prizes in

a bran tub. Going down the drear and aqueous street it was clear that if there are exalted moments in travel, as on the instant when we discover we really may prepare to go, yet exaltation implies the undistinguished flats from which, for a while, we are translated. This is a travel book for honest men. I am still on the flat. It will be to-morrow presently.

My chief fear was that my waterproof, rattling in the wind, would alarm silent and sleeping Swansea. I found a policeman standing at a street corner, holding out his cape to help away the rain. He could give me no hope. He knew where the dock was, but the way thither was difficult and tortuous. I had better follow the tram lines, and ask again, if I saw anybody. Therefore the tram lines I followed till my portable estate, by compound interest, had increased to untold tons; but the empty tram way went on for ever down the rows of frozen and desolate lamps, so that I surrendered all my chances of the seas of the tropics and the jungle of the Brazils, and turned aside from the course which the policeman said led to ships and the deep, entered the dark portico of a shop, where it was only half wet, and lit my pipe, there to wait for the shy gods to turn my luck. Hesitating footsteps fumbled to where I was hidden, and stopped at the flash of my match. "Could yer 'blige with a light, mister?"

He was a little elderly seaman in yellow oilskins and a so'wester. He was rather drunk. His oilskins gathered the reflected street shine, so that he looked phosphorescent, an old man risen wet and shining from the ocean. He was looking for Buenos Aires, he explained, and hadn't got any matches. Now he, for the Plate, and I, for ultimate Amazonas, set off down the Swansea tram lines. And the wind whined through overhead wires, and a lost dog followed us along the empty thoroughfare where the only sound was of waterspouts, and the elderly mariner sang bold and improper songs, so that I wondered there was not an irruption of nightcaps at upper Swansea windows to witness this disturbance of their usual peace.

We came at length to abandoned lagoons, where spectral ships were moored down the marges, and round the wide waters was the loom of uncertain monsters and buildings.

Railway metals waylaid us and caught us by the feet. There were many electric moons swaying in the gale, and they spilled showers of broken light, which melted on the black water, and betrayed to us our loneliness in outer night. The call of a vessel's syren across that inhospitable space was heard by us as the prolonged moan of the lost.

The old man of the sea took me under a stack of timber to light his pipe. He borrowed my box of matches, and malicious spurts of wind extinguished each match, steadily, as mine ancient struck them. It was now 4 a.m. He threw each bit of dead wood down, without irritation, as though it were the fate of man to strike lights for the gods to douse, but yet was he uplifted now beyond the hurt of cosmic mockery. The matches were not wasted. At least they lighted up his sorrowful face as he talked to me. I would not have had him any the less drunk, for it but softened his facial integument, which I could see had been hardened and set by bitter experience, masking the man; but now his jaded life, warmed by emotion, though much of the emotion was artificial and of the pewter born, was quick in his face again, and made him a human responsive to his kind, instead of a sober and warped shellback with a sour remembrance of his hardships, and of the futility of his endurance, and of the distance away of his masters with their bowels of iron.

He had seven children and the sea was a weary place. Had I any children?—and God keep them if I had. He was a troublesome old man ("that's another light gone") but he had just left his kids ("ah, to hell wi' the wind") and he had to talk to someone about them, and that was my rotten luck, said he. We got to the fifth child, and I heard something about her, when the wind reached round the wood stack at us, and snatched the last glim. So it was in the dark that I heard about the other two and the wife, while one of my pockets filled with rain. Only Milly, he said, was at work, and what was four pound a month for the rest? And he was sick of the sea and chief mates, and did I think a chap stood for a better time when he died, if he kept off drink and did his bit without grousing, like some of the parson fellers said? Then he indicated my ship, and disappeared in the dark. He is still waiting an answer to his last question, which I have saved for you to give him.

For me, I was in no mood to discuss whether balm is to be got in Gilead, when we come to the place; but stumbling among the lumber on the deserted deck of the s.s. "Capella," I found a cabin, fell into it, and remember nothing more but the smell of hot bread, eggs and bacon, and coffee, which visited me in a beautiful dream. Then I woke to the reveille of a tin whistle, which the chief engineer was playing in my ear; and it was daylight. The jumble of recollections of the night before were but dark insanities. But the smell of that aromatic food, I give grace, did not pass with the awakening, for next door I heard lively sizzling in the galley. Already Fleet Street was hull down.

If you are used only to the methods of passenger steamers and regular routes, then you know little of travel. You are but carried about. Insistent clocks and schedules keep that way, and the upholstered but rigid routine is a soporific. You never see the hither side of the hedge. The granite countenance of fortune, her eyes filmed like frozen pools, which keeps alert and bright the voyager who is unprotected from her unscheduled and unmoral acts except by his own ready buckler, is watched for you by others. You are never surprised into fear by the unlucky position of the planets, nor moved to sing Laus Deo, when now and then, the stars are propitious. I had been brought hastily to the "Capella," for it was said she was sailing instantly. This morning I learned at breakfast that nobody knew when she could sail. Our steamer sat two feet higher than her capacity. There was some galvanized iron to come from Glasgow, some machinery from Sheffield; and owing to labour difficulties we were short of several hundred tons of coal. A little mob of us, all strangers, shuffled after the Skipper's spry heels that morning to the Board of Trade offices, where an official mumbled over the ship's articles, to our shut ears, and we signed where we were told. A more glum and unromantic group of voyagers, each man twirling his shabby hat in his hands as he waited his turn for the corroded pen, was never

seen this side of the Elizabethan era. I became the purser of
the "Capella," with my wages lawfully recorded at a shilling
per month.

I was committed. There was no withdrawal now but
desertion. And desertion, at times, I seriously considered,
because for a week more the cargo dribbled down to us,
while I endured as a moucher about those winter docks with
their coal tips, and the muddy streets with their sailors' slop
marts, marine stores, and pawnshops having a cankered
display of chronometers, telescopes, and other flotsam of
marine failure and wreckage. Daily the quays and the dismal
waterside ways with their cheap shops were still more
depressed by additional snow mush and drives of sleet; and
it was no warmth for this idler that he saw the tradesmen,
because of the season, putting holly among their oranges and
wreathing beer bottles with chains of coloured paper. The
iron decks and cabins of my new home were as chill and
unfriendly as the empty grate, the marble tables, and the tin
advertisements of chemical slops of a temperance hotel. Am
I plain? Such are the conditions which compass the wayward
traveller. This is what chills one's rapid pulse when pursuing
at last the rosy visions of boyhood. The deplorable littoral of
our island kingdom is part of a life on the ocean wave, and
should help you in coming to a decision when next you see
a friendless and bestial sailorman. It becomes necessary to
declare that we shall really get down to the tropics presently;
have the courage to wait, like the crew of the "Capella." Our
ship did sail, when she was ready.

It was the afternoon before we sailed, and having listened
long enough to my messmates, who, after dinner, weighed
the probabilities of malaria, yellow fever and other alien
disasters into our coming strange voyage, that I went into
the town to take my last look round a book shop, and to get
some marine soap, dungarees, and things. Here was I at last
with my heart's desire. On the very next day I should sail, I
myself, and no other hero, veritably Me at last, for a place
not on the chart, because the place we should find, at the
journey's end, the map described with those words of magic:
"Forest" and "Unexplored." I made my way round crates

and barrels on that untidy deck, which had a thick mud of coal dust and snow, to the ladder overside. Coal dust and melting snow! But where was the uplifted heart, the radiant anticipation, as of one to whom the future was big with treasures to be born, which are the privilege of a young pilgrim, released from his usual obligations to pursue far horizons in the Spanish main, while his envious fellows in the city still cast ledgers under gas lamps? Here was another swindle of the romanticists. You may search their warm and golden pages in vain for coal tips, melting ice, delays, and steam heaters that will not work for cold cabins. Down they go here, though. These gallant affairs, I thought, as I descended the wet and gritty ladder, are much better done before the fire at home, in your slippers; for the large scale map, as you traverse its alluring blank areas, leaves out the conditions which now, when I am on the actual business, precipitate as frozen spicules, as would north winds, my warm, aerial, and cloudy enthusiasms that were wont to be dyed such wonderful hues by sunsets, poems, and tales of old travel. Another of these congealing draughts was now to catch me unbuttoned. Because of our unusual destination, and the wild stories that were told of it, we were a point of interest in Swansea docks, and had many interviewers and curious visitors. Some of them were on the quay then, inspecting our steamer, and I as stepped off the ladder one turned to me.

"Mister," he whispered, "are you going in her?"

"I am," I said.

"O gord," said he.

That night I met a number of my grave fellow shipmates in the town. The question was, Should we then go back to the ship?

"What," burst out one of us in surprise—his gold-laced cap was already resting on his right eyebrow—"Now? Not me. Boys, don't freeze the Carnival. Follow me!"

We followed him. The rest of the evening is more easily given in dumb show. There was a mechanical piano in a saloon bar, and it steadily devoured pennies, and returned to us automatic joy, fortissimo, over which our conversation

strenuously highstepped and vaulted. Later, there was a
search for cabs, and an engineer carried with him everywhere
two geese by their necks and sometimes trod on their loose
feet. When he did this he snatched a goose from his own
grasp, and then roundly abused us for our post-dated frivol-
ity. We learned our steamer was now moored in mid-dock.
We found a quay wall, and at the bottom of it, at a great
depth in the dark, the level of the water was seen only
because shreds of lamp-shine floated there. We understood a
boat was below, and found it was, and we loaded it till the
water brimmed at the gunwale. As we mounted the "Capella's" rope-ladder only one goose fell back into the dock.

The "Capella" started in her sleep, and she woke me. She
was still trembling. Resting my hand on her I felt her heart
begin to throb, though faintly. We were off.

It was a bright morning, early and keen. Those habitual
quays now were moving past us. The decks were cleared, the
carpenter and some sailors were fixing the hatches, and the
pilot, muffled in a thick white shawl, was on the bridge with
the Skipper. We stopped in the outer lock, the exhaust
humming impatiently while a pier-head jumper—for we
were a sailor short—was examined by our doctor. The
Skipper had some short words for an official who had
mounted the bridge, because the third mate had deserted,
and had taken his half pay; and the official, who had
volunteered to get us a substitute, had failed. There were
now but two mates for our big tramp steamer going a long
and arduous voyage which included the navigation for some
months of narrow inland waterways in the tropics. Our first
mate, passing amidships where the Purser was leaning
overside, stopped to tell me what this meant for him and the
second mate. I was mighty glad it was not the purser's fault.
I have never heard a short speech more passionate; and his
eyes were feral. Yet it became increasingly clear to me, as
the voyage lengthened, that his eyes no more than met the
case.

Out we drove at last. It was December, but by luck we
found a halcyon morning which had got lost in the year's

procession. It was a Sunday morning, and it had not been ashore. It was still virgin, bearing a vestal light. It had not been soiled yet by any suspicion of this trampled planet, this muddy star, which its innocent and tenuous rays had discovered in the region of night. I thought it still was regarding us as a lucky find there. Its light was tremulous, as if with joy and eagerness. I met this discovering morning as your ambassador while you still slept, and betrayed not, I hope, any greyness and bleared satiety of ours to its pure, frail, and lucid regard. That was the last good service I did before leaving you quite. I was glad to see how well our old earth did meet such a light, as though it had difficulty in looking day in the face. The world was miraculously re-newed. It rose, and received the new-born of Aurora in its arms. There was clouds of pearl above hills of chrysoprase. The sea ran in volatile flames. The shadows on the bright deck shot to and fro as we rolled. The breakfast bell rang not too soon. This was a right beginning.

The pilot was dropped, and a course was shaped to pass between Lundy and Hartland. A strong north-wester and its seas caught us beyond the Mumbles, and the quality of the sunshine thinned to a flickering stuff which cast only grey shadows. The "Capella" became quarrelsome, and began to strike the seas heavily. You may know the "Capella" when you see her. She is a modern three-thousand-ton freighter, with derrick supports fore and aft, and a funnel; and the three of them are so fearful of seeming rakish that they overdo the effect of stern utility, and appear to lean ahead. She is a three-island ship, the amidships section carrying the second mate's cabin, and the cabins of the four engineers, all of them, excepting the Chief's cabin, looking outwards overseas across a narrow sheltered alleyway; and on a narrower athwartship's alleyway there, and opening astern, are the Chief's place, and the cook's galley, the entrance to the engine-room, and the engineers' messroom. Above this structure is the boat deck. You may reach the poop, which contains the master's and chief mate's quarters, the doctor's and steward's berths, and the saloon, by descending a perpendicular iron ladder to the long main deck, or else, as all did at sea, by a flying trestle bridge, which is dismantled when in port. Her black funnel is relieved by a cryptic design in white, and her bows are so bluff that, as the chief mate put it, "her belly begins there." She might not take your eye, but a shipowner would see her points. She carries a large cargo on a comparatively low registered tonnage. The money that built her went mostly in hull and engines, and the latter do their work as sweetly as an eight-day clock, giving ten and a half knots, weather permitting, on a low coal consumption. There was not much money left, therefore, for balm in the cabins, and that is the reason we do not find it there.

At sundown the sky cleared. The wind, increased in violence, had swept it of the last feather. Lundy was over our starboard bow, a small dark blot in a clear yellow light which poured, with the gale and the rising seas, from the west. The glass was falling. Now, the Skipper has often told me how his "Capella" had faced hurricanes off Cape Hatteras, when laden with ore, and had kept her decks dry. There are other stories about her surprising buoyancy, when deeply laden, and I have heard them all at home, and they are fine stories. But what lies they are! For there below me, with Lundy not even passed, and the Bay of Biscay to come (Para not to be thought of yet) were tons and tons of salt wash that could not get time to escape by the scuppers, but plunged wearily amongst the hatches and winches.

"I've never seen her as dirty as this," grumbled the chief engineer apologetically, peeping from his cabin at cold green water lopping over casually on to the after deck. "It's that patent fuel—its stowed wrong. Now she'll roll—you can feel it—the cat she is, she's never going to stop. It's that patent fuel and her new load line."

Certainly she sat close to the sea. I had never seen so much lively water so close. She wallowed, she plunged, she rolled, she sank heavily to its level. I looked out from the round window of the Chief's cabin, and when she inclined those green mounds of the swell swinging under us and away were superior, in apparition, to my outlook.

"Listen to it," said the Chief. He stopped triturating some

shavings of hard tobacco between his huge palms, and sat quietly, hands clasped, as though in prayer. The surge mourned over the deck. The day, too, was growing towards the dusky hours of retrospection. That sombre monody outside was like the tremor and boom of the drums funebre. "That chap some of you talk about—Lloyd George!"—said the Chief, suddenly rubbing his tobacco again with energy. (Good God, I thought, and here we are at sea too. Now what has the misguided man done.) "If I had him here I'd hold him down in that wash on deck till it cleared. Then he'd know. He put it there, to break sailors' legs. This steamer, she had dry decks till her load line was altered. She carries more now than she was built for, two hundred tons more. If I had him here—but there you are! Popularity! There's a fine popular noise for you, isn't it? Sailors growled for better food. 'What about this improved food scale?' says Mr Lloyd George to the shipowners. 'Oh,' said they, 'we'll give 'em better food, the drunken insubordinate dogs, if you'll make overloading legal.' 'Why,' says Lloyd George, 'then it wouldn't be illegal, would it?' So it was done. What does the public know about a ship's buoyancy? Nothing. But it understands food. So the clever man heightens the Plimsoll mark, adds a million or so to shipowners' capital by dipping his pen in the ink, and gives Jack more jam. What you want ashore," the Chief added bitterly, "is not more voters, as some say, but more lunatic asylums."

Though I had left politics at home, to be settled by others, like the trouble with the drains, the dog licence, and the dispute about the garden fence, I glanced with interest at the Chief. I know him well. Not only is he a kindly man, but he himself is also a philosophic rebel. But his eye was hard, and he still ground the tobacco with forgetful energy, as though an objectionable thing were between his strong hands. Then impatiently he threw the tobacco loose on his log book, which was open on his deck, paused, and said, "Ah, maybe the man thought a little freeboard the less didn't matter. God give him grace," and picked his flute out of a bookshelf which was fastened above his bunk; sat down over the steam heater, and broke out like a blackbird. Yet was it a well-remembered air he fluted so well. I listened so long as respect for the artist demanded, then rose, filled my pipe from the fragrant grains on the log book, and left him. Presently I would listen to such airs; but his was too soon.

I repeat I had confidence in the "Capella" to gain. I went forward to get it, mounting the bridge, where my cabin mate, the youthful second officer, was in charge, in his oilskins. A cheerful sight he looked. "I think," said he briskly, "we're going to catch it." He was puckering his face over our course. Lundy was looming large—even Rat Island was plain—but it looked so frail in that flood of seas, wind, and wild yellow light streaming together from the evening west, that I looked for the unsubstantial island to spring suddenly from its foundations, and to come down on us a stretched wisp of thinned and ragged smoke. The sea was adrift from its old confines. The flood was pouring past, and the wind was the drainage of interstellar space. Lundy was the last delicate fragment of land. It still fronted the upheaval and rush of the ungoverned elements, but one looked for it to be swept away.

Yet that wild and scenic west, of such pallor and clarity that one shrank from facing its inhospitable spaciousness, with each shape of a wave there, black against the light as it reared ahead, a distinct individual foe in the host moving to the attack, was but the prelude. Night and the worst were to come. Just then, while the last of the light was shining on the officer's oilskins, I was only surprised that our bulk was such a trifle after all. Our loaded vessel looked so bluff and massive when in dock. She began to attempt, off Lundy, the spring and jauntiness of a trawler. The bows sank to the rails in an acre of white, and the spume flew past the bridge like rain. The black bows lifted and swayed, buoyant on submarine upheavals, to cut out segments of the sunset; then sank again into dark hollows where the foam was luminous. The cold and wind were bitter dolours.

We rolled. I grasped the rail of the weather cloth, in the drive of wind and spume, and rode down on our charger like a valiant man; like a valiant man who is uncertain of his seat. Something like a valiant man. We advanced to the attack, masts and funnel describing great arcs, and steadily our bows shouldered away the foe. I think sailors deserve large monies. Being the less valiant—for the longer I watched, the more grew I wet and cold—it came to my mind that where we were, but a few weeks before, another large freighter had her hatches opened by the seas, and presently was but a trace of oil and cinders on the waters. You will remember I am on my first long voyage. The officer was quite cheerful and asked me if I knew Forest Gate. There were, he said, some fine girls at Forest Gate.

We rounded Hartland. It was dusk, the weather was now directly on our starboard beam, and the waves were coming solidly inboard. The main deck was white with plunging water. We rolled still more.

"I can't make out why you left London when you didn't have to," said the grinning sailor. "I'd like to be on the Stratford tram, going down to Forest Gate."

This was nearly as bad as the Chief's flute. I held up two fingers over those hatches of ours, called silently on blessed Saint Anthony, who loves sailors, and went down the ladder; for night had come, and the prospect from the "Capella" was not the less apprehensive to the mind of a landsman because the enemy could not be seen, except as flying ghosts. The noises could be heard all right.

I shut my heavy teak door amidships, shut out the daunting uproar of floods, and the sensation that the night was collapsing round our heaving ship. There was a home light far away, on some unseen Cornish headland, rising and falling like a soaring but tethered star. Nor did I want the lights of home.

"I love the sea," a beautiful woman once said to me. (We, then, stood looking out over it from a height, and the sea was but the sediment of the still air, the blue precipitation of the sky, for it was that restful time, early October. I also loved it then.)

I was thinking of this, when the concrete floor of the cabin nearly became a wall, and I fell absurdwise, striking nearly every item in the cabin. Was this the way to greet a lover? Sitting on a sea-chest, and swaying to and fro because the ship compelled me to a figure of woe, I began to consider whether it was only the books about the sea which I had loved hitherto, and not the sea itself. Perhaps it is better not to live with it, if you would love it. The sea is at its best at London, near midnight, when you are within the arms of a capacious chair, before a glowing fire, selecting phases of the voyages you will never make. It is wiser not to try to realize your dreams. There are no real dreams. For as to the sea itself, love it you cannot. Why should you? I will never believe again the sea was ever loved by anyone whose life was married to it. It is the creation of Omnipotence, which is not of human kind and understandable, and so the springs of its behaviour are hidden. The sea does not assume its royal blue to please you. Its brute and dark desolation is not raised to overwhelm you; you disappear then because you happen to be there. It carries the lucky foolish to fortune, and drags the calculating wise to the strewn bones. Yet, thought I, that night off Cornwall, if I pray now as one of the privileged and lucky foolish, this very occasion may prove to be set apart for the sole use of the calculating wise. Because that is the way things happen at sea. What else may we expect from It, the nameless thing, new-born with each dawn, but as old as the night? Now for me had it degenerated into its mood of old night, behaving as it did in the lightless days, before poetry came to change it with flattery. It was again as inhuman as when the poet was merely a wonderfully potential blob on a warm mudbank.

Here, you see, is the whole trouble in appealing to Omnipotence. Picture me entering the wide western ocean at night, an inconspicuous but self-important morsel sitting on a sea-chest, at a time when it was perhaps ordained that hundreds of ships should have anxious passages. (Afterwards I learned very many ships did have anxious passages.) How could I expect to be spared, even though somewhere the hairs of my head were all numbered? It is plain that to spare me would be to extend beneficence to all. There only remained to me my liberty to hope that our particular steamer might miss all seventh waves, by luck. I was free to do that.

I turned up the dull and stinking oil lamp, and tried to read; but that fuliginous glim haunted the pages. That black-edged light too much resembled my own thoughts made manifest. There were some bunches of my cabin mate's clothes hanging from hooks, and I watched their erratic behaviour instead. The water in the carafe was also interesting, because quite mad, standing diagonally in the bottle, and then reversing. A lump of soap made a flying leap from the washstand, and then slithered about the floor like something hunted and panic-stricken. I listened to numerous little voices. There was no telling their origins. There was a chorus in the cabin, rustlings, whispers, plaints, creaks, wails, and grunts; but they were foundered in the din when the spittoon, which was an empty meat tin, got its lashings loose, and began a rioting fandango on the concrete. Over the clothes chest, which was also our table and a cabin fixture, was a portrait of the mate's sweetheart, and on its frame was one of my busy little friends the cockroaches; for the mate and I do not sleep alone in this cabin, not by hundreds. The cockroach stood in thought, waving his hands interrogatively, as one who talks to himself nervously. The ship at that moment received a seventh wave, lurched, and trembled. The cockroach fell. I rose, listening. I felt sure a new clamour would begin at once, showing we had reached another and critical stage of the fight. But no; the brave heart of her was beating as before. I could feel its steady pulse throbbing in our table. We were alive and strong, though labouring direfully.

It was when I was thinking whether bed would be, as I have so often found it, the best answer to doubt, that I heard a boatswain's pipe.

I fought one side of the door, and the wind fought the other. My hurry to open the door was great, but the obstinate wind jammed it firmly. Without warning the wind released its hold, the ship fell over to windward, the door flew open, and forth I went, clutching at the driving dark. Then up sailed my side of the ship, and the door shut with the sound of gunfire. I had never experienced such insensate violence. These were the unlawful noises and movements of chaos. Hanging to a rail, I was puzzling out which was the fore and which the rear of the ship, when a flying lump of salt water struck me in the face just as a figure (I thought it was the chief officer) hurried past me bawling "All hands."

The figure came back. "That you, purser? Number three hatch has gone," it said, and disappeared instantly.

So. Then this very thing had come to me, and at night! Our hatches were adrift. It was impossible. Why, we had only just left Swansea. It could not be true; it was absurdly unfair. This was my first long voyage, and it had only just begun. I stood like the cricketer who is out for a duck.

If I could tell you how I felt, I would. Somebody was shouting some where, but his words were cut off at once by the wind and blown away. I felt my way along a wet and dark iron alleyway which was giddily unstable, pressing hard against my feet, and then falling from under me. I got round by the engine-room entrance. Small gleams, shavings of light, were escaping from seams in the unseen structure, but they showed nothing, except a length of wet rail or a scrap of wet deck. The ship itself was a shade, manned by voices.

I could not see that anything was being done. Were they allowing her to fill up like an open barge? I became aware my surcharged feelings were escaping by my knees, which kept knocking in their tremors against a lower rail. I tried to stop this trembling by hardening my muscles, but my fearful legs had their own way. Yet it is plain there was nothing to fear. I told my legs so. Had we not but that day left Swansea? Besides, I had already commenced a letter which was to be posted at Para. The letter would have to be posted. They were waiting for it at home.

Somewhere below me a heavy mass of water plunged monstrously, and became a faintly luminous cloud over all the main deck aft, actually framing the rectangular form of the deck in the night. It was unreasonable. I was not really one of the crew either, though on the articles. I was there by chance. No advantage should be taken of that. A torrent poured down the athwartships alleyway, and nearly swept me from my feet.

One could not watch what was happening. That was another cruel injustice. The wind and sea could be heard, and the ship could be felt. But how could I be expected to know what to do in the dark in such circumstances? There ought to be a light. This should have happened in the daytime. My garrulous knees struck the lower rail violently in their excitement. I leaned over the rail, shading my eyes. I grew savagely indignant with something having no name and no shape. I cannot even now give a name to the thing that angered me, but can just discern, in the twilight which shrouds the undiscovered, a vast calm face the rock of which no human emotion can move, with eyes that stare but see nothing, and a mouth that never speaks, and ears from which assailing cries and questions fall as stone falls from it, as unavailing as your prayers; but we shall never cease to pray and fling stones, alternately, up there into the twilight.

Nevertheless, when the chief, with his hurricane lamp, found me, he says I was smiling. The youth who was our second mate ran up and stood by us, the better to shout to the deck below. He shouted, bending over the rail, till he was screaming through hoarseness. He turned to us abruptly. "They don't understand a word I say," he cried in despair. "There isn't a sailor or an Englishman in the crowd, the—— German farmers." This, I found afterwards, was nearly true. These men had been signed on at a Continental port. It was really our Dutch cook who saved us that night. It was the cook who first saw the hatch covers going.

The ship's head had been put to the seas to keep the decks as clear as possible, and being now more accustomed to the gloom I could make out the men below busy at the hatch. Most conspicuous among them was the cook, who had taken charge there, and he, with three languages, bludgeoned into surprising activity the inexperienced youngsters who were learning for the first time what happens to a ship when the carpenter's chief job on leaving port has its defects discovered by exceptional weather. They were wading through swirling waters as they worked, and once a greater wave sprang bodily over them, and when the hatch showed through the foam again some of the men had gone as though dissolved. But it was found they had kept the right side of the bulwarks, and the elderly carpenter, whose leg had got wedged in a winch, was the only one damaged.

If you ask me when I shall be pleased to allow the necessary sun to rise upon this narrative to give it a little warmth, then I must tell you it cannot be done till we have fastened down the "Capella's" number two hatch, at least. That hatch has gone now, and if hatches one and four give way while number two is getting attention from the weary, soaked, and frozen crowd which has just had an hour's desperate work at number three, then I fear the sun will never rise on this narrative. (How Bates got over to his wonderful blue butterflies in those forest paths under a tropical sun in thirty-eight words I do not know. He must have been thinking of nothing but his butterflies. I cannot do it, with the seas and the ship keeping my mind so busy.)

Luckily, the other hatches kept staunch. We were water-tight again. When the Old Man, the Chief, the Doctor, and the Purser, gathered late that night in the Chief's cabin to see what it was he had secreted in his cupboard, and boasted of, we sat where we could, being comfortably crowded, and I never knew tobacco could taste like that. I felt as if never before had I found such large leisure for extracting its full flavour. From being suddenly confined within a space which gave me a short outlook of a few hours, I was presently released into the open again and of what might remain to me of the usual gift of ample years. I had all that time to smoke in. Never did a pipe taste so sweet. It is idle for good and serious souls to think me graceless here with this talk of tobacco immediately after such a release. Let me tell them my sacrificial smoke rose up straight and accepted. Looking through the smoke I saw clearly how worthy, kind, and lovable were the faces of my comrades. I warmed to this voyage for the first time; as though, after a test, I had been initiated. This was the place for me, with men like these about me, and such great affairs to be met. I revelled in the thought of our valorous bluff, insignificant as we were in that malign desolation, sundered from our kind.

"Chief," said the Old Man, "it was my department that time. None of your old engines did it."

"You've got a good cook," said the Chief, "I saw that." Then the Chief, remembering something, turned in his seat to the picture hanging above his desk of a smiling and handsome matron. "Here's luck, old girl," he said, holding up his glass; "you can still send me some letters."

The Chief, in case of an emergency, slept in his clothes that night on the settee, and I climbed into his bunk. What a comfortable outline the man had, as he lay on his broad back, mildly snoring. There was a tangle of tense hair over a square copper coloured forehead. A long experience of such nights was written in many lines on that brow, and was shown in that indifferent snoring while chaos was without. The nose sprang out of the big face like an ejaculation, and beneath it was a moustache clipped short to show the red of the upper lip. The jaw was powerful, but its curves made it friendly. His body and limbs hid the settee and had a margin over. I quite believed what I had been told of his successful way with refractory stokers. There was confidence to be got from a mere look at that slumbering Jovian form. The storm assailed its hairy and fleshy ears in vain. I braced my knees against the bulkhead to keep myself still, the rolling was so violent, and went to sleep . . . waking to find us on a level keel; and was deceived into thinking the parallel lines of grey and gold in the upper air, seen as a picture framed by the port were the heights about a harbour into which we had run for shelter; but it was only cloudland over the western ocean. The stillness, too, was but a short reprieve. The wind was merely making a detour, to spring at us from another quarter.

The sun died at birth. The wind we had lost we found again as a gale from the south-east. The waters quickly increased again, and by noon the saloon was light and giddy with the racing of the propeller. I moved about like an infant learning to walk. We were 201 miles from the Mumbles, course S.W. ½ W.; it was cold, and I was still

looking for the pleasures of travel. The Doctor came to
introduce himself, like a good man, and tried me with such
things as fevers, Shaw, Brazilian entomology, the evolution
of sex, the medical profession under socialism, the sea and
the poets. But my thoughts were in retreat, with the black
dog in full cry. It was too cold and damp to talk even of sex.
When my oil lamp began to throw its rays of brown smell,
the Doctor, tired of the effort to exalt the sour dough which
was my mind, left me. It was night. O, the sea and the
poets!

By next morning the gale, now from the south-west, like
the seas, was constantly reinforced with squalls of hurricane
violence. The Chief put a man at the throttle. In the early
afternoon the waves had assumed serious proportions. They
soared by us in broad sombre ranges, with hissing white
ridges, an inhospitable and subduing sight. They were a
quite different tribe of waves from the volatile and malicious
natives of the Bristol Channel. Those channel waves had no
serried ranks in the attack; they were but a horde of
undisciplined savages, appearing to assault without design
or plan, but getting at us as they could, depending on their
numbers. The waves in the channel were smaller folk, but
more athletic, and very noisy; they appeared to detach
themselves from the sea, and to leap at us, shouting.

These western ocean waves had a different character.
They were the sea. We did not have a multitude of waves in
sight, but the sea floor itself might have been undulating.
The ocean was profoundly convulsed. Our outlook was
confined to a few heights and hollows, and the moving
heights were swift, but unhurried and stately. Your alarm, as
you saw a greater hill appear ahead, tower, and bear down,
had no time to get more than just out of the stage of surprise
and wonder when the "Capella's" bows were pointing
skyward on a long up-slope of water, the broken summit of
which was too quick for the "Capella"—the bows disappeared in a white explosion, a volley of spray, as hard as
shot, raked the bridge, the foredeck filled with raging water,
and the wave swept along our run, dark, severe, and immense; with so little noise too; with but a faint hissing of

foam, as in a deliberate silence. The "Capella" then began to run down a valley.

The engines were reduced to half speed; it would have been dangerous to drive her at such seas. Our wet and slippery decks were bleak, wind-swept, and deserted. The mirror of water on the iron surfaces, constantly renewed, reflected and flashed the wild lights in the sky as she rolled and pitched, and somehow those reflections from her polish made the steamer seem more desolate and forlorn. Not a man showed anywhere on the vessel's length, except merely to hurry from one vantage to another—darting out of the ship's interior, and scurrying to another hole and vanishing abruptly, like a rabbit.

The gale was dumb till it met and was torn in our harsh opposition, shouting and moaning then in anger and torment as we steadily pressed our iron into its ponderable body. You could imagine the flawless flood of air pouring silently express till it met our pillars and pinnacles, and then flying past rift, the thousand punctures instantly spreading into long shrieking lacerations. The wounds and mouths were so many, loud, and poignant, that you wondered you could not see them. Our structure was full of voices, but the weighty body which drove against our shrouds and funnel guys, and kept them strongly vibrating, was curiously invisible. The hard jets of air spurted hissing through the winches. The sound in the shrouds and stays began like that of something tearing, and rose to a high keening. The deeper notes were amidships, in the alleyways and round the engine-room casing; but there the ship itself contributed a note, a metallic murmur so profound that it was felt as a tremor rather than heard. It was almost below human hearing. It was the hollow ship resonant, the steel walls, decks, and bulkheads quivering under the drumming of the seas, and the regular throws of the crank-shaft far below.

It was on this day the "Capella" ceased to be marine engine to me. She was not the "Capella" of the Swansea docks, the sea waggon squatting low in the water, with bows like a box, and a width of beam which made her seem a wharf fixture. To-day in the Atlantic her bluff bows rose to meet the approaching bulk of each wave with such steady honesty, getting up heavily to meet its quick wiles, it is true, but often with such success that we found ourselves perched at a height above the gloom of the hollow seas, getting more light and seeing more world; though sometimes the hill-top was missed; she was not quick enough, and broke the inflowing ridge with her face. She behaved so like a brave patient thing that now her portrait, which I treasure, is to me that of one who has befriended me, a staunch and homely body who never tired in faithful well-doing. She became our little sanctuary, especially near dayfall, with those sombre mounts close round us bringing twilight before its time.

Your glance caught a wave passing amidships as a heaped mass of polished obsidian, having minor hollows and ridges on its slopes, conchoidal fractures in its glass. It rose directly and acutely from your feet to a summit that was awesome because the eye travelled to it over a long and broken up-slope; this hill had intervened suddenly to obscure thirty degrees of light; and the imagination shrank from contemplating water which overshadowed your foothold with such high dark bulk toppling in collapse. The steamer leaning that side, your face was quite close to the beginning of the bare mobile down, where it swirled past in a vitreous flux, tortured lines of green foam buried far but plain in its translucent deeps. It passed; and the light released from the sky streamed over the "Capella" again as your side of her lifted in the roll, the sea falling down her iron wall as far as the bilge. The steamer spouted violently from her choked valve, as it cleared the sea, like a swimmer who battles, and then gets his mouth free from a smother.

Her task against those head seas and the squalls was so hard and continuous that the murmur of her heart, which I fancied grew louder almost to a moaning when her body sank to the rails, the panic of her cries when the screw raced, when she lost her hold, her noble and rhythmic labourings, the sense of her concentrated and unremitting power given by the smoke driving in violence from her swaying funnel, the cordage quivering in tense curves, the seas that burst in her face as clouds, falling roaring inboard then to founder half her length, she presently to raise her heavy body slowly out of an acre of foam, the cascades streaming from her in veils,—all this was like great music. I learned why a ship has a name. It is for the same reason that you and I have names. She has happenings according to her own weird. She shows perversities and virtues her parents never dreamed into the plans they laid for her. Her heredity cannot be explained by the general chemics of iron and steel and the principles of the steam engine; but something counts in her of the moods of her creators, both of the happy men and the sullen men whose bright or dark energies poured into her rivets and plates as they hammered, and now suffuse her body. Something of the "Capella" was revealed to me, "our" ship. She was one for pride and trust. She was slow, but that slowness was of her dignity and size; she had valour in her. She was not a light yacht. She was strong and hard, taking heavy punishment, and then lifting her broad face over the seas to look for the next enemy. But was she slow? She seemed but slow. The eye judged by those assailing hills, so vast and whelmingly quick. The hills were so dark, swift, and great, moving barely inferior to the clouds which travelled with them, the collapsing roof which fell over the seas, flying with the same impulse as the waters. There was the uplifted ocean, and pressing down to it, sundered from it only by the gale—the gale forced them apart—the foundered heavens, a low ceiling which would have been night itself but that it was thinned in patches by some solvent day. And our "Capella," heavy as was her body, and great and swift as were the hills, never failed to carry us up the long slopes, and over the white summits which moved down on us like the marked approach of catastrophe. If one of the greater hills but hit us, I thought——

One did. Late that afternoon the second mate, who was on watch, saw such a wave bearing down on us. It was so dominantly above us that instinctively he put his hand in his pocket for his whistle. It was his first voyage in an ocean steamer; he was not long out of his apprenticeship in "sails," and so he did not telegraph to stop the engines. The

Skipper looked up through the chart-room window, saw the high gloom of this wave over us, and jumped out for the bridge ladder to get at the telegraph himself. He was too late.

We went under. The wave stopped us with the shock of a grounding, came solid over our forelength, and broke on our structure amidships. The concussion itself scattered things about my cabin. When the "Capella" showed herself again the ventilators had gone, the windlass was damaged, and the iron ends of the drum on the forecastle head, on which a steel hawser was wound, had been doubled on themselves, like tinfoil.

By day these movements of water on a grand scale, the harsh and deep noises of gale and breaking seas, and the labouring of the steamer, no more than awed me. At least, my sight could escape. But courage went with the light. At dusk, the eye, which had the liberty during the hours of light to range up the inclines of the sea to distant summits, and note that these dangers always passed, was imprisoned by a dreadful apparition. When there was more night than day in the dusk you saw no waves. You saw, and close at hand, only vertical shadows, and they swayed noiselessly without progressing on the fading sky high over you. I could but think the ocean level had risen greatly, and was see-sawing much superior to us all round. The "Capella" remained then in a precarious nadir of the waters. Looking aft from the Chief's cabin I could see of our ship only the top of our mainmast, because that projected out of the shadow of the hollow into the last of the day overhead; and often the sheer apparitions oscillating around us swung above the truck of it, and the whole length vanished. The sense of onward movement ceased because nothing could be seen passing us. At dusk the steamer appeared to be rocking helplessly in a narrow sunken place which never had an outlet for us; the shadows of the seas erect over us did not move away, but their ridges pitched at changing angles.

You know the Sussex chalk hills at evening, just at that time when, from the foot of them, they lose all detail but what is on the skyline, become an abrupt plane before you of unequal height. That was the view from the "Capella," except that the skyline moved. And when we passed a barque that evening it looked as looks a solitary bush far on the summit of the downs. The barque did not pass us; we saw it fade, and the height it surmounted fade, as shadows do when all light has gone. But where we saw it last a green star was adrift and was ranging up and down in the night.

This was the dark time when, struggling from amidships to the poop, you knew there was something organised and coherent under you, still a standing place in chaos, only because you could feel it there. And this was the time to seek your fellows in the saloon, where there was light, warmth, sane and familiar things, and dinner. The "Capella's" saloon was fairly large, and the Skipper's pride. It was panelled in maple and oak, with a long settee at the forward end upholstered in red velvet, the velvet protected by a calico cover. A brass oil lamp with an opaline shade hung over the table from a beam beneath the skylight. There was a closed American stove, with a rigorously polished brass flue running up through the deck. On two oak sideboards in corners of the saloon some artificial plants blossomed; from single stems each plant blossomed into flowers of aniline dyes and of different species. One of these plants, an imitation palm, and a better imitation of life than the others, was carefully watered throughout the voyage by the steward till it wilted into corruption and an offence, and became a count against the steward which the skipper never forgave, for he thought his floral ornaments lovely. When a pretty Brazilian lady visitor at Itacoatiara admired the magenta rays of one blossom, he culled it for her (five earnest minutes with a sharp knife, for there was wire behind the green bark) more as a sacrifice and a hard duty then a joy, and often spoke of it afterwards, shaking his head regretfully.

Ah! that saloon. I remember it first, shiny, cold, and repellent, with a handful of fire to its wide capacity for draughts, in the northern seas. It had curious marine odours then, with which I was not friendly till long after, odours that lamps, burnished brass, newly polished wood, food, and the steward's storeroom behind it, never fully accounted for; and I remember it as I found it in the still heat of the

Amazon, when it had the air of an oven; when, writing in it, the sweat ran off the fingers to soil the paper, strange insects crawling everywhere on its green baize table cover, and banging against its lamp. I remember it assiduously now, every trivial feature of it, and the men, now scattered over all the world, thrown together in it then for a spell to make the most of each other. It has the indelible impress of a room of that house where first the interest in existence awakened in us.

The Skipper, with stove behind him, took his seat before the soup tureen at the head of the table. You would as soon think of altering the chart-room clock, even were it wrong, as of touching the soup tureen without the Skipper's orders. It is his duty and his right to serve the soup, and to call the steward to inform him the density of the vegetables in it is too heavy. We have no market garden on board, you know.

The Doctor was on the Skipper's right hand, and the Purser next to the Doctor, and on the opposite side, the chief mate. There was the plump and bald-headed German steward, in white apron, the lid of one eye heavier than the other, serving us in his shirt sleeves, sometimes sucking his teeth with a noticeable click when he knew a dish deserved our approval. You kept the soup in the plate by holding it off the table and watching its tides. When her stern sailed up, and the screw raced, the glass shade of the lamp, being a misfit, took our eyes to watch the coming smash; the soup then poured over you, and trying to push your chair back from the mess, you found the chair was a fixture on the floor. This last fact was never remembered. I should try to push my "Capella" chair back now, if I were sitting in it.

The Doctor, who had been long enough tinkering careless bodies to have grown a little worn and grizzled, was often removed from us by a faint but impervious hauteur, though maybe he was only a little better and differently dressed. He was a patient listener, but his eyes could be droll. The Doctor's chuckle, escaping from his thoughts while he was unguarded, would sometimes make the captain look up from a narrative with question and a trace of resentment in his glance. The captain was a great traveller, but he was puzzled to find the memory of our surgeon following him to the most remote and unfamiliar strands. "Now how did that fellow come to be at a place like that?" the captain would whisper to me afterwards. "Can't make him out. Who is he?" The surgeon had a bottomless fund of short stories, to which he would sometimes go about the time when we were pushing away the banana skins and nutshells. He had an elisive and stimulating method with them. He knew his work. At the end of one the captain would explain the fun to the seriously interested mate (who had leaned forward to learn), placing spoons and crumbs to demonstrate the main points. Then the mate, too, would join us with his happy laugh. The late and giddy laughter of the mate, when he also arrived, became a welcome feature of a yarn by the surgeon. We expected it. The mate's own stories were usually bawdy; he always prefaced them with some unmanageable hilarity, which impeded his start.

MATE (*pushing over his plate for soup*). That big wave washed out the men's berths, sir.

CAPTAIN. Then is did some good. The dirty brutes.

MATE. Heard the men grumbling to-night. Said we'll never get the hawsers to run out with them bugs in the hawse pipes. Say the bugs don't belong to them, sir—ship's property.

DOCTOR. Any this end of the ship, captain? Good Lord!

CAPTAIN. Not a bug. And if there's any for'ard the men brought 'em. No bugs in my ship. Never saw one in my cabin.

MATE (*making a confused effort to master his emotion, not to spill his soup, and to be respectful*). Te-he! you will, sir, Te-he! (*Realises he may not laugh, but suffers internally.*)

CAPTAIN (*indicates an interrogation with frightful eyes and guttural noises*).

MATE (*controls himself by concentrating on a fork*). Well, sir—I'm just telling you—I heard it said the men annoyed with bugs—some of 'em said seein's believin'—said they had enough for everybody. (*His voice breaks into a stifled falsetto.*) So they emptied a match—match—they emptied a match box full down your ventilator this morning.

The captain would frequently keep his seat in the saloon after dinner till he had finished his cigar, and in the vein, would put a leg over the arm of his chair, which he had pushed back (his chair was cushioned, and was not a fixture), and frowning at his cigar, as if for defects, would voyage again his early seas. I suppose a sailor would call our skipper a hard case. He was an elderly man, tall, spare, and meagrely bearded. His eyes were set close into a knife-like nose, and they were opaque and bright, like two blue stones under a forehead which narrowed and tightened into a small shiny cranium. There were tufts of grey wool above his temples. No light came through his eyes to make them limpid, except when he was fondling Tinker, the dog. They shone from the surface, giving him a look of peering and intent suspicion. The skin of his face, neck and hands, now worked a little loose, was so steeped in the tincture of sunshine that it had preserved an unctious child-like quality. His dress and habits betrayed an appreciation of his own person. He kept his own medicines.

I guessed he would have a ruthless process in an emergency; he would identify the success and safety of the ship with his own. He laughed from his mouth only, throwing his head back, showing surprisingly perfect teeth, and laughter did not change the crystalline glitter of his eyes. There was something alien and startling in his merriment. As though his own mind were too cold for him at times he would seek out me, or the chief, to find warmth in an argument. He would irritate us into a disputation; and though he was a choleric man, quick at opposition, yet his vocabulary then was flinty and sparse. It stuck, and was delivered with pain. You could think of him labouring at his views of men and affairs with a creaking slate pencil. He set one's teeth. But he was a sailor, cautious and bold, with a knowledge of ships and the sea that was a mine to me. Let me say that, during the voyage, I found him busy making a canvas cot. He sat on the poop and worked there, bent and patient as a seamstress, for days. With a judgment made too readily I believed he was, naturally, making it for his own comfort, against the heat of the river. When it was finished he was rolling up his ball of yarn, surveying his job, and he said, mumbling and shy, that the cot was for me.

The Skipper, on this day that our decks were swept, swore about the men and the bugs during dinner, muttered with foreboding about the glass, which was still falling, and the coals, which were being burnt to no purpose. We were hardly doing more than holding our place on our course. The saloon was delirious, and when she flung up her heels, the varied noises rose with the racing propeller to a crescendo of furious castenets. The mate let us. The Skipper sat gloom-ing, eyeing his cigar resentfully, his leg over the arm of his chair. The Doctor was swaying with the ship, weary and forlorn. Tinker had an appeal in his eyes, and made timorous noises. The Purser wondered why he was there at all, and blamed his silly dreams. The night boomed without. What a night!

SKIPPER. If this southerly wind goes round to the west and north, look out. I saw porpoises today too.

DOCTOR. When are we due at Para?

SKIPPER. Huh! What's this talk of Para. You wait. All this talk about when we shall get there's no good. . . . Now in those Newfoundland schooners where I served my time—I wouldn't have no talk in them about getting anywhere. Seems as if somebody heard. You always run into it. There was the "Lizzie Polwith." She was about 80 tons. Those west country schooners in the fish trade are never more than 100 tons, else they'd have to carry more than a master and one mate. I was her master, and a kid of eighteen. We left Falmouth for Cadiz. Now look what happened. My mate was old Tregenna. He was a regular misery. I never knew such a dead homer, not so much as he was, always wanting to talk about his wife. I say, when you've cast off, it's best not to have a home. The ship wants all you can give her. Tregenna, he looked back a lot. You know what I mean. Couldn't keep his mind on his job, but wished he was through with it. There he'd be cutting bread at dinner, and it 'ud remind him, and he'd be wishing he was cutting it at home. When things began to go stiff, he'd say, "Who wouldn't sell his little farm to go to sea?" Used to figure out on paper how long we'd be before we'd be back. Why, you never know when you'll get back.

See what happened. We left Cadiz that year on the first of January, and got things just right. The winds chased us over. There were big following seas, but you know those schooners ride like ducks. Up and over they go. Never a drop did we ship. Though they're lively enough to bruise and sicken all but good sailors. And old Tregenna was rubbing his hands and making out his figures better and better.

We arrived off St Johns in a bit more than three weeks. I reckon I'd done it all right, being such a young chap too. Well, I was turning in that night and just as I got into the companion a man said. "There goes a lump of ice." I jumped out again. Why, there was ice all round us. The sea was full of it as far as I could see into the night. "This is all along of your figuring," I sang out to Tregenna. "But you'll have a lot of time to reckon it up afresh," I said.

So he had. Do you know when we got in? We got in on April 15. We were two months and a half getting in. And we came over in three weeks. There's something in that Jonah story. Always some fool who can't keep his mouth shut and his mind on his job.

We did have a time. Two and a half months, and our provisions ran out. We were living on a little meal and dried peas. The ice chafed the "Lizzie" till the rudder was worn down to the stock. It roughed up her wooden sides till they looked as if they were covered with long coarse hair. We were a sight when we got in. You wouldn't have known us, hardly. We looked as if we'd come up from the bottom. . . . Don't ask me when we shall get to Para. Wait till we're out of this. Listen to that dog. Shut up, you Tinker. Making that noise, sir! Go and lie down.

The Skipper clapped on his cap aggressively and went out. The Doctor had a long and eloquent silence. Then he turned to me. "This beats all," he said. "Come and have a drop of gin, old dear." He led the way to his berth, which smelt of varnish and of lamp, and we swayed in chorus as the ship rolled, and had a heartening mourn together. But for its accidental compensations travel would not be worth the trouble. In proof of that there is the entry in my diary some days after:

"December 22. Awoke at four a.m. with the ship rolling as brutally as ever. A great noise of waters and things banging. The seas huge at sunrise, when the light came over their tops. Depressing sight. The sky was blue at first, but was soon overcast with squalls. The horizon ahead gets slate coloured, and low clouds underneath, like ragged bales of dirty wool, come towards us heavy and fast. Then the squall and waves rush down on us express, and the ship buries herself. Constantly hearing engine-room bell sounded from bridge to slacken speed as a big sea appears. The captain popped in his head as I was deciding whether to get up or stay where I was. He gazed sternly at me and said he was looking for Jonah. I half believe he means it too. Everybody is weary of this. The men have been in oilskins since the start.

"Noon to-day, Lat. 42.6 N. Long. 11.10 W. Miles by engines since noon yesterday 222. Knots by revolutions 9.2. But the slip is 49.2 per cent. So actual distance 112 miles only, and knots 4.6. Bad going. Wind southly. Engines racing and engineer still at throttle.

"Night, and a full moon tearing past cloud openings. The ship occasionally shows like a pale ghost, the black shadows of the funnel guys and stanchions oscillating on the white paint-work as she rolls. I went into Chief's cabin, and from its open door—for it was sensibly milder—looked out astern over the way we had come. Up and down this side and that, went the steamer, and the Great Bear, in a wind clear patch of sky, was dancing on our wake. Polaris was making eccentric orbits round the main masthead light. Then the Skipper came in. He sat gazing astern. The look of his face was enough. It was quite plain he would like to be offended to-night, and attack anybody about anything. Presently he started intently as he looked astern, and jumped from his seat crying the ultimate anathema on the chap at the wheel;

and ran out. The Chief glanced astern and laughed. 'The old man comes in here because it's uncommon handy for watching the wake. Look at it. Somebody on the bridge writing letters on the ocean. Thinking of his sweetheart, and her name is Sue.' We gave the Skipper's voice time to reach the wheelhouse, and then saw the wake visibly tauten out.

"I went aft, balancing like a man learning the tight rope, along the trestle bridge. The moon was still falling precipitously through the broken sky, and areas of the great seas, where the sweeping searchlight of the moon showed monsters shaping and slowly vanishing, were frightful. There were sudden expansions of vivid green lightnings in the north and east. I found the Doctor in the chief mate's cabin. I sang some songs in a riving minor, accompanied by the mate on an accordion, for the doctor's amusement, and discovered why sailors always use the accordion, previously a mystery to me. It has a sad and reflective note, suited to men with memories when alone on the ocean. It ought to fit Celtic bards better than the harp. It has a fine expiring moan. The mate gave an imitation of a dying man with it.

"To bed at 11. Tried to read Henry James. My cockroach came out to wave his derisive hands at me. No wonder. The light was very bad, and I was pitched from side to side of the bunk. Nearly thrown out once. I might just as well have attempted to read the Bhagavad-Gita in the original. So I read the last letters from home instead and then fell asleep as a little child."

There was something of leisure in her movements next morning. I felt sure the glass must be rising at last. The air felt lighter and more expansive. A peep through the port showed me the ceiling had gone up considerably in the night. There was little wind, for the waves, though as great as ever, had lost their white ridges. Their summits were rounded and smooth. We were running south out of it, though the residue of the dreary northern seas was still washing about the decks. It was December yesterday, but April to-day. The engineers' mess-room boy, with bare fat arms, went by the cabin, singing.

At breakfast we heard that Chips, who had retired to his bunk for some days past to mend a leg damaged when the hatches were in danger, had met with a more serious misfortune. We fell into a mood of silent and respectful compassion. There was nothing to be said. Chips had lost his Victoria Cross. He was an old hero in trouble. The few of us who were British there—true, most of us were Germans, Dutchmen, Scandinavians, and Portuguese—felt we represented The Country. Chips limped about the forecastle with reproach in his face, and we felt we were petty in noticing his face was also dirty, though it certainly was difficult to avoid seeing that too, perhaps because, and this can be said for us, the dirt was of longer standing than the reproach. Then again it is common knowledge that Chips sleeps in straw, having no mattress.

Chips' story we knew. It had been whispered about the ship. He was at the Siege of Alexandria, and a shell fell near a group of men on his ship. Chips picked it up and dropped it overboard before the fuse was finished. The Doctor and I felt especially responsible, for a reason I cannot easily explain, it is so vague, and we told Chips we would help him in his search for his lost treasure. This took us to Chips' sea-chest, and amid a group of mask-like faces—for how could foreigners guess what this mattered to us?—we hunted carefully for Chips his aureole. We found—but I suppose even Victoria Cross heroes must dirty their socks. There were other things also. Yet it was out of one of these very other things, which were, I think, shirts, that there dropped, when the Doctor picked up the garment, a little package wrapped in newspaper. Chips, from his berth, gave a cry of joy. The Doctor and I, smiling too, looked upon the old man feeling that we had acted for you all. Chips, secretive with his sacrosanct emblem, was putting the little packet under his coverlet, when a low foreign sailor snatched it from him. The Cross fell to the deck. I recovered it from the feet instantly in a white passion, and chanced to look at it. It confirmed that one, who is named Chips here, was something in the Royal and Ancient Order of Buffaloes.

Coming back from the fo'castle, suddenly I felt as the man

of the suburbs does when, bowed with months of black winter and work in a city alley, he is, without any warning, transfigured on his own doorstep one morning. There as before is his familiar shrub, dripping with rain. Yet is it as before? It points a black finger at him. But the finger has a polished green nail.

He is translated. His ears are opened, and there comes for the first time that year the silver whistle of the starlings. A touch of South is in the air. His burden falls.

The cloudy sky was not grey now, but pearly, for it was translucent to the sun. More than day had come; life was born. There was ichor in the day. They were not dark northern waves that baffled us, but we were shoved and rocked by the send of a long nacreous ocean swell, firm but kind, from the south-west. The iron ship which had been repulsive to the touch, for its face had been glassy and cold, was now drying a warm rust red, like earth of Devon in spring, and was responsive. You could rest against its iron body and feel yourself grow. I saw the Chief outside his cabin in his shirt sleeves, gazing overseas between the stanchions of the boat deck, smoking in the evident luxury of full comfort and release. Involuntarily, he danced the two-step as she rolled. "Got anything to read?" he asked.

Now that reminded me. We have no library, of course, but we have a circulation of books on board. There are no common shelves; but the book you left thoughtlessly on the skylight five minutes ago, while you went to find some matches, is gone when you return. And you, if you see a book lying open and unprotected in a cabin, glance round warily, dash in, and take it; very often only to discover to your bitter disappointment that it is one of your own, and not an adventurous and unread stranger. The Chief's question reminded me that the day we left Swansea a lady (and a friend of poor Jack, the public is well aware) sent us a bale of literature. We blessed her when we saw its bulk, looking at it as oxen might look at a truss of hay, for that was its size and shape. Though it proved to be shavings and a cruel blow to the animals, as you shall hear.

Here was the very day to get at that bale, and impatiently

I rolled it into the open. It was trussed with great care, so I tore away a corner of the wrappings, dived in a hand, and hauled out a copy of "Joy Bells for Young Christians," the November number of 1899.

Well. Anyhow, it was a clean copy, and I put it by as the portion of our baldheaded German steward.

This disappointment made me pause, though. Here was going to be a long job for the Purser, sorting out this. Supposing there were anything nutritious in the bale I did not mind the labour of the unpacking and the distribution; but if the bulk of the consignment was hailed, so to speak, by "Joy Bells," then it would be better to call a deck hand and get the package overside before the ship was littered with too much of this joy. A Brazilian stoker, as he passed, saw me standing in thought, and I suppose imagined—for he could not ask—that I wanted to cut the string, but had no knife. Before I could stop him, he, smiling a knowing and friendly smile, whipped out a blade from his rear; and at once we stood ankle-deep in literature. There was a landslide near me of Infant Methodists (dates unknown) and I gave the Brazilian an armful for his kindness.

Our dear unknown friend at Swansea, with her eye on our sailor-like but yet immortal souls, had heard, no doubt, at the annual meeting of the Society for the Succor of Seamen, at Caxton Hall, Westminster (held on the 29th of every February), what simple and barbarous and yet, in the main, considering our origins and circumstances, what worthy fellows we were. But she was not told at the meeting that the wealthy shipowners, subscribers to the society, and whose presence there made Caxton Hall seem nautical, have a way of signing on crews at continental ports because wages rule lower there; and that consequently not one of our men was moved by Christian English, but only by mates English, and then not so very quickly. The officers and engineers were English, and there the sailors' friend was right in her surmise; but I do not see how she could have done more to put in awful jeopardy the soul of our wise and spectacled chief engineer, for instance, than by approaching him with a winning and philanthropic smile, under the impulse to do him good with a statement of her religion in words of one syllable. He would have met her politely, I know; but after she had gone——

Let her try to imagine her own feelings if our Chief, uninvited and blankly unmindful, invaded the exclusive inner circle of Swansea society, and approached her in the midst of her own with the childish notion of instructing her in the first principles of his pronounced Pyrrhonism; or say he went to her as a colporteur of the Society for Instructing the Intelligence and Manners of Leisured Folk. But I must say for our chief that this cannot be even supposed. He would never offer the lowliest being such an indignity.

We pulled and dragged at the escaped mass of periodicals, looking for something good, but found no pearls had been cast before us. There were parish magazines and temperance monthlies, there were religious almanacs for the years we have lost; by some sporting chance there were even a few back numbers of the "Monumental Mason." It is plain the latter could be considered an added grievance, even though they were put in as a kindly reminder of our narrow lease here. It was an aggravation of the original offence to sailors who, when their short term here closes, have to make shift with some fire-bars at their heels. What is Aberdeen granite and indelible gold lettering to such men but a hint of the hardships which follow them even beyond the end?

So overboard went the lot—I may as well tell the whole truth, overboard also went the evangelical hymn books, new though they were. I will only suppress the advice cried to the gulls astern as the literature went floating and flying in their direction. We had to rely for our reading on what had been brought aboard by our crowd, a collection which gradually revealed itself in single books and magazines.

There was, for example, the "Morphology of the Crypto-gamia," an exhaustive work which gave me much pleasure in wondering how it got aboard at all. The chief mate used it as a wedge between his open door and the bulkhead, to prevent the miserable knocking as the ship lolled about. He would not lend me that book, because it jammed into the opening nicely; but I borrowed from him "Three Fingered

Jack, the Terror of the Antilles," and I made him a complete gift in return of "Robert Elsmere" which I found marooned on a bunker hatch as I came along. There you see the delightful chance and hazardous character of our literature.

I prided myself on the select reading I had brought aboard with me. But what devilish black art the sea air worked on those choice volumes, however, I cannot explain. I have no means of knowing. But there they are, their covers bitten by cockroaches, and the words inside bleached and sterilised of all meaning. There they will stop; Henry James, too. For what is the use of him when big seas are running? He would be a magician indeed who could capture our minds then. You get the right amplitude of leisure and the flat undistracting circumstances he demands, the emptiness and the immobility necessary, when you are waiting for cargo long in coming at a low seaboard. I suppose we want the representation of life only when we are not very much alive. In heavy weather there is no doubt old newspapers make the best reading, especially if they have good bold advertisements. For I know it requires the same courage and concentration needed ashore for reading Another Great Speech by the Premier; indeed, the steel blue quality of deadly resolution used only by men of letters who write biographies and spin literary causeries, to manage even novels when great billows are moving. The mind is inclined to absent itself then. Then it is you put all reading aside with a promise of a long and leisurely festival of books when the ship is steaming uniformly down the unvarying "trades."

But when you get near the neighbourhood of the constant sun, during the day you fall asleep over "Three Fingered Jack" and the old magazines which you had on your knees while musing on the colours of the sea and the mounting architecture of the clouds; and beyond sundown listen to the mate's accordion or the engineer's flute. Perhaps, moved by the hu-s-s-h of the waves, the silky and purple dark, and the loneliness of your little company under the mid-ocean stars, tentatively (though your shipmates are very forgiving) lift a ballad yourself; for something is expected of you, and singing seems right.

Of all the books aboard the "Capella" I got most out of the Skipper's sailing directories and his charts. Talk of romance! There was that chart-room under the bridge, across its open doors on either side creaming waves going by in the moonlight, and the steamer inclining each side alternately, and the shadows of the rigging sliding back and forth on the pale deck. You cannot know what romance is till you are in seas you have never sailed before, where the marks will be few when landfall comes; that ocean where the Skipper is to find his own way by his lore of the sea, and may even ask your opinion about alternatives; and there read sailing directories. The romance of these books cannot be translated or quoted. It would leave them, as though a glimmer went out, if you attempted to take them from that chart-room where pendant things are swaying leisurely, where you can hear the bells tell the watches, and the skipper's gold-laced cap is on the mahogany table. The South Atlantic Sailing Directions, our own guide, is fine, especially when it gets down to the uninhabited islands in far southern latitudes. I do not think this noble volume is included in the best hundred books, but I know it can release the mind from the body.

But what's this talk of landfalls? as the old man would say. There will be no landfall yet for us; and this is Christmas Eve. I knew it was an auspicious occasion of some kind, for the steward just went aft with two big plum cakes cuddled in his apron. That made me look at the calendar. We are now 800 miles out, and the steamer has reached six knots. This was the best night we had yet found. The steamer was on an even keel, with but occasional spasms of sharp rolling, for there was no sea, but only old ocean breathing deeply and regularly in its sleep, and sometimes making a slight movement. The light of the full moon was the shining ghost of noon. The steamer was distinct but immaterial, saliently accentuated, as a phantom. A deep shadow would have detached the forecastle head but for a length of luminous bulwark which still held it, and some quiet voices of men who were within the shadow, yarning. The line of bulwark and the murmuring voices held us together. The prow as it dipped sank into drifts of lambent snow. The snow fled by the steamer's sides, melting and musical. Two engineers off duty leaned on the rails amidships, smoking, looking into the vacancy in which the moonlight laid a floor of troubled silver. As if drawn by its light a few little clouds were poised near the moon, grouped round the bright heart of the night. There was the moon and its small company of clouds, and ourselves below in our own defined allotment of sea. The only thing outside and far was Sirius, burning independently in the east, looking unwinking through the wall of night into our world.

On such a night and with Christmas morning but sixty minutes away it would have been wasting life to go to bed. I glanced expectantly at the door of the Chief's cabin, and saw indeed it was open, a yellow rectangle within which was the profile of the Chief beneath his lamp, talking to somebody. The Doctor was there, and he made room for me on the settee. Then the captain joined us, and I perched myself on the wash-stand.

"Well, we can undress to-night when we turn in," said the Chief. (None of us had, so far.) In a long silence which filled the cabin with tobacco smoke I could hear the engines below uplifted in confident song.

"Now they're walking round," said the Skipper, nodding his head. "Now she feels it."

When we met thus, between the hours of nine and midnight, as was our irregular habit, the talk first was always desultory, and about our own ship and our own circumstances, for the concerns of our little world strangely occupied our minds, as you would think, and the large affairs of that great world we had left, of which we heard now no sound nor rumour, had lessened in the mind, faded and vanished, all the huge consequence and loud clangour of it, so that now there was an empty horizon astern, and nothing between us and that void but a few gulls, like small and pursuing recollections. Our little microcosm, afloat and sundered in the wastes, was occupied in its own polity. We talked of the carpenter's bad leg; complained of the cook's bread; heard that Tinker the dog, being young, had the habit at night, while honest folk slept, of eating the saloon mats; grumbled that the ship's tobacco was mouldy. The deck was getting dry, the Skipper said, and now we could get the men chipping it, and then it could be tarred.

"That donkeyman," said the Skipper, "that man wastes the fresh water. I'll have a lock put on the pump handle. He works it as if we were laid on to the main. I spoke to him about it this morning." The fresh water is a vital affair with us. We may not drink the water of the country to which we are bound, so eighty tons of Welsh mountain spring is in our cleansed and whitewashed tanks. Woe to the man caught overflowing his can, if an officer sees him. "The handle can't be locked," said the Chief, "because its next to the galley. The cook wants it all day long."

"Well, let me catch anyone wasting it. We'd look all right with a lot of dysentery, drinking that river water out there."

This common meeting-place of ours, the Chief's cabin, is on a highway of the ship, being on the direct route from the poop to the bridge, and so it is a hostel, for the chief is a kindly and popular man, big and robust in body and mind; though he has a knack, at odd and unexpected times, of being candid in a way that shocks, treading on corns without ruth, the skipper's particularly, when their two departments are at a difference.

This cabin was one which I always visited first, for, especially in the morning when other folk had not rubbed the night out of their eyes, and so looked darkly upon their fellows, my friend the Chief had the early eye of a child and the soaring spirit of the lark. I never met him when he had got out of bed on the wrong side. His cabin became a refuge to me, for, unlike the Doctor's and my own place (we both were birds of passage, therefore our cabins were cold and stark), the Chief's was comfortable with settled furniture, cosy and habitable, like a fixed home. There was a wicker chair, with cushions, and a writing-desk where the engineer's log lay handy and bearing some plug tobacco, freshly cut, on its cover, and a pipe rack above the desk carrying a most foul assortment waiting their turns again for favour. Portraits of the Chief's family were on the walls, smiling boys and girls, with their mother in a chief place, looking upon daddy by proxy. There was a book-shelf bearing some engineering manuals, a few novels and magazines, a tape measure, some gauge glasses, some tin whistles, a flute, and a palm leaf fan. Above the wash-stand was a rack with glasses and a carafe. A settee ran along one side, and his bunk upon the other side. There we sat on Christmas Eve, while the wicker chair bent and complained with the Skipper's weight as he swayed to the leisurely rocking of the ship. The tobacco smoke floated in coils and blue smears in the room. A bottle of Hollands rested for security on the bed, and we held our glasses on our knees.

The pallid and puffy face of the steward, a very honest man secretly free with his small store of apples on my account because I am green and my palate not yet used to the flatness of tinned provisions, looked in on us from the right. "Vhere is der dog, sir? I haf not seen der dog." "Must be about," we cried. "We had seen him," we said "nosing about the poop for rats, or asleep on the saloon mat, or padding round the casing looking for friends." "But no, I haf looked. He is not found. Vhere is der dog?" A hole in our little community, it was apparent from our intent looks, could not be thought of with equanimity. Tinker's importance became quite large. The second engineer passed the door, caught the drift of our anxious converse, and turned to say the dog was then asleep in his room. "Ach! zat is all right." We struck matches for our pipes again.

"That dog, I shouldn't like to lose him," said the skipper, stroking his beard. "There's no luck in that. I shot a dog once on a ship; and the first we ran into a blow and lost a lot of gear, and then the mate got his hand smashed, and then everything got cross-grained till I'd have paid, ah, fifty pounds to have had the brute back again, and an ugly customer he was. Ah, you can smile, Doctor, but there it is. I'm not superstitious and never was. But you can't tell me. Look at the things that happen. When I was a youngster, my ship was off Rio, and I dreamt my father was dead. I took my bearings and the time. I dreamed my father died in a red brick house with a laylock tree by the door and that tree was in blossom plain enough to smell. I didn't know the house. There was a path of clean red bricks leading up to the porch, through a garden. I didn't see my father. But you know what dreams are like—no sense in them—there the house was and not a soul in sight. I knew he was dying inside it.

"How do you account for that? Have you got it down in your books? I lay you haven't. I forgot all about that dream. Long after I was at Cape Town and met my brother. That reminded me. After a bit I said to him, 'Father's dead.' 'Yes,' he said, 'but how did you know?' and I told him. 'Yes,' he said, 'it was like that. A place he was staying at in Essex. But how did you know?' I didn't tell him. What's the good? He wouldn't have believed it. People don't."

All through the anxious time when we were being soused and buffeted I noticed how our company, every man of them, even the Pyrrhonist, saw omens in all the chance variety of the vast menace under the frown of which we huddled in our iron box; porpoises alongside; one of mother Cary's dark brood accompanying us, glancing about the vagaries of the flowing hills with swift precision; the form of a cloud; a loom far out, as though day were there at least. The fall of a portrait in the Chief's room once set him wondering and melancholy. Again, when the dog whined and moped, the Skipper eyed the animal narrowly, as though the creature had prescience but could tell us what it knew only by drooping and quivering its hind quarters. You might have thought that Fate, dumb and cruel, but a little relenting for something inevitably to come to our mishap, were trying to stretch a point, and so induced the Skipper to put his shirt on inside out one morning, after dreaming he saw drowned rats, in case the horse were not too blind to see both the nod and the wink.

The Sphinx makes subtle dumb motions, as it were, when closely regarded. I do not wonder if it does. Sometimes in those dark days I thought I got a hint or two. I cannot tell you what they were. The weather grew brighter afterwards and I forgot them. From our narrow and weltering security, where the wind searched through us like the judgment eye, I know, looking out upon the wilderness in turmoil where was no help, and no witness of our undoing, where the gleams were fleeting as though the very day were riven and tumbling, that I saw the filmy shapes of those things which darken the minds of primitives. While the sky is changeful, and there are storms at sea when our fellows are absent, and mischance and death are veiled but here, we shall have gods and ghosts. The sharp-sighted collectors of old brain-lumber and such curios may still keep busy, and tie up their dry bundles of mythology and religions; but I myself could make plenty more.

So it was my shipmates' yarns were most of the dire kind, with some dim warning precedent. I do not recall a story that was gay, except those of the wanton sort. They were of close calls and of women, as, I suppose, have been those of all hard livers, from the cave men on.

Eight bells were rung on the bridge, and like a faint echo in a higher pitch, answered from the fo'castle. Christmas morning! By my pocket compass we toasted the folk at home. We had heard a good many stories of wreck this night, and the Chief was now at his contribution to the unseasonable memories. ("I've had enough of it. Here goes," said the Doctor; and he went.) "Don't leave us. It lets in the draught. Well, the compliments to you. This typhoon—I had had four others—but this one made me think it was good-bye. She was a small steamer, that 'Samuel Plimsoll,' and old, but well-behaved. But her light nearly went out in that blow. It was that dark you could find nothing but the noise, and we were just the same as a chunk of wood under a waterfall, because the Lord knows how many feet of water were in the engine-room, for she was rolling so. Her fires were out. She had a list of 22 degrees to port. She simply lay in it, and it went over her. Every time she rolled over on the deep side, thinks I, this is the last of her. All this, mind you, went on for two days, and the skipper was in the chart-room, waiting. I've found that when the danger is not much you get excited, but when there seems no chance you get cool and cunning and try to make one. One time I thought she seemed easier, and I was able to get the donkey engine going. I felt better as soon as I heard the steam, even though it was only in the donkey. Thinks I, there's power, and it's mine—a canful of steam to a typhoon. It was a chance to laugh at. Then I took the other engineers with me and we went below. The water there, full of cinders and trash, pouring through the gear as she turned from side to side, made it look a pretty poor show. You see, the donkey wouldn't work the pumps, for the coal and muck was sucked in. So I took a basket and got into the tank, holding the basket under the pump. The water was up to my neck, and every time she rolled I was ducked. But the dodge worked, and that list of hers to port was a bit of luck in its way, for it helped us to get the starboard boiler going. When I saw the throws moving, and the wash angry when it splashed on the hot metal, I said, 'So much for your old typhoon.' We were not counted out then. We crawled under the lee of an island, and lay for four days repairing her. The funny thing was when we got to Hong Kong the papers were full of our loss. ' "Samuel Plimsoll" lost with all hands.' It was funny to see a bill like that. I met the placard as it came running round a corner, and it made me stand and shuffle my feet on the ground to see if the earth was all right. I knew the editor of that paper, and I was then going up to give him something good. And here he was making money out of us like that. He stood at the door of his office and saw me coming. I went up laughing, waving his paper in my hand. He looked quite surprised. His mouth was wide open. 'You're a nice sort of chap,' I said."

Christmas Day. In case it has become necessary for me to show again the symbols of verity, as this is a book of travel, here they are: "Lat. 37.2 N., long. 14.14 W. Light wind and moderate swell from S.W. Vessel rolling heavily at intervals. 961 miles out. Miles by engines 226. Actual distance travelled (because of the swell on our star-board bow) 197 miles." I cannot see that these particulars do more than help me out with the book, but as they have been considered essential in narratives of voyaging, here they are, and much good may they do anybody. Thoreau, in one of his quaintly superior moods when speaking of travel, said, "It is not worth while going round the world to count the cats in Zanzibar." In nearly every book of travel this is proved to be true. They show it was not worth the while, seeing it was either to shoot cats or to count degrees of latitude. (As for me, I have no reason whatever for being at sea.) Consider Arctic travel. I have read long rows of books on that, but recall few emotional moments. The finest passage in any book of Arctic travel is in Warburton Pikes' "Barren Grounds," where he quotes what the Indian said to the missionary who had been speaking of heaven. The Indian asked, "And is it like the land of the Musk-ox in summer, when the mist is on the lakes, and the loon cries very often?"

You feel at once that the country the Indian saw around him would be easily missed by us, even when in the midst of it. For taking the bearings of such a land, the sextant, and the miles already travelled, would not be factors to help much. Now the Indian knew nothing of artificial horizons and the aids to discovering where they are which strangers use. But in summer the mists of his lakes were but the vapour of his musings, the penumbra of the unfathomed deeps of his mind whereon he paddled his own canoe; and when the wild-fowl called, it was his memory heard; it was his thought become vocal then while he dreamed on. I myself learned that the treasures found in travel, the chance rewards of travel which make it worth while, cannot be accounted beforehand, and seldom are matters a listener would care to hear about afterwards; for they have no substance. They are no matter. They are untranslatable from their time and place; and like the man who unwittingly lies down to sleep on the tumulus where the little people dance on midsummer night, and dreams that in the place where man has never been his pockets were filled with Fairy gold, waking to find pebbles there instead, so the traveller cannot prove the dreams he had, showing us only pebbles when he tries. Such fair things cannot be taken from the magic moment. They are but filmy, high in the ceiling of your thoughts then, rosy and sunlit by the chance of the light, transitory, melting as you watch. You come down to your lead again. These occasions are not on your itinerary. They are like the Indian's lakes in summer. They have no names. They cannot be found on the best maps. Not you nor any other will ever discover them again. Nor do they fill the hunger which sent you travelling; they are not provender for notebooks. They do not come to accord with your mood, but they come unaware to compel, and it is your own adverse and darkling atoms that are changed, at once dancing in accord with the rare incidence of that unreasonable and transcendent moment of your world, the rhythm of which you feel, as you would the beat of drums.

And what are these things?—but how can we tell? A strip of coral beach, as once I saw it, which was as all other coral beaches; but the ship passed close in, and by favour of the hour and the sun this strand did not glare, but was resplendent, and the colours of the sea, green, gold, and purple, were not its common virtues, but the emotional and passing attar of those hues. There was the long, slow labouring of our burdened tramp in the Atlantic storm. Or one April, and a wild cherry-tree in blossom by an English hedge, a white cloud tinctured with rose, and in it moving a dozen tropical chaffinches; the petals were on the grass.

And now, this is Christmas morning. I am in the Chief's bunk, and he still sleeps on the settee. We fell asleep where we lay yarning on our backs after midnight. I wake at the right moment, opening my eyes with the serene and secure conviction that things are very well. The slow rocking of the ship is perfect rest. There is no sound but the faint tap-tap of something loose on the desk and responding to the ship's movements. The cabin is strangely illuminated to its deepest corner by an extraordinary light, as though the intense glow of a rare dawn had penetrated even our ironwork. On the white top of the cabin a bright moon quivers about, the shine from live waters sent up through the round of our port. When we lean over, the port shows first the roof of the alleyway dappled with bright reflections; then a circle of sky, which the horizon soon halves; and then the dazzling white and blue of the near waves; we reverse.

This is life. This is what I have come for. I do not repose merely in a bunk. I am prone and easy in the deepest assurance of good. This conviction has penetrated even the unconsciousness of the Chief; he snores in profound luxury.

If in a ship you are brought sometimes too cruelly close to the scrutiny of the terms of your narrow tenure, expecting momentarily to see the document torn across by invisible fingers, yet nowhere else do you feel those terms to be so suddenly expanded in the sun. And nowhere else is got such release, secure and absolute, from the nudging of insistent trifles. There is nothing between your eyes and the confines of your own place. Empty day is all round. In the entire circle there is not the farthest impertinent interruption— through all the degrees there is not one fool standing in the light; and you yourself are on nobody's horizon. No history stains that place. There is not a black doubt anywhere. It is the first day again, and no need yet for a rubbish heap.

Yet when, singing to myself, I went outside to matins, I found Sandy our third engineer with the toothache. So much of truth is got from being a gymnosophist and regarding your own toes with aloof abstraction on a sunny Christmas morning. I became Sandy's courage for him instead, took his arm firmly, and led him aft to the doctor. We would start a rubbish heap for a pristine world with a decayed tooth. Something to be going on with.

Seeing we were almost off Madeira we had some amount of right to the July sun under which we had run. For the first time since the Mumbles our decks were quite dry, and cherry red with rust. There were glittering crusts of salt in odd places. At eight bells (midday) the captain ordered a general holiday, except for the routine duties; and the donkey-man appeared to startle us as the apparition of a stranger on the ship, for he had a clean face, though his eyes still were dark and spectral, and he wore a suit of new dungarees, stiff and creased from a paper parcel, but just opened, out of a Swansea slop shop. His mates were some seconds realising him. Then they made derisive signs, and the boldest some ribald cries. I thought their resentment was really aroused by Donkey's new shirt; it was that touch which pushed matters too far, and made him unfriendly. He saw this himself. Soon he changed the new shirt for one that had been rendered neutral in the stoke-hold and the bucket.

There was something neutral, like Donkey's old shirt,

about most of our crowd. Each one of the mob which gathered with mess kits a little before midday about the galley door seemed reduced, was faded in a noticeable measure from the sharp and strong pattern of a man. Their conversation about the galley was always in subdued mutterings, not direct, but out of the mouth corners, sideways. Their only independence was in the negligence of their attitudes. They might have been keeping in mind an austere and invisible presence, whose swift words from nowhere might at any time cleave their soft babble. If I made to pass through them the babble ceased, and from limp poses they sprang upright in the narrow way to let me pass, their eyes cast down. A man who had not seen me coming, but still sprawled on the rail, talking quietly, would be nudged by his neighbour. It struck me this attitude would change when they knew us better; but it never did. These deckhands and firemen were mostly youngsters, steadied by a few older hands. Chips and Donkey were the veterans. In that crowd the boatswain was the admirable figure. He was a young Britisher, tall, upright, and weighty, with a smiling, respectful eye in which sometimes, I thought, there was a faint hint of mockery. He had an easy balance and confidence in his movements which made him worth watching when about his business. Clean shaven when he came aboard, he now had a tawny beard which caught gold lights, and it was singularly good on his weather-darkened face. He seldom wore a cap, for it could have added little protection to the taut vigour of his hair, and would have spoilt, as perhaps he himself guessed, that proper flourish and climax to the poise of his head.

Donkey was an Irishman, and he was the huge frame of what, maybe thirty years before, had been a powerful man. This morning his big cadaverous face, white only on the bony ridges surrounding the depressions of the temples, the cheeks, and the dark pits of the eyes, and with the shadowy hollow of the mouth which gaped through the weight of the massive jaw, would have resembled, from a little distance, that of the skeleton head of one of the monsters in a geological gallery, but for the dewlap sustained by sinews running from his chin down his throat. Donkey was a silent man, and never caught your glance as you passed him, but lumbered along with so much of the surprising celerity of a gaunt elephant that you thought you might hear the rasp of his loose clothes. He was a simple and docile fellow. I never heard him speak, but he used to come to the Chief, fill the door with his massive front, his small eyes which expressed nothing and were but sparks of life, looking nowhere in particular, and making guttural sounds; and the Chief, being used to him, understood. At sea Donkey did his small duties like a plain but cumbersome mechanism that had some-where in it an obscure point of rationality. When ashore, though, he was said to go mad, and to roll trampling and trumpeting through the squalid littoral of the world; being brought aboard afterwards an enormity of lax bones and flesh, with the cogitating glim in his bulk quite doused.

Of the others, there was a Teutonic bunch of lads, deck-hands, which I never succeeded in segregating, they looked so much alike. They had pimpled, idle faces, and neutral eyes, cast down when they sidled by one, thin down on their chins, and grimy raiment which, by the look of it, was an integument never cast after we left port. One name would have covered that lot, and frequently I heard the mates use it. But Olsen, the Norwegian with a blond moustache which covered his mouth like a fog-protector, and stern blue eyes, was a sailor. The firemen made a better bunch. There was among them a swarthy Brazilian, whose constant smile seemed ever on the point of breaking into song, but that he was always chewing the end of a sweat rag he wore twisted round his neck. The happy feature of our firemen was a Dutchman, whose hollow face was full of silent woe and endurance. He was our chief joy. When once we found the sun, he then appeared in a single garment, trousers and braces cut in one piece of brown canvas, hauled up well under his arms, leaving his slab feet remote and forlorn. His torso was bare, a dancing girl in red and blue tattooed on his chest. He wore a bowler hat without a brim.

We will get Christmas over. It was a pagan festival, Looking back at it, I see—with the astonishment of the sedate who is native to a geometrical suburb where the morning train follows the night and every numbered house shelters a moral agnostic—I see a dancing baccanal with free gestures who fades, as I look back intently, doubting my senses, in a roseous haze. The lawless movements of that wild, bright and laughing figure, its exultant blasphemy, its confident mockery, are remembered by me as though once I had been admitted to the green room of heaven. Surely I have seen a god whose deathless knowledge derides the solemn gods, behind the curtain. It was Christmas night, and our little "Capella," our point of night shine, a star moving through the void to its dark destiny, filled the vault with its song, while its fellows in the heavens stood round. Christmas is over.

The day following was Sunday, a grey day of penance, the men soberly washing their shirts in buckets under the forecastle head, smoking moody pipes. The garments were tied to any convenient gear where they could hang free. The sky was leaden. This grey day was distinguished by the strange phenomenon of an horizon which was almost level; the skyline and the clouds did not slant first this way, then that. The swell had almost gone. Already I began to feel the large patience and tranquillity of a mind losing its shadows, and contemplating the light and space of a long voyage in which the same men do the same things in the same place daily under the centre of the empty sky. Sitting on a hatch with the Doctor, smoking, we confessed, with ease at the heart, and with minds in which nervous vibrations had ceased, that we must have reached the place that was nowhere, and that now time was not for us. We had escaped you all. We were free. There was not anything to engage us. There was nothing to do, and nobody who wanted us. Never before had I felt so still and conscious of myself. I realised, with a little start of surprise, that it was Me who felt the warm air, and who looked at the slow pulse of the waters, and the fulgent breaks in the roof, and heard the droning of the wake, and not that mere skin, eyes and ears which, as in London, break in upon our preoccupied minds with agitating sensations; and I took in this newly-discovered world of ocean and cloudland and my own sure identity centred therein with the complacency of an immortal who will see all the things which do not matter pass away. When we left England we were tense, and sometimes white (though there were others who went red) about a Great Crisis in our Country's History. The Doctor and I arrived on board, detached from the opposing armies in the impending conflict, and at first put our hands swiftly to our swords every ten minutes or so during meals. Of that crisis only one small gull now was left, and he was following us astern with a melancholy cry at intervals, of which we took no more notice. (And that gull departed, I see by my diary, the very next day.)

So ended the Great Crisis. I did not even note the ship's position at the time, though I can see now that was a serious fault for which future historians may blame me. I can but state vaguely that it was about sixty miles north-west of the Fortunate Isles. The change in the quality of the sun and air became most marked; I remember that. The horizon expanded to a surprising distance. According to letters from home, sent about that date, which I received long afterwards, I am unable to find that similar phenomena were witnessed in England. Probably they were but local. These manifestations in the heavens filled the few of us privileged to witness them with awe, and a new faith in the power and compassion of God. Nothing further of note occurred on this day, except that Chips, as a further miracle, suddenly was raised whole from where he lay in his bunk with a useless leg. His leg, you may remember, was damaged in the gale off Cornwall. The Doctor, going his rounds, was surprised to find Chips dancing the hoola-hoola in the forecastle, and a stoker, with a cut eye, wailing for a lost half bottle of gin taken from his box while he was on duty. Thereafter Chips returned to work, his leg becoming halt again only when he knew we saw him stepping it too blithely.

"*Decr.* 27. Distance run for past 24 hours to midday 219. Total distance 1177 miles. Fine weather. Glass rising."

Have you ever heard of the monotony of a long voyage?

The same sky you know, the same waters, the same deck; and now I can see it should be added, the same old self, dismayed by the contemplation of its features daily, week after week, within that spacious empty hall, where is no escape from the bright stare overhead which reveals your baldness and blemishes without ruth. You get found out. You want to mix with the mob again, to get lost in the sameness of your fellows. He who goes travelling should leave his self at home, or as much of it as is not wanted on the voyage. It is surprising to find how little you want of yourself. The ideal traveller would venture out merely as a disembodied thought, or, at most, as an eye.

A mere eye would see no monotony, for the sky may be the same sky, but its moods are like those of the same woman; and the ocean, though young as the morning, is older than Asia—you never know what to expect from that profound enigma. As for the sunny deck, I see the Doctor sitting on a spare spar, waiting for someone to sit beside him. The Chief is filing a piece of small gear outside his cabin. The Skipper is overlooking, with a hard frown, a group of men busy repairing his chart-room, which is just forward of the engine-room casing (I could get a job from him at once for the asking, though I shall not ask). The first mate is trying to be in three places at once. The second mate patrols the bridge. The German steward, who tells curious stories in a Teutonised dialect of Shadwell, is hanging mattresses and bed clothes over a boom. The men are chipping and tarring the deck; and the boatswain, bare-legged, wildly bearded, a sheath knife on his hams, looks like a fine pirate brought to menial tasks.

I have watched this day's monotonous sky onwards from the dawn. We are in the neighbourhood of the Hesperides. For some early hours of the morning it was grey. But the grey roof soon broke with the incumbent weight of light, letting sunshine through narrow fractures to the sea, far out. There were partitions of thin gold in the dim hall. The moving floor was patterned in day and night. The low ceiling was fused where the day poured through, became a candent vapour, volatilised. We had over us before breakfast the ultimate blue, where a few cirrus clouds showed its great height.

Then it was August. The sea ran in broad heavy mounds, blue-black and vitreous, which hardly moved our bulk. In the afternoon, the ocean, a short distance from the ship, grew filmed and opaque, a milky blue shot with purple shadows. Its surface, though heaving, was smooth and flawless. No light entered its deeps, but the radiant heat was mirrored on it as on the pallor of fluid lava. The water ploughed up by the bows did not break, but rolled over viscidly. The sun dropped behind the sea about a point west of our course. Night was near. Yet still the high dome with its circular floor the sea was magically illuminated, as by the proximity of a wonderful presence. We, solitary and privileged in the theatre, waited expectant. The doors of glory were somewhere ajar. The western wall was clear, shining and empty, enclosed by a proscenium of amber flames. In the north-east, astern of us, were some high fair-weather clouds, like a faint host of little cherubs, and from their superior galleries they watched a light invisible to us; it made their faces bright. Beneath them the glazed sea was coral pink. Even our own prosaic iron gear was sublimated; our ship became lustrous and strange. We were the Argonauts, and our world was bright with the veritable self-radiance of a world of romance where the things that would happen were undreamed of, and we watched for them from our argosy's side, calm and expectant; my fellows were transfigured, looked huge, were rosy and awful, immortals in that light no mortal is given to see.

Now had been given me fellowship with the ship and her men; we were one body. I had been absorbed by our enterprise. For a long while our steamer was a harsh and foreign thing to me, unfriendly to the eye, difficult to understand. But now she had become intelligible and proper. She and her men were all my world, and I could find my way about that world in the dark. Getting used to a ship has the process of the growth of a lasting friendship. Chance begins it. You regard your luck askance, as you accept a new acquaintance with no joy, to make the best of him. But presently, to put the matter at its lowest, you arrive at an understanding. You have learned your friend's worth. Familiarity would breed contempt only in the mouse-hearted. You never have to account him afresh, or he is no comrade; there can be no surprises again, no encounters with a stranger in him. His value, at the least reckoning, is that you know his value. Any hour of the day or night you can guess with assurance where his mind would be found. And here my "Capella" has no strange doors and startling declivities and traps for me any more. I know her. She is not exactly all she should be, but I apprehend exactly what she is. If I hurt myself against her it is my own fault. She is as familiar to me as home now. I should resent any alteration. Having learned to know her faults I like her as she is; the trestle bridge with its sagging hand-ropes and wobbling stanchions (look out, you, when she rolls) which crosses the main deck aft on the port side from the amidships section, where I live, to the poop, where the Doctor lives. The two little streets of three doors each, to port and starboard of her amidships, the doors that open out under the shade of the boat deck to sea. There, amidships also, are the Chief's room and the galley, the engineers' messroom, and the engine-room entrance; but these last do not open overside, but look aft, from a connecting alley which runs across the ship to joint the side alleyways. Forward of these cabins is the engine-room casing, where the 'midship deck broadens, but is cumbered with bunker hatches (mind your feet, at night, there); and beyond, again, is the chart-room, and over the chart-room the bridge and the wheel-house, from which is a sheer long drop to the main deck foreward. At the finish of that deck is an iron wall, with the entrance to the mysterious forecastle in its centre; and over that is the uplifted head of our world watching our course, a bleak wind-swept place of rails, cable chains, and windlass. The poop has a timber deck, and there in fine weather the deck chairs are. The poop is a place needing exact navigation at night. Long boxes enclosing the rudder chains are on either side of it. In the centre is the saloon skylight, the companion, the steward's ice chest, and the hand-steering gear. Also there are two boats. I gained my night knowledge of the poop deck by assault, and retained my gains with sticking plaster. I am really proud of the privilege which has been given me to roam now this rolling shadow at night, this little dark cloud blowing between the stars and the deep, the unseen abyss below us with its profound reverberations, and the height above with its scattered lights as remote as the sounds in the deeps. With calm faith in our swaying shadow I place my feet where nothing shows, sure that my angel will bear me up. I put out my hands and a support comes to them; the pitfalls have ladders for me, and by touching at some places in the black shadow, as by magic, a lighted and comfortable room at once materialises for my rest in the void.

I think I liked her better as a formless shadow after sundown. Whether it was then a noise in my head, my tranquil thoughts murmuring in their sleep, or whether the sound I heard was the deep humming of the world's speed, I don't know; whatever it was, it was the only sound. Our mainmasthead light was but a nearer star of the host. I was not surprised to see one of the stars so close. I was within the luminous porch of the Milky Way.

It was midnight. In that silence, where I was alone in space, adrift on a night cloud in the constellations, the stars were really my familiars; once, when in London, though they had been named to me and were constant there, they were far in the place to which one lifts one's eyes from the dust and traffic, nothing to do with London and with me. But now there was no more dust and traffic. I was among them at last. Splendid Orion was near and vast in his hunting. The Pleiades no longer dimmered on the very limit of vision, but were separate points of delicate light. The night moved with diamond fire.

I was so far absent from the body that a human voice beside me was like a surprising concussion with something invisible in space. Turning, there was the glow of Sandy's pipe. Sandy is an elderly man, and an engineer. He was leaning over the rail, cooling after his watch below. The magic of the star shine had got into his mind too. He began with guesses about the things which are not known, parrying doubt with, "Ah—but it's hard to say; there are things——"; and, "you bright young fellers don't know everything"; and "somebody told me a queer thing now."

"There was a bright young feller, same as yourself, and he was first mate of the 'Abertawe,' out of Cardiff. Jack Driscoll was his name. It was a funny thing happened to him. I heard about it afterwards.

"All the girls thought Jack Driscoll was so nice. One of the girls was his owner's daughter, and she was the best of the bunch, anyway, for she was an only child, and her father would have given her the earth. He was a good owner, was her father, as things go in Cardiff. Do you know Cardiff? Well, a little goes a long way on the Welsh coast. Jack was a smart sailor, with the first chance of the next new boat, if he watched out. I reckon Jack was a fool. Why, he needn't have gone to sea any more. But what did he do?

"Jack was one of them fellers who think if they put a gold-laced cap saucy over one ear, and laugh with the eyes, they can whistle up a duchess. And I daresay Jack could in summer, in his white suit, when he'd just shaved. He was a bit of all right was Jack. He was a proper tall lad, and the way he carried himself— It was a treat to see him move about a ship. His black hair was like one of the big fiddler chap's, and his smile would take in one of his pals.

"Well, it was happy days for Jack. He got good things to come to him. He didn't have to look for 'em, like me and you. He could get off the mark, at the first word, like a bird, and he never left a job while there was a loose bit to it. Sometimes when there was nothing doing it was pretty rotten, Jack would say, to be stuck there in a Welsh tramp with a crowd of dagoes, and drink coffee essence and condensed milk out of a pint mug, and never go to a music hall only once in six months. Jack reckoned it would be fine to be brass-bound always, in one of the liners, and have a deck like a skating rink, and a lot of lady passengers who wanted a chap like him to talk to them.

"He could tell stories, too, on the quiet, could Jack. They were pretty blue, though. Sailor stories. They were all about himself in the West Coast ports. Do you know the Chili coast? Well, it's mind your eye there, and no half larks. They're pretty handy with knives out there. But when Jack was out for fun you couldn't stop him. He was like all you young chaps. He wouldn't listen to sense.

"The 'Abertawe' went light ship to Barry, one trip, from Buenos Aires, and Jack saw her snug, and told all the men to be at the shipping office early and sober in the morning, because they got in on a Sunday, and Jack saw the old man safe on his way to Cardiff, and then shaved, and sang while he was shaving. He got himself up west-end style, new yellow boots and all, and tied his red tie Spanish fashion. And he went down the quay, looking for anything that was about, and he felt like the best man on the Welsh coast.

"But Barry is a dull place. Do you know Barry? Well, it's a one-eyed God-forsaken town, made out of odds and ends stuck down anywhere, all new houses, docks, coal tips, and railway sidings, and nowhere to go. It's best to stay aboard, in Barry. Jack began to feel like the only bird on a mud-bank. He got out of the town, and walked along a road till he came to an old woman sitting in the hedge, with her back up against a telegraph post. Her face was brown and wrinkled, and she had an orange-coloured handkerchief round her face, and tied under her chin. She was smoking a pipe, and looking at her blucher boots. As Jack came along, she said, 'Tell your fortune, pretty gentleman?' Jack laughed, and told her his face was his fortune.

" 'What do you see when you look in the glass?' said she.

"Now that was dead easy to Jack, because he knew as well as the girls; and he told her. There was none of your silly modesty about Jack. Then the old woman laughed; but I reckon Jack thought she was only pleased with him, because he made it a point to make the mothers and the grandmothers smile, the same as the girls.

" 'What do you see in this glass?' said she to Jack. She was fumbling in her dress, and hauls out a mirror like you see in the old-fashion shops, a mirror made of silver, and it had a frame of ebony. She polished it on her skirt, and gave it to him, and told him to pass a bit of silver with the other hand. Well, Jack saw sport, and he could always pay for that, and he did what she said. But he only saw himself in the mirror.

" 'Hi,' said Jack, 'here, what's your little game now. None of your larks now,' he said, 'or I'll ask a policeman what he can see in this tin glass of yours.'

" 'You and your policeman,' she said. 'Look now, my dandy boy, and see more than your money's worth.' And she rubbed the glass again. Then Jack took another look. It was a dull day, but that mirror was bright with sunshine. There was something funny about that mirror. He saw a fine place in it, all cool and white and gold, like you see out East. It was a palace, I reckon. There was a fountain in the middle, and some girls with not a lot on, like some of the Amsterdam postcard girls, were lying around, just anyhow. And there was Jack's own self among 'em, and they were laughing and talking to him. It was fine. Jack turned his head, just like you would do, to see if the real place was behind him. But, of course, there was the funnels and topmasts of Barry, and the sky looked like rain. I bet it gave him a shock.

" 'Now you've seen what'll be your luck, honey, if you're not careful,' said the old woman. 'Mind your eye,' she said, 'mind your eye, you with the saucy face. What's more,' she called after him, 'don't you speak to the girl with the odd eyes in Cardiff, though I know you will, and sorry you'll be.'

" 'Go to the devil,' said Jack.

"He was just like all you young chaps. Thought she was an artful old shark who'd got his money dead easy. That's what you always think. If you don't understand anything, then there's nothing in it. You call in at the next pub and chatter to the barmaid. What happened? Why, the very next day the skipper came back, and told him the new boat was near ready, and the owner wanted to see him. Jack went, and forgot about everything, except that he was going to be the handsome boy all right with the owner's own daughter to look at him. A pretty girl she was too. I saw her once, holding up her skirts off the deck while she looked around. The Skipper introduced me. 'Good morning, Mr Brown,' she said to me.

"Coming out of the Great Western Station at Cardiff Jack saw a place he'd never noticed before. It wasn't Cardiff style. 'It's a new place,' Jack thinks to himself, 'and a ripping good place it looks,' for he was thirsty, and there was plenty of time. 'It must have been run up since I was here last,' says Jack to himself, 'though that's queer, for I reckon it'd take years to rig up a dandy show of this sort.' But in he went.

"He was surprised, when he got in, and so would you have been. It was like the place I saw on the stage in London once. It was in Aladdin, at a place in the Mile End Road. You know what those things are like, when the curtain goes up. You can see a long way, but you can't see all the way. You expect something to happen there. It was full of pillars, all white and gold, in a pink light. There was a lot of ladies and gentlemen sitting on sofas full of cushions, talking, and they were too grand to even notice Jack as he stood there looking round for a chair. But it took a lot to get on Jack's nerves. There was one girl in a white silk dress, with red roses in her golden belt, and she had a white hat with red roses in that, and she looked like a summer day. Jack was glad to see that the only vacant chair was at a table where she sat alone. Of course, over there goes Jack. The place was as quiet as a church before the service begins. There was only a faint whispering. He got to where the girl sat, as if she was waiting for him. She looked up and smiled at Jack. Jack sat down beside her and said what a fine day it was. She had a face the colour of moonlight, and her eyes were odd. But there wasn't a girl who could make Jack wonder if his tie was straight, in those days, and he began to order things, and talk.

"Once he took a look round, leaning back in his chair, feeling pretty large, and he noticed the other people were looking at him artful-like, out of the corners of their eyes, as if he was talking too loud. But Jack thought he'd jolly well talk as he liked, and he'd got just the best girl in that room or anywhere else. He looked at his watch. It was near twelve o'clock. He had to be at his owner's by one. There was plenty of time.

"The drink had a funny taste, but it was the best liquor

he'd ever had. He marked down that place. He didn't know there was a show like that in Cardiff. He caught hold of the girl's hand, which he noticed was white, and very cold, and pretended he wanted to look at her ring. There was a stone in the ring, just like a bit of soda. She asked him to try it on his own finger, because the stone changed colour then, but Jack couldn't get the ring off till he'd placed her finger to his lips, to moisten the ring. He was the boy, was Jack, to see things didn't drag along. When he got the ring on his finger the stone was full of red fire. So the time went; but he forgot all about time, and the owner, and the owner's daughter, and everything. The girl's hair was scented, too, and it was close to him.

"Presently he looked up, and saw what he'd never noticed before. He could see further into the building than ever. There seemed to be a garden beyond, full of sunshine, and all the men and women were walking that way, talking loud, and laughing. His own girl got up too, and said, 'Come along, Jack Driscoll,' and he never even wondered how she knew his name, nor why her face was like snow by moonlight, nor why she smiled like that.

"No. Not Jack. All he thought was what a ripping garden it was, with palms, and marble courts, like you see in the East. There was music far away, two notes and a drum, like you hear in a native dance, before the dancers come. It made Jack feel like a millionaire or a lord, able to do anything, but just then only wanting a good time. Then he noticed they were alone in the garden, which was full of trees in blossom. All the other people had gone. There was only that music. The place was very quiet. He could hear water tinkling in a fountain, and he reckoned he would stay there till closing time. The girl talked to him in whispers, and he put his arm round her. I don't know how long he stayed there, but he kept telling the girl she was the best girl he'd ever had, and he'd never had such a good time in his life.

"It was funny the way he got out. Jack reckoned in there that the world would never come to an end, like young fellers do, when they're enjoying themselves proper. But once he took her ring off his finger, to have another look at it.

Then he was in the street again, looking up at a building which had its door shut, and Jack only thought he was looking there for a number he wanted.

"It had started to rain. He looked at his watch. It was just twelve o'clock. He didn't know what he wanted with an address in that street, so he started off in a hurry for his owner's house, feeling pretty stiff, as if he'd been sleeping rough. When he got to his owner's house, he rang the bell.

"The owner's daughter came to the door, and looked at him like she didn't know him, and was a bit afraid of him. 'No thank you,' she said kindly, 'not to-day.' And shut the door at once.

"What puzzled Jack was that he didn't feel surprised and angry. He turned and went down those steps again, and down the street, thinking it over. He looked back at the house. Yes, that was the house all right. And that was Annie all right. Well, what the devil was the matter with him? There was a public-house at the corner, and he stopped there, thinking things over, and staring at the window. Then he saw his face in a mirror, and shouted so that the barman came and ordered him out of that, sharp now. But he kept looking at the glass, not believing his eyes. He knew his own face again, but only just knew it. His eyes were dull and red and gummy, same as those old men have who've lived too long, and his fact was puffed and pimpled, and he had a lousy white beard."

II

DECEMBER 28. Lat. 39.10 N., long. 16.3 W. Course, S.W. ½ west. We are nearing the tropics. Now the ship has such a complete set of grumblers, good fellows who know their work better than anyone less than God, that our great distance at sea is plain. Our men, casually gathered and speaking divers tongues, detached from earth and set afloat on a mobile islet to mix on it if they can, have become one body to deal with the common enemy. We are corporate to face each trouble as it meets us, and free to explain afterwards how much better we should have done under another captain. The skipper knows this broad spirit now possesses us, and so is contented and blithe, wearing only on deck that weary look which is the sober badge of high office, as though he were an unfortunate man to have us about him, we being what we are, but that he would do his best with the fools, seeing we are in his charge.

This morning at six, hearing the men at the hose-pipes giving the decks their daily wash, I tumbled out for a cold tub. This is a simple affair. You leave the cabin with a towel about you, stand in a clear space, and rotate before the hydrant, to general cheering. A hot bath on the "Capella" is not so easy, because, although there is a bath-room aboard, it has become a paint locker. One must descend into the engine-room, after warning the engineer on duty, who then will have ready a barrel, filled from the boilers. The ingenious man will fix a shower bath also. This is a perforated meat tin, hanging from a grating above the tub, and connected with a pump. After a hot bath in the engine-room, where the temperature was often well over 120°, that shower of cold sea water would strike loud cries from any man whose self-control was uncertain.

This morning was the right prelude to the tropics. This

was the morning when, if our planet had been till then untenanted, a world unconsummated and waiting approval, the divine approval would have come, and a child would have been born, an immortal, the offspring of Aurora and the Sea God, flame-haired and lusty, with eyes as bright as joy, and a rosy body to be kissed from toes to crown. The dancing light, and the warm shower suddenly born alive in it from one ripe cloud, the golden air, the waves of the north-east trades, the seas of the world in the first dawn, moving along like a multitude released to play, their blue passionate and profound, their crests innocent and dazzling, made me think I might hear faint cheering, if I listened intently. In the west was a steep range of cloudland rising from the sea, and against it was inclined the flame of a rainbow. There was that rainbow, as constant as the pennant hoisted over an uplighted occasion. The world's noble emblem was aloft. I demanded of the Skipper if he would run up our ensign in reply to it; but he only peered at me curiously.

The heat increased with the day. We had run well down from the bleak apex of the world with its nimbus of fogs. Here was the entrance to the place where our youthful dreams began. I recognised it. Every feature was as we both have seen it from afar, across the roofs from our outlook in the arid city when the path to it had appeared as hopeless to our feet as the path to the moon. This pioneer can assure his fellows whose bright illusions grow fainter with age that their dreams must be followed up, to be reached.

At midday we began to cast clothes. As to the afternoon, of that I remember the less. There was the chief's empty bunk, so much more alluring than my own. Into that I climbed, my mind steeled against drowsy weakness. I would digest my dinner with a book, eyes sternly alert.

The "Capella" rocked slowly, a big cradle. My body was lax and responsive. There was about us the silent emptiness which is far from the centres where many men believe it is necessary to get lots of things done. The Chief suspired on his settee. The waves were singing to themselves. A ray of light laughed in my eyes, playing hide and seek across the wisdom of my book. . . . I put the book down.

As you know, where I had come from we do not dare to sleep during daylight without first arguing with the conscience, which usually we fail to convince. This comes of our mental trick which takes a pleasure we wholly desire and puts on it a prohibitive label. Self-indulgence, you understand; softening of the character; courage, brothers, do not stumble. The solemn forefinger wags gravely in our faces. Before I fell asleep, my habit, born of the hard grey weather which makes an Englishman hard and prosperous, did come with its admonitory forefinger. Remembering that I was secure in a sunnier world I cried out with ribald mockery across the abyss I had safely crossed, knowing my old self could not follow, and shut my eyes happily. And also, let me say—sitting up again with an urgent afterthought, which I must get rid of before I sleep—if this were not a plain narrative of travel without any wise asides I would get off the "Capella" here to argue that what all you fellows want in the place I have luckily left is not more self-restraint, in which wan virtue you have long shown yourselves to be so proficient that our awards for your merit have overcrowded the work-houses, but more rollicking self-indulgence and a ruddy and bright eyed insistence on the means to it. Look at me now in this bunk! Not since I was last in a cradle have I felt the world would buoy me up if I dared to shut my eyes to affairs while the sun was shining. But I am going to try it again now, and risk my future. I repeat, I would argue this with you, only I want to sleep. . . .

It is worth recording that when I woke I found nothing had happened to me, except benefit. The venture can be made safely. Others had kept the course for me. The ship had not stopped. Through the door I could see a half-naked, blackened, and sweating stoker, who had been keeping the fires while I slept, and he was getting back his breath in loud sobs. Something had made him sick. These stupid and dirty men will drink too much while they are attending to the furnaces. They have been warned of the danger, of which they take no heed, and so they have to suffer. On the poop was the second officer, busy in the hot sun with a gang, overhauling a boat. And I found, on enquiry, that a man was still at the wheel. So thereafter, while in the land of the constant sun, I slept every afternoon, and was never a penny the worse. Somehow, you know, things went on. I think I shall become one of the intelligent leisured class.

It was within an hour of midnight. The moon had set. I was idling amidships about the ship's shadowy structure when I was asked to take charge of the bridge till eight bells. The second mate was ill, and the first mate was asleep through overwork. The skipper said he would not keep me up there long. I had but to call if a light came into view, and to keep an eye on the wheelhouse. Ah, but it is long since I played at ships, and was a pirate captain. I remembered there are dull folk who wonder what it feels like to be a king. The king does not know. Ask the small boy who is surprised with an order to hold a horse's head. I took my promotion, mounting the steep ladder to the open height in the night.

I felt then I was more than sundered from my kind. I had been taken and placed remotely from the comfort of the "Capella's" isolated community also. There was me, and there were the stars. They were my nearest neighbours. I stood for you among them alone. When the last man hears but does not see the deep waters of this dark sphere in that night to which there shall be no morning sun, he shall know what was my sensation aloft in the saddle of the "Capella"; the only inhabitant of a congealed asteroid off the main track in space, with the sun diminished to a point through travel, and the Milky Way not reached yet; though I could see we were approaching its bay of light. An appreciable journey had been made. But by the faintness of its shine there was a timeless vacancy to be travelled still. We should make that faint glow, that congregation of suns, that archipelago of worlds; though not yet. But had we not all the night to travel in? The night would be long. We should not be disrupted any more by the old day. The final morning had passed. I had no doubt the drift of the dark lump to which I clung in space, while my hair streamed with our speed, would at length reach the bright fraternity, no more than a dimmer of removed promise though it seemed.

A bell rang beside me in the night. It was answered at once

from somewhere ahead. Others, then, were journeying with me. The void was peopled, though the travellers were all invisible; and I heard a confident voice call, "Lights are burning bright." The lights were. I could see that. But when the profundities are about you, and you think you are alone in outer night, that is the kind of word to hear. Joyously I shouted into what seemed to be boundless nothing, "All Right!"

One dayfall we saw the Canary Islands a great distance on the port beam. I do not know which day it was. The Hesperides were as blurred as the place in the calendar. The days had run together into a measureless sense of well-being. We had passed the last of the trivial allotments of time. The islands loomed, and I wondered whether that land was the hint of something in a past life which the memory saw but could not shape. Whatever was there it was too long forgotten. That apparition which a whisper told me was land faded as I gazed at it overseas, lazily trying to remember what it once meant. It was gone again. It was no matter now. Perhaps I was deceiving myself. Perhaps I had had no other life. This "Capella," always under the height of a blue dome, always the centre of a circular floor of waters, waters to be seen beating against the steep and luminous walls encompassing us, though nowhere finding an outlet, was all my experience. I could recall only the faintest shadows of a past into that limpid present. I could see nothing clearly that was not confined within the dark faultless line where the sky was inseparably annealed to the sea. Here I had been always. All I knew was this length of sheltered deck, and those doors behind me where I leaned on a rail between the stanchions, doors which sheltered a few familiars with their clothes on hooks, their pipe racks, and photographs of women, a length of deck finishing on either hand in two iron ladders, the ladder forward, just past the radiation and coal grit by the engine-room casing, descending to a broad walk which led to the forecastle head, that bare outlook always at a difference with the horizon; and the ladder aft going down to another broad walk, sticky with new tar, where the bulwarks were as high as the breast, and Tinker the dog, glad of a word from you, trotted about the rusty winches and around the hatches; and that walk aft finished in the door of the alley-way opening upon the asylum of the doctor's cabin, and the saloon, the skipper's sanctum, and the domain of the friendly steward. There was the smell of the cargo drawing from the ventilators on the deck, when you went by their trumpet mouths. There was the warm oily gush of air from the engine-room entrance. And in the saloon alley-way I used to think the store of potatoes, right behind, was generating gases. (But nobody knows every origin of the marine smells.) Well, here were all the things my senses apprehended. I could walk round my universe in five minutes. And when I had finished I could do it again. Here I had been always. Nothing could be clearer than that. Looking out from my immediate circumstances I saw no entrance to the place where we were rocking, the place where the "Capella" was alone. The walls of the enclosure were flawless. There was not a door through them anywhere. There was not a rift in the precision of the dark circle about us where one could crawl out between the sky and the sea.

There we indubitably were though, and I dwelt constantly on the miracle of that lucky existence. I could not doubt that we were there. Yet how had we got there? I leave that to the metaphysicians. There we were; and no man who merely trusted his experience could explain our presence. There was some evidence to my simple mind that such a life in such surroundings perchance was the gift of the gods, and that we could never get any nearer the limits of the world in which we had been placed to see what was beyond, could never approach that enclosure of blue walls where the distant waves,which beat against them, could not get out. Morning after morning I watched them, the dark leaping shapes of the far rebels, mounting their prison at its base, and collapsing, beaten.

The seas never changed. They followed us and the wind, a living host, the blue of their slopes and hollows as deep as ecstasy, their crests white and lambent. They were buoyant, they were leisurely, they were the right companions of travel. They just kept pace with us. They ran after us like happy children, as though they had been lagging. They came a-beam to turn up to us their shining faces, calling to us musically, then dropping behind again in silence. When I looked overside into the pellucid depths, peering below the surface in long forgetfulness, leaving the body and gliding the mind in that palpable and hyacinthine air beneath us where the sunken foam dimmered in pale clouds, I felt myself not afloat but hovering in the midst of a hollow sphere filled with light. The blue water was only a heavier and a darker air. I had no weight there. I was only a quiet thought tinctured with the royal colour of the space wherein I drifted.

The upper half of the sphere was blue also, but of a different blue. The rarer and more volatile ether was above us. The sea was its essence and precipitate. The sea colour was profound and satisfying; but the colour of the sky was diffused, as though the heaven were an idea which was beyond you, which you stood regarding, and azure were its symbol, and that by concentration you might fathom its meaning. But I can report no luck from my concentrated efforts on that symbol. The colour may have been its own reward.

Every morning after breakfast the Skipper and the Doctor made a visit to the forecastle. Then, after the Doctor had carefully searched his dress for insects, we spent the day together. We mounted the forecastle to begin with, watching the acre of dazzling foam which the "Capella's" bows broke around us. Out of that the flying fish would get up, just under us, to go skimming off, flights of silver locusts. This reminded the surgeon that we might try for albacore and bonito, which would be a change from tinned mutton. The Skipper found a long fir pole, to which was attached sixty fathoms of line, with a large hook which we covered with a white rag, lapping a cutting of tin round the shank. When this object was dropped over the stern in its leaps from wave to wave it bore a distant resemblance to a flying fish. The weight of the trailing line, breaking a cord "tell-tale," frequently gave us false alarms and long tiring hauls. But on the second day the scaffold pole vibrated to some purpose, and we knew we were hauling in more than the bait. We got aboard a coryphene, the dolphin of the sailors. It gave us in its death agony the famous display, beautiful, but rather painful to watch, for the wonderful hues, as they changed, stayed in the eye, and sent to the mind only a message of a creature in a violent death struggle.

The contours of this predatory fish express extraordinary speed and power, and its armed mouth has been upturned by Providence the better to catch a flying fish as they drop back to sea after an effort to escape from it. But Providence, or evolution, had never taught the coryphene that there are times when the little flying fish, as it falls back exhausted, may be a rag of white shirt and a scrap of bright tin ware with a large hook in its deceptive little belly. So there the dolphin was, glowing and fading with the hues of faery. Its life really illuminating it from within. As its life ebbed, or strove convulsively, its colours waned and pulsed. It was gold when it came on board, and darkened to ultramarine as it thrashed the deck, and its broad dorsal fin showed violet eyes. Its body changed to a pale metallic green; and then its light went out.

Now as I look back upon the "Capella" and her company as they were in that period of our adventure when our place was but somewhere in mid-ocean between Senegambia and Trinidad, I see us but indifferently, for we are mellowed in that haze in which retrospection just discerns those affairs, long since accomplished, that were not altogether wearisome. It is better to go to my log again, for there the matter was noted by the stub of a pencil at the very time, and when, unless a beautiful mist was seen, it had not the remotest chance of being recorded. When I turn to the diary for further evidence of those days of blue and gold in the north-east trades its faithfulness is seen at once.

"30 *Decr.* A grey day. The sun fitful. Wind and seas on the port quarter, and the large following billows occasionally lopping inboard as she rolled. The decks therefore are sloppy again. We had a sharp reminder at six bells that we are not bound to any health resort, as Sandy put it. We were told to go aft, where the doctor would give each of us five grains of quinine. This is to be a daily rite. To encourage the men to take the quinine it is to be given to them in gin. Being foreigners, they did not understand the advice about the quinine, but they caught the word gin quite well, and they were outside the saloon alley-way, a smiling queue, at the stroke of eleven. I went along to see the harsh truth dawn on them. The first man was a big German deckhand. He took the glass from the doctor. His shy and puzzled smile at this unexpected charity from the skipper dissolved instantly when the quinine got behind it. His eyes opened and stared at nothing. To the surprise of his fellows he turned violently to the ship's side, rested his hands on it, and spat; spat carefully, continuously, and with grave deliberation.

"Distance run since noon yesterday 230 miles. Actual knots 9.5. Total distance 2072 miles. There was not a living thing in sight to-day; not even a flying fish.

"The night is fine and starlit, the Milky Way a brilliant arch from each to west, under which we are steaming. When Venus rose she was a tiny moon, so refulgent that she gave a faint pallor to a large area of sky, outlined the coast of a cloud, and made a broad shining path on the sea. The moon rose after nine, veiled in filmy air, peeping motionless at the edge of a black curtain.

"The moon later was quite obscured, and the steamer ceased to exist except where in my heated cabin the smoky oil lamp showed me my dismal cubicle. I went in and sat on the mate's sea chest. The mate was on duty. On the washstand was his mug of cocoa, and on top of the mug two thick sandwiches of bread and meat. That food was black with cockroaches. The oil lamp stank but gave little light. The engines were throbbing, and out of the open door I saw the gleam of the wash, and heard its harassing note. I could not read. I loathed the idea of getting into the hot bunk and lying there, stewing, a clear keen clangour of thoughts making sleep impossible. The mate appeared, drove off the cockroaches cheerfully, examined the sandwiches for incon-spicuous deer, opening each to make sure, and then muffled himself with one. My God! I could have killed him with these two hands. What right had he to be cheerful? But he is such a ginger-headed boy, and to break that unconsciously happy smile of his would be sacrilege. Besides, he began to tell me about his sweetheart. Her portrait hangs in our cabin. It is an enlargement. You pay for the frame, and the photographer, overjoyed I suppose, gives you the enlargement. I prefer the second engineer's sweethearts, who are in colours, and are Dutch picture postcards and cuttings from French comic papers; and he calls them his recollections of Sundays at home. I listened, patient and kind, to the second mate's reminiscences of rapturous evening walks under the lamps of Swansea with this girl in the picture—no doubt it eased his heart to tell me—till I could have howled aloud, like the dog who hears music at night. Then I broke away, and ran to the chief's cabin for sanctuary.

"The Chief was making an abstract, and was searching through his log for ten tons of coal which were missing. In the hunt for the lost coal I lost myself. I grew excited wherever a thick bush of figures promised the hidden quarry; and in an hour's search found the strayed tons in hiding at the bottom of a column. They had been left there, and not transported into the next. Again the dread of that bunk had to be faced and dealt with. I stood at the chief's door, knocking out my pipe, looking astern into the night, looking to where Ursa-Major, our celestial familiar of home, was low down and preparing to leave us altogether to the strange and perhaps unlucky gods of other skies. O the nights at sea!

"31 *Decr.* Wakened with my heart jumping because of a devastating sound without. In the early morning, Tinker was being thrashed by the Old Man for eating the saloon mats. When at 11.30 the men congregated amidships with their tins for dinner the sun was a near furnace and the breeze a balm. The white of the ship is now a glare, and the sea foam cannot be looked at. Donkey lumbered out of his place where he attends to the minor boiler, his face the colour of putty, and held to a rail, gazing out with dead eyes overside, gasping. He declared he couldn't stick his job. The flying fish are getting up in flights all day long. I saw one fish go a distance of about fifty yards in a semi-circle, making a bight in the direction of the wind. We caught another large coryphene to-day, and had him in steaks for tea. He was much better cooked than the last, which had the texture of white wool; and to increase our happiness the cook had not given us sour bread. At midday we were 17.22 N. and 33.27 W.

"I had a lonely evening with the chief. This is New Year's eve. We talked of the East India Dock Road, and of much else in London Town. At eight bells, when we held up our glasses in the direction of Polaris, the moon was bright and the waters hushed. Then we took each a hurricane lamp, and went about the decks collecting flying fish for breakfast, finding a dozen of them.

"1 *Jan.* The uplifted splendour of these days persists; but the splendour sags now a little at midday with the weight of the heat. The poop deck is now sheltered with an awning; and lying there in lazy chairs, with a wind following and barely overtaking us, idly watching the shadows of the overhead gear move on the bright awning as the ship rolls, is to get caught in the toils of the droning wake, and to sleep before you know you are a prisoner. The wake itself, in these seas, when the sun is on it, a broad road going home straight and white over the hills, the road which is not for us, is one of the good things of the voyage. Straight beneath the rail the wake is an upheaval of gems, sapphires, emeralds, and diamonds, always instantly melting in the sun, always fusing and fleeting in swift coils of malachite and chryso-prase, but never gone. As you watch that coloured turmoil it draws your mind from your body. You feel your careless gaze snatched in the revolving hues speeding astern, and your consciousness is instantly unwound from your spinning brain, and you are left standing on the ship, an empty spool.

"Under the awning at night, to the Doctor and to me, the first mate played his accordion. He is a little Welshman, this mate, with a childish nose and a brutish moustache, and in his face is blended a girlish innocence of large affairs, and the hirsute nature of the adult male animal, a nature he relieves on the "Capella" with bawdy talk and guffaws. He played 'Come, Birdie, Come,' and things like that, and then told us some Monte Videan stories. As they were true stories about himself and other young sailors they ought really to be included in a faithful diary of a sea voyage, yet as I cannot reproduce the Doctor's antiseptic judgment, of which I know nothing but the glow of his pipe in the unresponding dark at the end of the stories—the last titter of the mate had died away—it is better to leave this matter alone.

"3 *Jan.* The hottest day we have had. I descended at midday to the engines to see Sandy at work with his shining giants. Standing on the middle platform, while he was shouting his greetings to me over the uproar, I felt the heat of the grating through my boot soles, and shifted. The temperature there was 122°. Sandy was but in his drawers and a pair of old boots, and the tongues of the boots, properly, were hanging out. His noble torso was glistening with moisture, and as I talked, energetically vaulting my words above the roar of the crank throws in that hot and oleaginous place, the perspiration began a sudden drop from my own face and hands, and in a copious way which startled me. For a time I had some difficulty in breathing, as though in a vacuum, but gradually forgot this danger of suffocation in the love of the artist Sandy showed while offering me the spectacle of 'his job.' I think I understood him. At first one would see no order in that haze of rioting steel. The massive metal waves of the shaft were walloping and plunging in their pits with an astonishing bird-like alacrity; about fifteen tons of polished steel were moving with swift and somewhat awful desperation. The big room shook and hummed with the vigour of it. But order came as Sandy talked, and presently I found the continuous thunder, that deadening bass of the crank throws, seemed to lessen as we conversed, sitting together on a tool chest. Our voices easily penetrated it. And listening more attentively at length I found what Sandy said was true, that each tossing and circling part of the room-full could be heard contributing its strident or profound note to the chorus, and each became constant and expected, a singing personality which was heard through the others whenever listened for. Above all, at regular intervals, a rod rang clear, like the bell in Parsifal;

yet, curiously enough, Sandy declared he could not catch
that note, though it tolled clear and resonant enough in my
ears. The skylight was so far above us that we got little
daylight. Hanging from the gratings in a few places, some
black iron pots, shaped like kettles, had cotton rags in their
spouts, and were giving us oil flares instead. The terrific
unremitting energy of the ponderous arms, moving thunder-
ously, and still with a speed which made tons as aery as
flashes of light; and Sandy in the midst of it, quick in
nothing but his eyes, moving about his raging but tethered
monsters cock-sure and casual, rubbing his hands on a pull
of cotton waste, putting his ear down to listen attentively at
a bearing, his face turned from a steel fist which flung
violently at his head, missed him, and withdrew to shoot at
him again, gave me the first distinct feeling that our enterprise had its purpose powerfully energised and cunningly
directed. I felt as I watched the dance of the eccentrics and
the connecting rods that our ship was getting along fa-
mously. I think I detected in Sandy himself a faint contempt
for the chap at the upper end of the telegraph. I stayed two
hours, and then my shirt was as though I had been overboard;
and ascending a greasy and almost perpendicular series of
ladders to the upper world, I discovered, from the drag of my
feet and the weight of my body, that I had had just as much
of an engineer's watch in the tropics as I could stand. There
was a burst of cool light. The tumult ceased; and again there
was the old "Capella" rocking in the singing seas, for ever
under the tranquil clouds. We had stopped again.

"4 *Jan.* A moderate north-east wind and sea, and a bright
morning; but far out a dark cloud formed, and grew, and
driving towards us, covered us presently with a blue-black
canopy. The warm torrent fell with outrageous violence, and
for all we could see of our way the 'Capella' might have been
in a dense fog. The mosquito curtains were served out to-
day, and we amused ourselves draping our bunks. Later, the
weather cleared. The night was stiflingly hot; and in that
reeking bunk, with an iron bulkhead separating me from
the engine room, it was like lying on the shelf of an oven.
Though wide open on its catch, the door admitted no air, but

did allow a miserable tap-tapping as the ship rolled. At eleven o'clock a pale face floated in the black vacancy of the door, and I could see the Doctor peering in to find if I were awake. 'I say, Purser, I can't sleep. Will you come and have a gossip, old dear?' We went aft in our pyjamas, the Doctor cleared away bottles and things from his settee, and we disembarked from the 'Capella,' visiting other and distant stars, returning to our own again not before three next morning.

"5 *Jan.* We seem to have got to a dead end of the trade winds. The heat of the forenoon was oppressively humid and dinner was nearly lost through it. The cook, a fair and plump Dutchman, broke down in the midst of his pans, and was carried out to find his breath again. This poor chef is up at four o'clock every morning coffee making; is working in the galley, which is badly ventilated, all day, getting two hours rest in the early afternoon. Then he goes on till the saloon tea is over; when he begins to bake bread. He fills in his leisure in peeling potatoes.

"All round the horizon motionless and permanent storm clouds are banked. Their forms do not alter, but their colours change with the hours. They seem to encompass us in a circular lake, a range of precipitous and intricately piled Alps, high and massive. Cleaving those steeps of calamitous rock—for so they looked, and not in the least like vapour—are chasms full of night, and the upper slopes and summits are lucent in amber and pearl. In the south and east the ranges are indigo dark and threatening, and the water between us and that closed country is opaque and heavy as molten lead. Across the peaks of the mountains rest horizontal strata of mist. Some petrels were about to-day. The evening is cool, with a slight head breeze."

After weeks at sea, imprisoned within the walls of the sky, walls which have not opened once to admit another vessel to give the assurance of communion, you begin to doubt your direction and destination, and the possibility of change. Only the clouds change. The ship is no nearer breaking that rigid circle. She cannot escape from her place under the centre of the dome. The most cheering assurance

I had was the pulse of the steamer, felt whenever I rested against her warm body. Purposeful life was there, at least. Though the day may have been brazen, and without a hint of progress, and the sea the same empty wilderness, yet when most disheartened in the blind and melancholy night I felt under me the beatings, energetic and insistent, of her lively heart, some of that vitality was communicated, and I got sleep as a child would in the arms of a strong and wakeful guardian.

Poised between two profundities—though nearer the clouds, cirrus and lofty though they are, than the land straight beneath the keel—and with morning and night the only variety in the round, the days flicker by white and black like a magic lantern working without a story. Tired of watching for the fruits of our enterprise I went to sleep. Old Captain Morgan must have lived a dull life, monotonous with adventure. What is the use of travel, I asked myself. The stars are as near to London as they are to the Spanish main. In their planetary journey through the void the passengers at Peckham see as much as their fellows who peer through the windows in Macassar. The sun rises in the east, and the moon is horned; but some of the passengers on the mudball, strangely enough, take their tea without milk. Yet what of that?

In the chart room some days ago I learned we had 3000 fathoms under us. Well; these waves of the tropics, curling over such abysmal deeps, look much the same as the waves off Land's End. I began to see what I had done. I had changed the murk of winter in London for the discomforts of the dog days. I had come thousands of miles to see the thermometer rise. Where are the Spanish Main, the Guianas, and the Brazils? At last I had discovered them. I found their true bearings. They are in Raleigh's "Golden City of Manoa," in Burney's "Buccaneers of America," with Drake, Humboldt, Bates, and Wallace; and I had left them all at home. We borrow the light of an observant and imaginative traveller, and see the foreign land bright with his aura; and we think it is the country which shines.

*   *   *

At eight this morning we crossed the equator. I paid my footing in whisky, and forgot all about the equator. Soon after that, idling under the poop awning, I picked up the Doctor's book from his vacant chair. I took the essays of Emerson carelessly and read at once—the sage plainly had laid a trap for me—"Why covet a knowledge of new facts? Day and night, a house and garden, a few books, a few actions, serve as well as all trades and spectacles." So——. At this moment the first mate crossed my light, and presently I heard the sounding machine whirring, and then stop. There was a pause, and then the mate's unimportant voice, "Twenty-five fathoms, sir, grey sand!"

Emerson went sprawling. I stood up. Twenty-five fathoms! Then that grey sand stuck to the tallow of the weight was the first of the Brazils. The circle of waters was still complete about us, but over the bows, at a great distance, were thunder clouds and wild lights. The oceanic swell had decreased to a languid and glassy beat, and the water had become jade green in colour, shot with turquoise gleams. The Skipper, himself interested and almost jolly, announced a pound of tobacco to the first man who spied the coast. We were nearing it at last. Those far clouds canopied the forests of the Amazon. We stood in at slow speed.

I know those forests. I mean I have often navigated their obscure waterways, rafting through the wilds on a map, in my slippers, at night. Now those forests soon were to loom on a veritable skyline. I should see them where they stood, their roots in the unfrequented floods. I should see Santa Maria de Belem, its aerial foliage over its shipping and squalor. It was quite near now. I should see Santarem and Obydos, and Ita-coatiara; and then, turning from the King of Rivers to his tributary, the Madeira, follow the Madeira to the San Antonio falls in the heart of the South American continent. We drew over 23 feet, with this "Capella." We were going to try what had never been attempted before by an ocean steamer. This, too, was pioneering. I also was on an adventure, going two thousand miles under those clouds of the equatorial rains, to live for a while in the forests of the Orellana. And our vessel's rigging, so they tell me, sometimes shall drag the foliage in showers on our decks, and where we anchor at night the creatures of the jungle will call.

Our nearness to land stirs up some old dreads in our minds also. We discuss those dreads again, though with more concern than we did at Swansea. Over the bows is now the prelude. We have heard many unsettling legends of yellow fever, malaria, blackwater fever, dysentery, and beri-beri. The mates, looking for land, swear they were fools to come a voyage like this. They ought to have known better. The Doctor, who does not always smile when he is amused, advises us not to buy a white sun umbrella at Para, but a black one; then it will do for the funerals.

"Land O!" That was the Skipper's own perfunctory cry. He had saved his pound of tobacco. It was two in the afternoon. There was America. I rediscovered it with some difficulty. All I could see was a mere local thickening of the horizon, as though the pen which drew the faint line dividing the world ahead into an upper and a nether opalescence had run a little freely at one point. That thickening of the horizon was the island of Monjui. Soon, though, there was a palpable something athwart our course. The skyline heightened into a bluish barrier, which, as we approached still nearer, broke into sections. The chart showed that a series of low wooded islands skirted the mainland. Yet it was hard to believe we were approaching land again. What showed as land was of too unsubstantial a quality, too thin and broken a rind on that vast area of water to be of any use as a foothold. Where luminous sky was behind an island groups of diminutive palms showed, as tiny and distinct as the forms of mildew under a magnifying glass, delicate black pencillings along the foot of the skywall. Often that hairlike tracery seemed to rest upon the sea. The "Capella" continued to stand in, till America was more than a frail and tinted illusion which sometimes faded the more the eye sought it. Presently it cast reflections. The islands grew into cobalt layers, with vistas of silver water between them, giving them body. The course was changed to west, and we cruised along for Atalaia point, towards the pilot station. Over the thin and futile rind of land which topped the sea—it might have undulated on the low swell—ponderous thunder clouds towered, continents of night in the sky, with translucent areas dividing them which were strangely illuminated from the hither side. Curtains as black as bitumen draped to the waters from great heights. Two of these appalling curtains, trailing over America, were a little withdrawn. We could look beyond them to a diminishing array of glowing cloud summits, as if we saw there an accidental revelation of a secret and wonderful region with a sun of its own. And all, gigantic clouds, the sea, the far and frail coast, were serene and still. The air had ceased to breathe. I thought this new lucent world we had found might prove but a lucky dream after all, to be seen but not to be entered, and that some noise would presently shatter it and wake me. But we came alongside the white pilot schooner, and the pilot put off in a boat manned by such a crowd of grinning, ragged, and cinnamon skinned pirates as would have broken the fragile wonder of any spell. Ours, though, did not break, and I was able to believe we had arrived. At sunset the great clouds were full of explosions of electric fire, and there were momentary revelations above us of huge impending shapes. We went slowly over a lower world obscurely lighted by phosphorescent waves.

It was not easy to make out, before sunrise, what it was we had come to. I saw a phantom and indeterminate country; but as though we guessed it was suspicious and observant, and its stillness a device, we moved forward slowly and noiselessly, as a thief at an entrance. Low level cliffs were near to either beam. The cliffs might have been the dense residuum of the night. The night had been precipitated from the sky, which was clearing and brightening. Our steamer was between banks of these iron shades.

Suddenly the sunrise ran a long band of glowing saffron over the shadow to port, and the vague summit became remarkable with a parapet of black filigree, crowns and fronds of palms and strange trees showing in rigid patterns of ebony. A faint air then moved from off shore as though under the impulse of the pouring light. It was heated and

humid, and bore a curious odour, at once foreign and
familiar, the smell of damp earth, but not of the earth I
knew, and of vegetation, but of vegetation exotic and wild.
For a time it puzzled me that I knew the smell; and then I
remembered where we had met before. It was in the palm
house at Kew Gardens. At Kew that odour once made a
deeper impression on me than the extraordinary vegetation
itself, for as a boy I thought that I inhaled the very spirit of
the tropics of which it was born. After the first minute on
the Para river that smell went, and I never noticed it again.

Full day came quickly to show me the reality of one of my
early visions, and I suppose I may not expect many more such
minutes as I spent when watching from the "Capella's"
bridge the forest of the Amazon take shape. It was soon over.
The morning light brimmed at the forest top, and spilled into
the river. The channel filled with sunshine. There it was
then. In the northern cliff I could see even the boughs and
trunks; they were veins of silver in a mass of solid chrysolite.
This forest had not the rounded and dull verdure of our own
woods in midsummer, with deep bays of shadow. It was a
sheer front, uniform, shadowless, and astonishingly vivid. I
thought then the appearance of the forest was but a local
feature, and so gazed at it for what it would show me next. It
had nothing else to show me. Clumps of palms threw their
fronds above the forest roof in some places, or a giant exogen
raised a dome; but that was all. Those strong characters in
the growth were seen only in passing. They did not change the
outlook ahead of converging lines of level green heights rising directly from a brownish flood.

Occasionally the river narrowed, or we passed close to one
wall, and then we could see the texture of the forest surface,
the microstructure of the cliff, though we could never look
into it for more than a few yards, except where, in some
places, habitations were thrust into the base of the woods, as
in lower caverns. An exuberant wealth of forms built up that
forest which was so featureless from a little distance. The
numerous palms gave grace and life to the façade, for their
plumes flung in noble arcs from tall and slender columns, or
sprayed directly from the ground in emerald fountains. The

rest was inextricable confusion. Vines looped across the front of green, binding the forest with cordage, and the roots of epiphytes dropped from upper boughs, like hanks of twine.

In some places the river widened into lagoons, and we seemed to be in a maze of islands. Canoes shot across the waterways, and river schooners, shaped very like junks, with high poops and blue and red sails, were diminished beneath the verdure, betraying the great height of the woods. Because of its longitudinal extension, fining down to a point in the distance, the elevation of the forest, when uncontrasted, looked much less than it really was. The scene was so luminous, still, and voiceless, it was so like a radiant mirage, or a vivid remembrance of an emotional dream got from books read and read again, that only the unquestionable verity of our iron steamer, present with her smoke and prosaic gear, convinced me that what was outside us was there. Across a hatch a large butterfly hovered and flickered like a flame. Dragon flies were suspended invisibly over our awning, jewels in shimmering enamels.

We anchored just before breakfast, and a small launch flying a large Brazilian flag was soon fussing at our gangway. The Brazilian customs men boarded us, and the official who was left in charge to overlook the "Capella" while we remained was a tall and majestic Latin with dark eyes of such nobility and brooding melancholy that it never occurred to me that our doctor, who has travelled much, was other than a fellow with a dull Anglo-Saxon mind when he removed some loose property to his cabin and locked his door, before he went ashore. So I left my field glasses on the ice-chest; and that was the last I saw of them. Yet that fellow had such lovely hair, as the ladies would say, and his smile and his courtesy were fit for kings. He carried a scented pink handkerchief and wore patent leather boots. Our surgeon had but a faint laugh when these explanations were made to him, taking my hand fondly, and saying he loved little children.

Para, a flat congestion of white buildings and red roofs in

the sun, was about a mile beyond our anchorage, over the
port bow; and as its name has been to me one that had the
appeal of the world not ours, like Tripoli of Barbary, Macassar, the Marquesas, and the Rio Madre de Dios, the agent's
launch, as it took us towards the small craft lying immediately before the front of that spread of houses between the
river and the forest, was so momentous an occasion that the
small talk of the dainty Englishmen in linen suits, a gossip-
ing group around the agent and the Skipper, hardly came
into the picture, to my mind. The launch rudely hustled
through a cluster of gaily painted native boats, the dingiest
of them bearing some sonorous name, and I landed in Brazil.

There was an esplanade, shadowed by an avenue of mangoes. We crossed that, and went along hot narrow streets, by
blotched and shabby walls, to the office to which our ship
was consigned. We met a fisherman carrying a large turtle by
a flipper. We came to a dim cool warehouse. There, some
negroes and half-breeds were lazily hauling packages in the
shadows. It had an office railed off where a few English
clerks, in immaculate white, overlooked a staff of natives.
The warehouse had a strange and memorable odour, evasive,
sweet, and pungent, as barbaric a note as I found in Para, and
I understood at once I had come to a place where there were
things I did not know. I felt almost timorous and yet
compelled when I sniffed at those shadows; though what the
eye saw in the squalid streets of the riverside, where brown
folk stood regarding us carelessly from openings in the walls,
I had thought no more than a little interesting.

What length of time we should have in Belem was
uncertain, but presently the Skipper, looking most morose,
came away from his discussion with the agent and told us,
at some length, what he thought of people who kept a ship
waiting because of a few unimportant papers. Then he
mumbled, very reluctantly, that we had plenty of time to see
all Para. The Doctor and I were out of that office before the
Skipper had time to change his mind. Our captain is a very
excellent master mariner, but occasionally he likes to test
the security of his absolute autocracy, to see if it is still
sound. I never knew it when it was not; but yet he must, to

assure himself of a certainty, or to exercise some devilish choler in his nature, sometimes beat our poor weak bodies against the adamant thing, to see which first will break. I will say for him that he is always polite when handing back to us our bruised fragments. Here he was giving us a day's freedom, and one's first city of the tropics in which to spend it and we agreed with him that such a waste of time was almost unbearable, and left hurriedly.

Outside the office was a small public square where grew palms which ran flexible boles, swaying with the weight of their crowns, clear above the surrounding buildings, shadowing them except in one place, where the front of a ruinous church showed, topped by a crucifix. The church, a white and dilapidated structure, was hoary with ficus and other plants which grew from ledges and crevices. Through the crowns of the palms the sunlight fell in dazzling lathes and partitions, chequering the stones. An ox-cart stood beneath.

The Paraenses, passing by at a lazy gait—which I was soon compelled to imitate—in the heat, were puzzling folk to one used to the features of a race of pure blood, like ourselves. Portuguese, negro, and Indian were there, but rarely a true type of one. Except where the black was the predominant factor the men were impoverished bodies, sallow, meagre, and listless; though there were some brown and brawny ruffians by the foreshore. But the women often were very showy creatures, certainly indolent in movement, but not listless, and built in notable curves. They were usually of a richer colour than their mates, and moved as though their blood were of a quicker temper. They had slow and insolent eyes. The Indian has given them the black hair and brown skin, the negro the figure, and Portugal their features and eyes. Of course, the ladies of Para society, boasting their straight Portuguese descent, are not included in this insulting description; and I do not think I saw them. Unless, indeed, they were the ladies who boldly eyed us in the fashionable Para hotel, where we lunched, at a great price, off imported potatoes, tinned peas, and beef which in England would be sold to a glue factory; I mean the women in those Parisian costumes erring something on the side of emphasis, and whose remarkable pallor was even a little greenish in the throat shadows.

After lunch some disappointment and irresolution crept into our holiday. . . . There had been a time—but that was when Para was only in a book; that was when its mere printed name was to me a token of the tropics. You know the place I mean. You can picture it. Paths that go at noon but a little way into the jungle which overshadows an isolated community of strange but kindly folk, paths that end in a twilight stillness; ardent hues, flowers of vanilla, warm rain, a luscious and generative earth, fireflies in the scented dusk of gardens; and mystery—every outlook disappearing in the dark of the unknown.

Well, here I was, placed by the ordinary moves of circumstance in the very place the name of which once had been to me like a chord of that music none hears but oneself. I stood in Para, outside a picture postcard shop. Electric cars were bumping down a narrow street. The glitter of a cheap jeweller's was next to the stationer's; and on the other side was a vendor of American and Parisian boots. There have been changes in Para since Bates wrote his idylls of the forest. We two travellers, after ordering some red earthenware chatties, went to find Bates' village of Nazareth. In 1850 it was a mile from the town. It is part of the town now, and an electric tram took us there, a tram which drove vultures off the line as it bumped along. The heat was a serious burden. The many dogs, which found energy enough to limp out of the way of the car only when at the point of death, were thin and diseased, and most unfortunate to our nice eyes. The Brazilian men of better quality we passed were dressed in black cloth suits, and one mocked the equator with a silk hat and yellow boots. I set down these things as the tram showed them. The evident pride and hauteur, too, of these Latins, was a surprise to one of a stronger race. We stopped at a street corner, and this was Nazareth. Bates' pleasant hamlet is now the place of Para's fashionable homes—pleasant still, though the overhead tram cables, and the electric light standards which interrupt the avenues of trees, place you there, now your own turn comes to look for the romance of the tropics, in another century. But the villas are in heliotrope, primrose, azure, and rose, bowered in extravagant arbors of papaws, mangoes, bananas, and palms, with shrubberies beneath of feathery mimosas, and cassias with orange and crimson blooms. And my last walk ashore was in Swansea High Street in the winter rain! From Nazareth's main street the side turnings go down to the forest. For, in spite of its quays, its steamers, and its electric trams, Para is but built in a larger clearing of the wilderness. The jungle stood at the bottom of all suburban streets, a definite city wall. The spontaneity and savage freedom of the plant life in this land of alternate hot sun and warm showers at last blurred and made insignificant to me the men who braved it in silk hats and broadcloth there, and the trams, and the jewellers' shops, for my experience of vegetation was got on my knees in a London suburb, praying things to come out of the cold mud. Here, I began to suspect, they beseiged us, quick and turbulent, an exhaustible army, ready to reconquer the foothold man had hardly won, and to obliterate his works.

We passed through by-ways, where naked brown babies played before the doors. We happened upon the cathedral, and went on to the little dock where native vessels rested on garbage, the tide being out. Vultures pulled at stuff beneath the bilges. The crews, more Indian than anything, and men of better body than the sallow fellows in the town, sprawled on the hot stones of the quays and about the decks. There was a huge negress, arms akimbo, a shapeless monument in black indiarubber draped in cotton print, who talked loudly with a red boneless mouth to two disregarding Indians sitting with their backs to a wall. She had a rabbit's foot, mounted in silver, hanging between her dugs. The schooners, ranged in an arcade, were rigged for lateen sails, very like Mediterranean craft. The forest was a narrow neutral tinted ribbon far beyond. The sky was blue, the texture of porcelain. The river was yellow. And I was grievously disappointed; yet if you put it to me I cannot say why. There was something missing, and I don't know what. There was something I could not find; but as it is too intangible a matter for me to describe even now, you may say, if you like, that the fault was with me, and not with Para. We stood in a shady place, and the doctor, looking down at his hand, suddenly struck it. "Let us go," he said. He showed me the corpse of a mosquito. "Have you ever seen the yellow fever chap?" the Doctor asked. "That is he." We left.

Near the agent's office we met an English shipping clerk, and he took us into a drink shop, and sat us at a marble-topped table having gilded iron legs, and called for gin tonics. We began to tell him what we thought of Para. It did not seem much of a place. It was neither here nor there.

He was a pallid fellow with a contemplative smile, and with weary eyes and tired movements. "I know all that," he said. "It's a bit of a hole. Still—you'd be surprised. There's a lot here you don't see at first. It's big. All out there"—he waved his arm west inclusively—"it's a world with no light yet. You get lost in it. But you're going up. You'll see. The other end of the forest is as far from the people in the streets here as London is—it's farther—and they know no more about it. I was like you when I first came. I gave the place a week, and then reckoned I knew it near enough. Now, I'm —well, I'm half afraid of it . . . not afraid of anything I can see . . . I don't know. There's something damn strange about it. Something you never can find out. It's something that's been here since the beginning, and it's too big and strong for us. It waits its time. I can feel it now. Look at those palm trees, outside. Don't they look as if they're waiting? What are they waiting for? You get that feeling here in the afternoon when you can't get air, and the rain clouds are banking up round the woods, and nothing moves. 'Lord,' said a fellow to me when I first came, 'tell us about Peckham. But for the spicy talk about yellow fever I'd think I was dead and waiting wide awake for the judgment day.' That's just the feeling. As if something dark was coming and you couldn't move. There the forest is, all round us. Nobody knows what's at the back of it. Men leave Para, going up river. We have a drink in here, and they go up river, and don't come back.

"Down by the square one day I saw an old boy in white

ducks and a sun helmet having a shindy with the sentry at the barracks. The old fellow was kicking up a dust. He was English, and I suppose he thought the sentry would under-stand him, if he shouted. English and Americans do.

"You have to get into the road here, when you approach the barracks. It's the custom. The sentry always sends you off the pavement. The old chap was quite red in the face about it. And the things he was saying! Lucky for him the soldier didn't know what he meant. So I went over, as he was an Englishman, and told him what the sentry wanted. 'What,' said the man, 'walk in the road? Not me. I'd sooner go back.'

"Go back he did, too. I walked with him and we got rather pally. We came in here. We sat at that table in the corner. He said he was Captain Davis, of Barry. Ever heard of him? He said he had brought out a shallow-draught river boat, and he was taking her up the Rio Japura. The way he talked! Do you know the Japura? Well, it's a deuce of a way from here. But that old captain talked—he talked like a child. He was so obstinate about it. He was going to take that boat up the Japura, and you'd have thought it was above Boulter's Lock. Then he began to swear about the dagoes.

"The old chap got quite wild again when he thought of that soldier. He was a little man, nothing of him, and his face was screwed up as if he was always annoyed about something. You have to take things as they come, here, and let it go. But this Davis man was an irritable old boy, and most of his talk was about money. He said he was through with the boat running jobs. No more of 'em. It was as bare as boards. Nothing to be made at the game, he said. Over his left eye he had a funny hairy wart, a sort of knob, and whenever he got excited it turned red. I may say he let me pay for all the drinks. I reckon he was pretty close with his money.

"He told me he knew a man in Barry who'd got a fine pub—a little gold-mine. He said there was a stuffed bear at the pub and it brought lots of customers. Seemed to think I must know the place. He said he was going to try to get an alligator for the chap who kept the pub. The alligator could stand on its hind legs at the other side of the door, with an electric bulb in its mouth, like a lemon. That was his fine side. He reckoned that would bring customers. Then old Davis started to fidget about. I began to think he wanted to tell me something, and I wondered what the deuce it was. I thought it was money. It generally is. At last he told me. He wanted one of those dried Indian heads for that pub. 'You know what I mean,' he said. 'The Indians kill somebody, and make his head smaller than a baby's, and the hair hangs down all round.'

"Have you ever seen one of those heads? The Indians bone 'em, and stuff 'em with spice and gums, and let 'em dry in the sun. They don't look nice. I've seen one or two.

"But I tried to persuade him to let the head go. The Government has stopped that business, you know. Got a bit too thick. If you ordered a head, the Johnnies would just go out and have somebody's napper.

"I missed old Davis after that. I was transferred to Man-aõs, up river. I don't know what became of him. It was nearly a year when I came back to Para. Our people had had the clearing of that boat old Davis brought out, and I found some of his papers, still unsettled. I asked about him, in a general way, and found he hadn't arrived. His tug had been back twice. When it was here last it seemed the native skipper explained Davis went ashore, when returning, at a place where they touched for rubber. He went into the village and didn't come back. Well, it seems the skipper waited. No Davis. So he tootled his whistle and went on up stream, because the river was falling, and he had some more stations to do in the season. He was at the village again in a few days, though, and Davis wasn't there then. The tug captain said the village was deserted, and he supposed the old chap had gone down river in another boat. But he's not back yet. The boss said the fever had got him, somewhere. That's the way things go here.

"A month ago an American civil engineer touched here, and had to wait for a boat for New York. He'd been right up country surveying for some job or another, Peru way. I went up to his hotel with the fellows to see him one evening. He was on his knees packing his trunks. 'Say, boys,' he said, sitting on the floor, 'I brought a whole lot of truck from way up, and now it hasn't got a smile for me.' He offered me his collection of butterflies. Then the Yankee picked up a ball of newspaper off the floor, and began to peel it. 'This goes home,' he said. 'Have you seen anything like that? I bet you haven't.' He held out the opened packet in his hand, and there was a brown core to it. 'I reckon that is thousands of years old,' said the American.

"It was a little dried head, no bigger than a cricket ball, and about the same colour. Very like an Indian's too. The features were quite plain, and there was a tiny wart over the left eye-brow. 'I bet you that's thousands of years old,' said the American. 'I bet you it isn't two,' I said."

We returned to the steamer in the late afternoon, bringing with us two Brazilian pilots, who were to take us as far as Ita-coatiara. We sailed next morning for the interior. Para, like all the towns on the Amazon, has but one way out of it. There is a continent behind Para, but you cannot go that way; when you leave the city you must take the river. Para stands by the only entrance to what is now the greatest region of virgin tropics left in the world. Always at anchor off the city's front are at least a dozen European steamers, most of them flying the red ensign. A famous engineering contractor, also British, is busy constructing modern wharves there; and Thames tugs and mudhoppers, flying the Brazilian flag, as the law insists, but bawling London compliments as they pass your ship, help the native schooners with their rakish lateen sails, blue and scarlet, to make the anchorage brisk and lively. Looking out from the "Capella's" bridge she appeared to be within a lagoon. The lake was elliptical, and so large it was a world for the eye to range in. It was bound by a low barrier of forest, a barrier distant enough to lose colour, nature, and significance. Para, white and red, lay reflecting the sunset from many facets in the south-west, with a cheerful array of superior towers and spires. From the ship Para looked big, modern, and prosperous; and with those vast rounded clouds of the rains assembling and mounting over the bright city, and brooding there, impassive and dark, but with impending keels lustrous with the burnish of copper and steel, and seeing a rainbow curving down from one cloud over the city's white front, I, being a new-comer, and with a pardonable feeling of exhilaration which was of my own well-being in a new and a wide and radiant place, thought of man there as a conqueror who had overcome the wilderness, builded him a city, bridled the exuberance of a savage land, and directed the sap and life, born in a rich soil of ardent sun and rain, into the forms useful to him. So I entered the chart-room, and looked with a new interest on the chart of the place. Then I felt less certain of the conqueror and his taming bridle. I saw that this lagoon in which the "Capella" showed large and important was but a point in an immense area of tractless islands and meandering waterways, a region intricate, and, the chart confessed, little known. The coast opposite the city, which I had taken for mainland, was the trivial Ihla des Oncas. The main channel of the river was beyond that island, with the coast of Marajo for the farther shore; and Marajo also was but an island, though as large as Wales. The north channel of the Amazon was beyond again, with more islands, about which the chart confessed less knowledge. One of the pilots was with me; and when I spoke of those points in the ultimate Amazons, the alluring names on maps you read in England, here they were, at Para, just what they are at home, still vague and far, journeys thither to be reckoned by time; a shrug of the shoulders and a look of amusement; two months, Senhor, or perhaps three or four. The idea came slowly; but it dawned, something like the conception of astronomy's amplitudes, of the remoteness of the beyond of Amazonas, that new world I had just entered.

I crept within the mosquito curtain that night, and the still heated dark lay on my mind, the pressure of an unknown full of dread. I thought of the pale shipping clerk and his tired smile, and of Captain Davis, his face no bigger than a cricket ball, and the same colour, with a wart over his eye; and recalled the anxious canvass I had heard made for news of sickness up-river. A ship had passed outwards that morning, the consul told us, with twenty men on board down with fever.

And Thorwaldsen. I forgot to tell you about Thorwaldsen. He was a trader, and last rainy season he took his vessel up some far backwater, beyond Manaōs, with his wife and his little daughter. News had just come from nowhere to Para that his wife had died in childbirth in the wilds, and Thorwaldsen had been murdered; but nothing was known of his daughter. There it was. I did not know the Thorwaldsens. But the trader's little girl who might then be alone in the gloom of the jungle with savages, helped to keep me awake. And the wife, that fair-haired Swede; she was in the alien wilderness, beyond all gentlehood, when her time came. I could see two mosquitoes doing their best to work backwards through the curtain mesh. They were after me, the emissaries of the unknown, and their pertinacity was astonishing.

"*Jan. 9.* The 'Capella' left Para at three o'clock this morning, and continued up the Para River. Daylight found us in a wide brownish stream, with the shores low and indistinguishable on either beam. When the sun grew hot, the jungle came close in; it was often so close that we could see the nests of wasps on the trees, like grey shields hanging there. Between the Para River and the Amazon the waters dissipate into a maze of serpenting ditches. In width these channels usually are no more than canals, but they were deep enough to float our big tramp steamer. They thread a multitude of islands, islands overloaded with a massed growth which topped our mast-heads. Our steamer was enclosed within resonant chasms, and the noise and incongruity of our progress awoke deep protests there.

"The dilated loom of the rains, the cloud shapes so continental that they occupied, where they stood not so far away, all the space between the earth and sky, bulged over the forest at the end of every view. The heat was luscious; but then I had nothing to do but to look on from a hammock under the awning. The foliage which was pressed out over the water, not many yards from the hurrying 'Capella,' had a closeness of texture astonishing, and even awful, to one who knew only the thin woods of the north. It ascended directly from the water's edge, sometimes out of the water, and we did not often see its foundation. There were no shady aisles and glades. The sight was stopped on a front of polished emerald, a congestion of still leaves. The air was still. Individual sprays and fronds, projecting from the mass in parabolas with flamboyant abandon and poise, were as rigid as metallic and enamelled shapes. The diversity of forms, and especially the number and variety of the palms, so overloaded an unseen standing that the parapets of the woods occasionally leaned outwards to form an arcade above our masts. One should not call this the jungle; it was even a soft and benignant Eden. This was the forest I really wished to find. Often the heavy parapets of the woods were upheld on long colonnades of grey palm boles; or the whole upper structure appeared based on low green arches, the pennate fronds of smaller palms flung direct from the earth.

"There was not a sound but the noise of our intruding steamer. Occasionally we brushed a projecting spray, or a vine pendent from a cornice. We proved the forest then. In some shallow places were regiments of aquatic grasses, bearing long plumes. There were trees which stood in the water on a tangle of straight pallid roots, as though on stilts. This up-burst of intense life so seldom showed the land to which it was fast, and the side rivers and paranas were so many, that I could believe the forest afloat, an archipelago of opaque green vapours. Our heavy wash swayed and undulated the aquatic plants and grasses, as though disturbing the fringe of those green clouds which clung to the water because of their weight in a still air.

"There was seldom a sign of life but the infrequent snowy herons, and those curious brown fowl, the ciganas. The sun was flaming on the majestic assembly of the storm. The warm air, broken by our steamer, coiled over us in a lazy flux. I did not hear the bell calling to meals. We all hung over the 'Capella's' side, gaping, like a lot of boys.

"Sometimes we passed single habitations on the water side. Ephemeral huts of palm-leaves were forced down by the forest, which overhung them, to wade on frail stilts. A canoe would be tied to a toy jetty, and on the jetty a sad woman and several naked children would stand, with no show of emotion, to watch us go by. Behind them was the impenetrable foliage. I thought of the precarious tenure on earth of these brown folk with some sadness, especially as the day was going. The easy dominance of the wilderness, and man's intelligent morsel of life resisting it, was made plain when we came suddenly upon one of his little shacks secreted among the aqueous roots of a great tree, cowering, as it were, between two of the giant's toes. Those brown babies on the jetties never cheered us. They watched us, serious and forlorn. Alongside their primitive hut were a few rubber trees, which we knew by their scars. Late in the afternoon we came to a large cavern in the base of the forest, a shadowy place where at last we did see a gathering of the folk. A number of little wooden crosses peeped above the floor in the hollow. The sundering floods and the forest do not always keep these folk from congregation, and the comfort of the last communion.

"There was a question at night as to whether our pilots would anchor or not. They decided to go on. We did not go the route of Bates, *via* Breves, but took the Parana de Buyassa on our way to the Amazon. It was night when we got to the parana, and but for the trailing lights, the fairy mooring lines of habitations in the woods, and what the silent explosions of lightning revealed of great heads of trees, startlingly close and monstrous, as though watching us in silent and intent regard, we saw nothing of it."

Once I knew a small boy, and on a summer day too much in the past now to be recalled without some private emotion, he said to his father, on the beach of a popular East Anglian resort, "And where is the sea?" He stood then, for the first time, where the sea, by all the promises of pictures and poems, should have been breaking on its cold grey crags. "The sea?" said the father, in astonishment, "why, there it is. Didn't you know?"

And that father, being an exact man, there beyond appeal

the sea was. And what was it? A discoloured wash, of mean limit, which flopped wearily on some shabby sands littered with people and luncheon papers. Such a flat, stupid, and leaden disillusion surely never before fell on the upturned, bright and expectant soul of a young human, who, I can vouch, began life, like most others, believing the noblest of everything. It was an ocean which was inferior even to the bathing-machines, and could be seen but in division when that child, walking along the rank of those boxes on wheels, peeped between them.

You will have noticed with what simple indifference the people who really know what they call the truth will shatter an illusion we have long cherished; though, as we alone see our private dreams, those honest folk cannot be blamed for poking their feet through fine pictures they did not know were there.

I had a picture of the Amazon, which I had long cherished. I was leaning to-day over the bulwarks of the "Capella" watching the jungle pass. The Doctor was with me. I thought we were still on the Para River, and was waiting for our vessel to emerge from that stream, as through a narrow gate, dramatically, into the broad sunlight of the greatest river in the world, the king of rivers, the Amazon of my picture. We idly scanned the forest with binoculars, having nothing to do, and saw some herons, and the ciganas, and once a sloth which was hanging to a tree. Para, I felt, was as distant as London. The silence, the immobility of it all, and the pour of the tropic sun, were just beginning to be a little subduing. We had come already to the wilderness. There was, I thought, a very great deal of this forest; and it never varied.

"We shall be on the Amazon soon," I said hopefully, to the doctor.

"We have been on it for hours," he replied. And that is how I got there.

But the Amazon is not seen, any more than is the sea, at the first glance. What the eye first gathers, is, naturally (for it is but an eye), nothing like commensurate with your own image of the river. The mind, by suggestive symbols, builds something portentous, a vague and tremendous idea. What I saw was only a very swift and opaque yellow flood, not much broader, it seemed to me, than the Thames at Gravesend, and the monotonous green of the forest. It was all I saw for a considerable time.

I see something different now. It is not easily explained merely as a yellow river, with a verdant elevation on either hand, and over it a blue sky. It would be difficult to find, except by luck, a word which would convey the immensity of the land of the Amazons, something of the aloofness and separation of the points of its extremes, with months and months of adventure between them. What a journey it would be from Ino in Bolivia, on the Rio Madre de Dios, to Conception in Colombia, on the Rio Putumayo; there is another "Odyssey" in a voyage like that. And think of the names of those places and rivers! When I take the map of South America now, and hold it with the estuary of the Amazon as its base, my thoughts are like those might be of a lost ant, crawling in and over the furrows and ridges of an exposed root as he regards all he may of the trunk rising into the whole upper cosmos of a spreading oak. The Amazon then looks to me, properly symbolical, as a monstrous tree, and its tributaries, paranas, furos, and igarapes, as the great boughs, little boughs, and twigs of its ascending and spreading ramifications, so minutely dissecting the continent with its numberless water-courses that the mind sees that dark region as an impenetrable density of green and secret leaves; which, literally, when you go there, is what you will find. You enter the leaves, and vanish. You creep about the region of but one of its branches, under a roof of foliage which stays the midday shine and lets it through to you in the dusk of the interior but as points of distant starlight. Occasionally, as we did upon a day, you see something like Santarem. There is a break and a change in the journey. Moving blindly through the maze of green, there, hanging in the clear day at the end of a bough, is a golden fruit.

"*Jan.* 10. The torrid morning, tempered by a cooling breeze which followed us up river, was soon overcast. Disappointingly narrow at first, the Amazon broadened later, but not to one's conception of its magnitude. But the greatness of this stream, I have already learned, dawns upon you in time, and if you sufficiently endure. It persists about you, this forest and this river, like the stark desolation of the sea. The real width of the river is not often seen because of the islands which fringe its banks, many of them of considerable size. The side channels, or paranas-miris, between the islands and the shores, are used in preference to the main stream by the native sailing craft, to avoid the strength of the current. We have the river to ourselves. The 'Capella' was taken by the pilots, first over to one side and then to the other, dodging the set of the stream. The forest has changed. It has now a graceless and savage aspect when we are close to it. There are not so many palms. At a little distance the growth appears a mass of spindly oaks and beeches, though with a more vivid and lighter green foliage. But when near it shows itself alien enough, a front of nameless and congested leaves. I suppose it would be more than a hundred feet in altitude. Sometimes the forest stands in the water. At other times a yellow bank shows, a narrow strip under the trees, rarely more than four feet high, and strewn with the bleaching skeletons of trees and entanglements of vine. There is rarely a sign of life. Once this morning a bird called in the woods when we were close. Butterflies are continually crossing the ship, and dragon-flies and great wasps and hornets are hawking over us. The sight of one swallowtail butterfly, a big black and yellow fellow, sent the cook insane. The insect stayed its noble flight, poised over our hatch, and then came down to see what we were. It settled on a coil of rope, leisurely pulsing its wings. The cook, at the sight of this bold and bright being, sprang from the galley, and leaped down to the deck with a dish cloth. To our surprise he caught the insect, and explained with eagerness how that shattered pattern of colours, which more than covered his gross palm, would improve his fire-screen in a Rotterdam parlour.

"Early in the forenoon sections of the forest vanished in grey rain squalls, though elsewhere the sun was brilliant. The plane of the dingy yellow flood was variegated with transient

areas of bright sulphur and chocolate. We were hugging the
right bank, and so saw the mouth of the Xingu as we passed.
At midday some hills ahead, the Serra de Almerim, gave us
relief from the dead level of the wearying green walls. The
sight of those blue heights with their flat tops—they were
perhaps no more than 100 feet above the forest—curiously
stimulated the eye and lifted one's humour, long depressed by
the everlasting sameness of the prospect and the heat. Later
in the day we passed more of the welcome hills, the Serra de
Maranuaqua, Velha Pobre, and Serras de Tapaiunaquara and
Paranaquara, their cones, truncated pyramids, knolls and hog
backs, ranging contrary to our course. Bates says some of
them are bare, or covered only with a short herbage; but all
those I examined with a good telescope had forest to the
summits; though a few of the inferior heights, which stood
behind the island of Jurupari (the island where dreams come
at night) were grassy. Those cobalt prominences rose like
precipitous islands from a green sea. We were the only spec-
tators. One high range, as we passed, was veiled in a glittering
mesh of rain. The river, after we left Jurupari, bent round and
brought the heights astern of us. The sun set.

"The river and the forest are best at sundown. The serene
level rays discovered the woods. We saw trees then distinctly, almost as a surprise. Till then the forest had been
but a gloom by day. Behind us was the jungle front. It
changed from green to gold, a band of light between the river
and the darkling sky. Some greater trees emerged majesti-
cally. It was the first time that day we had really seen the
features of the jungle. It was but a momentary revelation.
The clouds were reflectors, throwing amber lights below. In
the hills astern of us ravines hitherto unsuspected caught
the transitory glory. The dark heights had many polished
facets. One range, round-shouldered and wooded, I thought
resembled the promontories about Clovelly, and for a few
minutes the Amazon had the bright eyes of a friend. On a
ridge of those heights I could see the sky through some of its
trees. The light quickly gave out, and it was night.

"We continued cruising along the south shore. The usual
pulsations of lightning made night intermittent; the forest

was not more than 150 feet from our vessel, and sitting under the awning the trees kept jumping out of the night, startlingly near. The night was still and hot, and my cabin lamp had attracted myriads of insects through the door which had been left open for air. A heap of crawlers lay dead on the desk, and the bunk curtain was smothered with grotesque winged shapes, flies, cicadas, mantis, phasmas, moths, beetles, and mosquitoes."

Next morning found us running along the north shore. Parrots were squawking in the woods alongside. A large alligator floated close by the ship, its jaws open in menace. At breakfast time a strip of white beach came into view on the opposite coast, a place in that world of three colours on which one's tired eyes could alight and rest. That was Santarem. Sharp hills rose immediately behind the town. The town is in a saddle of the hills, slipping down to the river in terraces of white, chrome, and blue houses. The Rio Tapajos, a black water tributary and a noble river, enters the main stream by Santarem, its dark flood sharply contrasted with the tawny Amazon. But the Amazon seeps right across its mouth in a masterful way. There is a definite line dividing black from yellow water, and then no more Tapajos.

We passed numerous floating islands (Ilhas de Caapim) and trees adrift, evidence, the pilots said, that the river was rising. These grass islands are a feature of the Amazon. They look like lush pastures adrift. Some of them are so large it is difficult to believe they are really afloat till they come along-side. Then, if the river is at all broken by a breeze, the meadow plainly undulates. This floating cane and grass grows in the sheltered bays and quiet paranas-miris, for though the latter are navigable side-channels of the river in the rainy season, in the dry they are merely isolated swamps. But when the river is in flood the earth is washed away from the roots of this marsh growth, and it moves off, a flourishing, mobile field, often twenty feet in thickness. Such islands, when large, can be dangerous to small craft. Small flowers blossom on these aquatic fields, which shelter snakes and turtles, and sometimes the peixe-boi, the manatee.

Obydos was in sight in the afternoon, but presently we lost it in a violent squall of rain. The squall came down like a gun burst, and nearly carried away the awnings. It was evening before we were abreast of that most picturesque town I saw on the river. Obydos rests on one of the rare Amazon cliffs of rufus clay and sandstone. The forest mounts the hill above it, and the scattered red roofs of the town show in a surf of foliage. The cliffs glowed in cream and cherry tints, with a cascade of vines falling over them, though not reaching the shore. The dainty little houses sit high in a loop of the cliffs. We left the city behind, with a huge cumulus cloud resting over it, and the evening light on all.

But Obydos and sunsets and rain squalls, and the fireflies which flit about the dark ship at night in myriads, tiny blue and yellow glow-lamps which burn with puzzling inconstancy, as though being switched on and off, though they help me with this narrative, yet candour compels me to tell you that they take up more space in this book than they do in the land of the Amazon. They were incidental and small to us, dominated by the shadowing presence of the forest.

We have been on the river nearly a week. But our steamer's decks, even by day, are deserted now. We lean overside no longer looking at this strange country. The heat is the most noteworthy fact, and drives every one to what little leeward to the glare there is. Our cook, who is a salamander of a fellow, and has no need to fear the possibilities of his future life—though I do not remember he ever told me he was really thoughtful for them—feeling a little uncomfortable one day when at work on our dinner, glanced at his thermometer, and fled in terror. It registered 134°. He begged me to go in and verify it, and once inside I was hardly any time doing that. We have such days, without a breath of air, and two vivid walls of still jungle, and between them a yellow river serpentining under the torrid sun, and a silence which is like deafness.

Under the shadow of the awning aft, in his deck chair, the

Doctor is preparing our defences by sounding a profound volume on tropical diseases. This gives us but little confidence; though, as to our surgeon, recently I overheard one fireman to another, "I tell yer the—doc's a Man. That's what he is." (This is the result of the gin with the quinine.) Yet, good man as he is, his book on the consequences of the tropics is so large that we fear we all cannot escape so many impediments to joy. But our health's guardian is careful we do not anticipate anything from peeps into the mysteries. He never leaves his big book about, much as some of us would like to see the pictures in it, after what the donkey-man told us.

This is how it was. Donkey, in spite of instructions, and I know how emphatic the Skipper usually is, slept on deck away from his mosquito bar a few nights ago. He said at the time that he wasn't afraid of them little fanciful biters, or something of the kind. I have no doubt the Doctor would have had some trouble in making clear to Donkey's understanding exactly what are the links, delicate but sure, between mosquitoes and dissolution and decay in man. So he showed Donkey a picture. I wish I knew what it was—but the surgeon preserves the usual professional reticence in the affairs of his patients. For now Donkey is convinced it is very bad to sleep outside his curtain, and when he tries to tell us how unwholesome such sleeping can be, just at the point when he gets most entertaining his vocabulary wears into holes and tatters. You could not conjure that man from his curtain now, no, not if you showed him, in a vision, Cardiff, and the fairy lights of all its dock hotels. I know that in the Doctor's book there is a picture of a negro who acquired, in a superb way, a wonderful form of elephantiasis, for the Doctor showed it to me once, as a treat, when he thought I was growing slack and bored.

We require now such childish laughter at each other's discomfiture to break the spell of this land into which we are sinking deeper. Still the forest glides by. It is a shadow on the mind. It stands over us, an insistent riddle, every morning when I look out from by bunk. I watch it all day, drawn against my will; and as day is dying it is still there, paramount, enigmatic, silent, its question implied in its mere persistence—meeting me again on the next day, still with its mute interrogation.

We have been passing it for nearly a week. It should have convinced me by now that it is something material. But why should I suppose it is that? We have had no chance to examine it. It does not look real. It does not remind me of anything I know of vegetation. When you sight your first mountains, a delicate and phantom gleam athwart the stars, are you reminded of the substance of the hills? I have been watching it for so long, this abiding and soundless forest, that now I think it is like the sky, intangible, an apparition; what the eye sees of the infinite, just as the eye sees a blue colour overhead at midday, and the glow of the Milky Way at night. For the mind sees this forest better than the eye. The mind is not deceived by what merely shows. Wherever the steamer drives the forest recedes, as does the sky at sea; but it never leaves us.

The jungle gains nothing, and loses nothing, at noon. It is only a sombre thought still, as at mid-night. It is still, at noon, so obscure and dumb a presence that I suspect the sun does not illuminate it so much as reveal our steamer in its midst. We are revealed instead. The presence sees us advancing into its solitudes, a small, busy, and impudent intruder. But the forest does not greet, and does not resent us. It regards us with the vacancy of large composure, with a lofty watchfulness which has no need to show its mind. I think it knows our fears of its domain. It knows the secret of our fate. It makes no sign. The pallid boles of the trees, the sentinels by the water with the press of verdure behind them, stand, as we pass, like soundless exclamations. So when we go close in shore I find myself listening for a chance whisper, a careless betrayal of the secret. There is not a murmur in the host; though once a white bird flew yauping from a tree, and then it seemed the desolation had been surprised into a cry, a prolonged and melancholy admonition. Following that the silence was deepened, as though an indiscretion were regretted. A sustained and angry protest at our presence would have been natural; but not that infinite line of lofty trees, darkly superior, silently watching us pass.

One night we anchored off the south shore in twenty fathoms, but close under the trees. At daybreak we stood over to the opposite bank. The river here was of great width, the north coast being low and indistinct. These tacks across stream look so purposeless, in a place where there are no men and all the water looks the same. You go over for nothing. But this morning, high above the land ahead, some specks were seen drifting like fragments of burnt paper, the sport of an idle and distant wind. Those drifting dots were urubus, the vultures, generally the first sign that a settle-ment is near. To come upon a settlement upon the Amazons is like landfall at sea. It brings all on deck. And there, at last, was Ita-coatiara or Serpa. From one of the infrequent, low, ferruginous cliffs of this river the jungle had been cleared, and on that short range of modest, undulating heights which displaced the green palisades with soft glowings of rose, cherry, and orange rock, the sight escaped to a disorder of arboured houses, like a disarray of little white cubes; Serpa was, in appearance, half a basketful of white bricks shot into a portico of the forest.

That morning was no inducement to exertion, but when an Indian paddled his canoe alongside our anchored steamer the Doctor and the Purser got into it, and away. The hot earth would be a change from hot iron. Besides, I was eager for my first walk in equatorial woods. Our steamer was anchored below the town, off a small campo, or clearing. The native swashed his canoe into a margin of floating plants, which had rounded leaves and inflated stalks, like buoys. I looked at them, and indeed at the least thing, as keenly as though we were now going to land in the moon. Nothing should escape me; the colour of the mud, the water tepid to my hand, the bronze canoeman in his pair of old cotton pants split just where they should have been scrupu-lous, and the weeds and grass. I would drain my tropics to the last precious drop. I myself was seeing what I had thought others lucky to have seen. It was like being born into the world as an understanding adult. We got to a steep bank of red clay, fissured by the heat, and as hard as brick-work. Green and brown lizards whisked before us as we broke the quiet. From the top of the bank the anchored steamer looked a little stranger. Aboard her, and she is a busy village. Now she appeared but a mark I did not recognise in that reticent solitude. The Amazon was an immensity of water, a plain of burnished silver, where headlands, islands, and lines of cliff were all cut in one level mass of emerald veined with white. The canoe going downstream appeared to dissolve in candent vapour. Cloudland low down over the forest to the south, a far disorder of violet heights, waiting to fill the sky at sunset and to shock our unimportance then with convul-sions of blue flames, did not seem more aloof and inaccessible to me than our immediate surroundings.

The clearing was a small bay in the jungle. A few statuesque silk-cotton trees, buttressed giants, were isolated in its centre. A bunch of dun-coloured cattle with twisted horns stood beneath them, though the trees gave them no shade, for each grey trunk was as bare of branches for sixty feet of its length as a stone column. The wall of the jungle was quite near, and as I stood watching it intently, I could hear but the throb of my own life. The faint sibilation of insects was only as if, in the silence, you heard the sharp rays of the sun impinge on the earth; your finer ear caught that sound when you forget the ring and beat of your body. It was something below mere silence.

We approached the wall to the west, as a path went through the harsh swamp herbage that way, and entered the jungle. The sun went out almost at once. It was cellar cool under the trees. We had no idea where the path would lead us. That did not matter. No doubt it would be the place desired. The Doctor walked ahead, and I could just see his helmet, the way was so narrow and uncertain. I kept missing the helmet, for everything in the half-lighted solitude was strange. One could not keep an eye on a white hat on one's first equatorial ramble, and only when the quiet was heavy enough to be a burden did I look up from a puzzling leaf, or some busy ants, to find myself alone. There was a feeling that you were being watched; but there were no eyes, when you glanced round quickly. Do you remember that dream which sometimes came when we were children? There were, I remember, empty corridors prolonging into the shadows of a nameless house where not a sign showed of what was there. We went on, and no words we could think of when we woke could tell what we felt when we looked into those long silent aisles of the house without a name; for we knew something was there; but there was no telling what the thing would be like when it showed. That is your sensation in a first walk in a Brazilian forest.

I stopped at lianas, and curious foliage, trying to trace them to a beginning, but rarely with any success. There were some mantis, which commenced to run on a tree while I was examining its bark. They were like flakes of the bark. For a moment the tree seemed to quiver its hide at my irritating touch. Then the Doctor called, and I pushed along to find him stooping over a land snail, the size of a man's fist, which rather puzzled him, for it had what he called an operculum; that is, a cap such as a winkle's, only in this case it was as large as a crown piece. I do not know if it was the operculum, for my knowledge of such things is small; but I did feel this was the only twelfth birthday which had come to me for many years.

Presently we saw light, as you would from the interior of a tunnel. Some beams of sunshine slanted from a break in the roof to where a tree had fallen, making a bridge for us across an igaripe, a stream, that is, large enough to be a way for a canoe. The sundered, buttressed roots of the tree formed a steep climb to begin with, but the buttresses going straight along the trunk as handrails made crossing the bridge an easy matter. Raising my hand to a root which was hot in the sun, and watching a helicon butterfly, a black and yellow fellow, which settled near us, slowly open and shut his wings, I jumped, because it felt as though a lighted match had dropped into my sleeve. But I couldn't douse it. It burned in ten places at once. It was a first lesson in constant watchfulness in this new world. I had placed my hand in a swarm of inconspicuous fire ants. The dead tree was alive

with them, and our passage quickened. We rubbed ourselves
hysterically, for the Doctor had got some too; and there was
no professional reserve about him that time.

After crossing the igaripe the character of the forest
changed. It was now a growth of wild cacao trees. Nothing
grew beneath them. The floor was a black paste, littered
with dead sticks. The woods were more open, but darker and
more dank than before. The sooty limbs of the cacao trees
grew low, and filled the view ahead with a perplexity of
leafless and tortured boughs. They were hung about with
fruit, pendent lamps lit with a pale greenish light. We saw
nothing move there but two delicate butterflies, which had
transparent wings with opaque crimson spots, such as might
have been served Titania herself; yet the gloom and black
ooze, and the eerie globes, with their illusion of light hung
upon distorted shapes, was more the home of the fabulous
sucuruja, the serpent which is forty feet long.

A dry stick snapping underfoot had the same effect as that
crash which resounds for some embarrassing seconds when
your umbrella drops in a gallery of the British Museum. The
impulse was to apologise to something. We had been so long
in the twilight, recoiling at nameless objects in the path, a
monstrous legume perhaps a yard long and coiled like a
reptile, seeing things only with a second look, that the
sudden entrance into a malocal, a forest clearing, which, as
though it were a reservoir, the sun had filled with bright
light, was like a plunge into a warm, fluid, and lustrous
element.

In the clearing were the huts of an Indian village. Only the
roofs could be seen, through some plantations of bananas.
Around the clearing, a side of which was cut off by a stream,
was the overshadowing green presence. Some chocolate
babies, as serious as gnomes, looked up as we came into
daylight, opened their eyes wide, and fled up the path
between the plantains.

If I could sing, I would sing the banana. It has the loveliest
leaf I know. I feel intemperate about it, because I came upon
it after our passage through a wood which could have been
underground, a tangle of bare roots joining floor and ceiling

in limitless caverns. We stood looking at the plantation till our mind was fed with grace and light. The plantain jets upwards with a copious stem, and the fountain returns in broad rippled pennants, falling outwardly, refined to points, when the impulse is lost. A world could not be old on which such a plant grows. It is sure evidence of earth's vitality. To look at it you would not think that growing is a long process, a matter of months and natural difficulties. The plantain is an instant and joyous answer to the sun. The midribs of the leaves, powerful but resilient, held aloft in generous arches the broad planes of translucent green substance. It is not a fragile and dainty thing, except in colour and form. It is lush and solid, though its ascent is so aerial, and its form is content to the eye. There is no green like that of its leaves, except at sea. The stout midribs are sometimes rosy, but the banners they hold well above your upturned face are as the crest of a wave in the moment of collapse, the day showing through its fluid glass. And after the place of dead matter and mummied husks in gloom, where we had been wandering, this burst of leaves in full light was a return to life.

We continued along the path, in the way of the vanished children. Among the bananas were some rubber trees, their pale trunks scored with brown wounds, and under some of the incisions small tin cups adhered, fastened there with clay. In most of the cups the collected latex was congealed, for the cups were half full of rain-water, which was alive with mosquito larvae. The path led to the top of the river bank. The stream was narrow, but full and deep. A number of women and children were bathing below, and they looked up stolidly as we appeared. Some were negligent on the grass, sunning themselves. Others were combing their long, straight hair over their honey- and snuff-coloured bodies. The figures of the women were full, lissom, and rounded, and they posed as if they were aware that this place was theirs. They were as unconscious of their grace as animals. They looked round and up at us, and one stayed her hand, her comb half through the length of her hair, and all gazed intently at us with faces having no expression but a little surprise; then they turned again to proceed with their toilets and their gossip. They looked as proper with their brown and satiny limbs and bodies, in the secluded and sunny arbour where the water ran, framed in exuberant tropical foliage, as a herd of deer.

I had never seen primitive man in his native place till then. There he was, as at the beginning, and I saw with a new respect from what a splendid creature we are derived. It was, I am glad to say, to cheer the existence of these people that I had put money in a church plate at Poplar. Poplar, you may have heard, is a parish in civilisation where an organised community is able, through its heritage of the best of two thousand years of religion, science, commerce, and politics, to eke out to a finish the lives of its members (warped as they so often are by arid dispensations of Providence) with the humane Poor Law. The Poor Law is the civilised man's ironic rebuke to a parsimonious Creator. It is a jest which will ruin the solemnity of the Judgment Day. Only the man of long culture could think of such a shattering insult to the All Wise who made this earth too small for the children He continues to send to it, trailing their clouds of glory which prove a sad hindrance and get so fouled in the fight for standing room on their arrival. But these savages of the Brazilian forest know nothing of the immortal joke conceived by their cleverer brothers. They have all they want. Experience has not taught them to devise such a cosmic mock as a Poor Law. How do these poor savages live then, who have not been vouchsafed such light? They pluck bananas, I suppose, and eat them, swinging in hammocks. They live a purely animal existence. More than that, I even hear that should you find a child hungry in an Indian village, you may be sure all the strong men are hungry too. I was not able to prove that; yet it may be true there are people to-day to whom the law that the fittest must survive has not yet been helpfully revealed. (This is really the Doctor's fault. I should never have thought of Poplar if he had not wondered aloud how those bathers under the palms managed without a workhouse.)

Behind us were the shelters of these settled Indians, the "cabaclos," as they are called in Brazil (literally, copper coloured). Each house was but a square roof of the fronds of a species of attalea palm, upheld at each corner by poles seven feet high. The houses had no sides, but were quite open, except that some had a quarter of the interior partitioned off with a screen of leaves. There was a rough attempt at a garden about each dwelling, with rose bushes and coleas in the midst of gourds and patches of maize. The roses were scented, and of the single briar kind. We entered one of the dwellings, and surprised a young woman within who was swinging in a hammock smoking a native pipe of red clay through a grass stem. One fine limb, free of her cotton gown to the thigh, hung indolently over the hammock, the toes touching the earth and giving the couch movement. Her black hair, all at first we could see of her head, nearly reached the ground.

A well-grown girl, innocent from head to feet, saw us enter, and cried to her mother, who rose in the hammock, threw her gown over her leg, smiled gravely at us, and alighted, to vanish behind the screen with the child, reappearing presently with the girl neatly attired. Other children came, and soon had confidence to examine us closely and critically, grave little mortals with eyes which spoke the only language I understood there. The men and women who gathered stood behind the children, smiling sadly and kindly. They were gentle, undemonstrative, and observant, with features of the conventional Indian type. The men were spare and lithe, of medium height, wearing only shorts tied with string below their bronze busts. The women were of fuller build, with heavier but more cheerful features, and each was dressed in a single cotton garment, open above, revealing the breasts.

The noon shadows of the hut, and the trees, were deep as the stains of ink. A tray of mandioca root, farinha, was set in the hot sun to dry. Under a gourd tree was a heap of turtle shells. A little game, a capybara, and a bird like a crow with a brown rump, were hung on the screen. But the most remarkable feature of the house in the forest was its pets. A pair of parraquets ran in and out the bushes like green mice. My helmet was tipped over my eyes, and, looking upwards, there was an audience of monkeys in the shadow, quite beside themselves with curiousity. My sudden movement sent them off like fireworks. One was a most engaging little fellow, a jet-black tamarin slightly larger than a squirrel. Presently he found courage to come closer, with a companion, a brown monkey of his own size. As they sat side by side the Doctor pointed out that the expressions in the faces of these monkeys showed temperaments separating them even more widely than they were separated by those physical differences which made them species. I saw at once, with some pleasure and a little vanity, that I might be more nearly related to the friendly cabaclos than I am to some people in England. The brown chap would be no doubt a master of industry on the tree tops, keeping a whole tree to himself, and living on nuts which others gathered. You could see it in his keen and domineering look, and in the quick, casual way he crowded his fellow, who always made room for him. I have seen such a face, and such manners, in great industrial centres. They are the marks of the ablest and best, who get on. His hard eager eyes showed censoriousness, cruelty, and acquisitiveness. But his companion, with a sooty and hairless face, and black hair parted in the middle of a frail forehead, was a pal of ours, and knew it. The brown midget showed angry distrust of us, knowing what devilry was in his own mind. But the black, though more delicate and nervous a monkey, his mind being innocent of secret plots, had gentleness and faith in his looks, and showed a laughable and welcome curiosity in us. He made friendly twitterings—not the harsh and menacing chatter of the other—and perfectly self-possessed, his pure soul giving him quiethood, examined us in a brotherly way with an ebon paw which was as small and fragile as a black fairy's.

A jabiru stork stood on one leg, beak on breast, meditating, caring nothing for all that was outside its ruminating mind. There were parrots on the cross-ties of the roof, on the floor, on the shoulders of the women, and in the hands of the children, and they were getting an interesting time through the monkeys when their faces were not cocked sideways at us in a knowing fashion. And what looked like a crow was giving bitter and ruthless chase to a young agouti, in and out of the bare feet of the company. I have never seen creatures so tame. But Indian women, as I learned afterwards, have a fine gift for winning the confidence of wild things, and that afternoon they took hold of the creatures, anyhow and anywhere, to bring them for our inspection, without the captives showing the least alarm or anger. There were the dogs, too. But they were like all the dogs we saw in Brazil, looking sorry for themselves; and they sat about in case they should fall if they attempted to stand. Our audience broke up suddenly, in an uproar of protests, to chase the brown monkey, who was towing a frantic parrot by the tail.

We continued our walk, entering the forest again on another path. Here the growth was secondary, and the underbush dense on both sides of the trail. The voices of the village stopped as we entered the shades, and there was no more sound except when a bird scurried away heavily, and again, when some cicadas, the "scissors grinders," suddenly sprang an astonishing whirring from a tree. The sound was as loud as that of a locomotive letting steam escape in a covered station. At a clearing so small that the roof of the jungle had been but little broken, where a hut stood as though at a well-bottom sunk in a depth of trees, we turned back. That deep well in the trees contained but little light, for already it was being choked with vines. The hut was of the usual light construction, though its sides were of leaves, as well as its roof. I think it was the most melancholy dwelling I have ever happened on in my wanderings. It did not look as though it had been long deserted. There were ashes and a broken flesh-pot outside it. The entrance was veiled with gross spiders' webs. On the earth floor within were puddles of rain. Round it the forest stood, like night in abeyance. The tree tops overhung, silently intent on what man had been doing at their feet. A child's chemise was stretched on a thorn, and close by was a small grave, separated by little sticks from the secular earth. A dead plant was in the centre of the grave, and a crude wooden crucifix.

We had plenty of opportunities for exploring Serpa, for the Amazon that rainy season was slow in rising, and consequently it would have been unsafe for us to venture into the Madeira. The tributary would have been full, but it was necessary for the waters of the main stream to dam and heighten the flood of its tributary before we could trust our draught there. We were nine days at Serpa. The Amazon would rise as much as a foot one day, and our distance from the shore would increase perceptibly, with strong whirling eddies which made the trip ashore more difficult. Then it would fall again. Some of the yellow Amazon porpoises showed alongside occasionally, and alligators floated about, though nothing was seen of them but their snouts.

Serpa is a small but growing place. It was but a missionary settlement of Abacaxis Indians from the Madeira in 1759, and was called Itacoatiara. When I was there it was renewing its old importance, because the Madeira-Mamoré railway undertaking had placed a depot a little to the west of the village. The Doctor and I spent many memorable days in its neighbourhood, butterfly-hunting and sauntering. Though mosquitoes, anopeline and culex, are as common here as elsewhere in the Brazils—the lighters which came alongside with cargo for us conveyed clouds of them, and they took possession of every dark nook of the "Capella"—it is noteworthy that Serpa has the reputation, in Amazonas, of a health resort. I could find no explanation of that. There was malaria at Serpa, of course; but compared with the really lethal country, a country not so different in appearance and climate, of the upper Madeira, the salubrity of Serpa is perplexing. That virulent form of malaria peculiar to some tropical localities is a phenomenon which medical research has not yet explained. In the almost unexplored region of the Rio Madeira the fever is certain to every traveller, though the land is largely without inhabitants; and it is almost equally certain that it will be of the malignant type. Yet at an old settlement like Serpa, where probably every inhabitant has had malaria, and every mosquito is likely to be a host, the fever is but mild, and the traveller may escape it entirely.

By now you will be asking what Itacoatiara is like, that

community contentedly lost in the secret forest. I am afraid you will not learn, unless, in the happy future, you and I select a few friends, a few books, and erect some houses of palm leaves to protect us from all the really urgent and important matters which do not matter a twinkle to the eternal stars, noon it far and secure until the time comes for the gentle villagers to carry us out and forget us; remembering us again when the annual Day of the Dead comes round. They will leave some comfortable candles above us that night.

There the earth is a warm and luscious body. The lazy paths are cool with groves, and in the middle hours of the sun, when only a few butterflies are abroad, and the grass-hoppers are shrilling in the quiet, you swing in a hammock under a thatch—the air has been through some tree in blossom—and gossip, and drink coffee. Beyond the path of the village there is—nobody knows what; not even the Royal Geographical Society. One heard of a large and mys-terious lake a day's journey inland. Nobody knew anything about it. Nobody cared. One old man once, when hunting, saw its mirror through the forest's aisles, and heard the multitude of its birds.

The foreshore of the village is rugged with boulders richly tinctured with iron oxide, and often having a scoriaceous surface. There we would land, and scramble up to a street which ends on the height above the river. It is a broad road, with white, substantial, one-story houses on either side. The dwellings and stores have no windows, but are built with open fronts, for ventilation. This is Serpa's main street. It is shaded with avenues of trees. In the narrower side turnings the trees meet to form arcades. One day we saw such an avenue covered with yellow, trumpet-shaped blossoms. Ox-carts with solid wheels stand in the walks. The sunlight, broken in the leaves of the trees, patterned the roads with white fire, and so dappled the cattle that they were obscure; you saw the oxen only when they moved. There is a large square, grass-grown, in the centre of the village, where stands the church, a white, simple building with an open belfry in which the bell hangs plain, bright with verdigris. About here the merchants and tradesmen of Serpa have their places. The men, hearty and friendly souls, walk abroad in clean linen suits and straw hats, and their ladies, pallid, slight, but often singularly beautiful, are dressed as Europeans, but without hats; sometimes, when out walking late in the day, a lady would have a scarlet flower in her hair.

By the foreshore were the cabins, of mud and wood, of the negroes. Beyond the town, the roads run through the clearings, and end on the forest. In the clearings were the huts, wattle and daub, and of leaves, of the settled Indians and half-breeds. These were often prettily placed beneath groups of graceful palms. It was in the last direction that most often we made our way with our butterfly nets while other folk were sleeping during the sun's height. The humid heat, I suppose, was really a trial. One did perspire in an alarming way and with the least exertion. The Doctor, who carries substance, would have dark patches in his khaki uniform, and would wonder, with foreboding, whether any more in this life he would catch hold of a cold jug which held a straight pint in which ice tinkled. But to me the illumination, the heat, the odour, and the quiethood of those noons made life a great prize. I will say that my comrade, the Doctor, did much to make it so, with his gentle fun, and his wide knowledge of earth-lore. There was so much, wherever we went, to keep me on the magic side of time, and out of its shadow. On the west of the town were some huts, with plantations of bananas, pineapples, pawpaws, and maize, where blossomed cannas, mimosas, passion-flowers, and where other unseen blooms, especially after rain, made breathing a sensuous pleasure. There we tried to intercept the swallow-like flight of big sulphur and orange butterflies, though never with success. We had more success with the butterflies in the clearings, where some new huts stood, beyond the village. Over the stagnant pools in those open spaces dragon-flies hovered, fellows that moved, when we approached, like lines of red light. The butterflies, particularly a vermilion beauty with black bars on his wings, and a swift flier, used to settle and gem the mud about these pools. Other species frequented the flowering shrubs which had grown over the burnt wreckage and stumps of the forest.

That area was full of insects and birds. There we saw daily
the Sauba ants, sometimes called the parasol ants, in endless
processions, each ant hold a piece of leaf, the size of a
sixpenny bit, over its tiny body. Tanagers shot amongst the
bushes like blue projectiles. We saw a ficus there on one
occasion, of fair size, with large leathery leaves, which carried
a colony of remarkable caterpillars, each about seven inches
long, thick in proportion, blue black in colour with yellow
stripes, and a coral head, and filaments at the latter end.
They were pugnacious worms, fighting each other desperately when two met on a leaf. The larvae stripped that tree
in a day. We were not always sure that the people in this part
of Serpa were friendly. Mostly they were half-breeds, varying
mixtures of Indian and negro, and no doubt very superstitious. The rodent's foot was commonly worn by the women,
who, if we took notice of their children, sometimes would
spit, to avert the evil eye. But when the thunder clouds
banked close, and the air, being still, became loaded with the
scent of the wood fires of the villagers, promising rain, we
would enter a hut, and then always found we were welcome.

Even when kept to the ship for any reason this country
offered constant new things to keep our thoughts moving. A
regatão, the river pedlar, would bring his roomy montario,
the gypsy van of the river, his family aboard—the wife, the
grandmother, and the sad, shy, little children—and offer us
fruits, and perhaps his monkey and parrots. Gradually the
"Capella" added to her company. The Chief bought a parrot
which had many Indian and Portuguese phrases. It tried to
climb a funnel guy, in escaping the curiosity of our terrier,
and fell into the river. We fished her out with a bucket. The
vampire bats came aboard every night. They were not very
terrible creatures to look at; but we discovered they frequented the forecastle to no good purpose. Again, stories
filtered through to us of sickness on the Madeira, and
abruptly they gave the palms and the sunsets a new light.
One man was brought in from beyond and died of beri-beri.
This shook the nerves of one of our Brazilian pilots, and he
refused to go beyond where we were. As for me, there at
Serpa the "Capella" was at anchor, and we were not near the

Madeira, and seemed never likely to go. I watched the sunsets. The brief, cool evenings prompted me (fever in the future or not) to praise and grace. Crickets chirped everywhere on the ship then, and the air was full of the sparks of fireflies. You could smell this good earth.

There was one sunset when the overspreading of violet clouds would have shut out the day quite, but that the canopy was not closely adjusted to the low barrier of forest to the westward. Through that narrow chink a yellow light streamed, and traced shapes on the lurid walls and roof which narrowly enclosed us. This was the beginning of the most alarming of our daily electrical storms. There was no wind. Serpa and all the coast facing that rift where the light entered our prison, stood prominent and strange, and surprised us much as if we had not looked in that direction till then. The curtain dropped behind the forest, and all light was shut out. We could not see across the ship. Knowing how strong and bright could be the electrical discharges (though they were rarely accompanied by thunder) when not heralded in so portentous a way, we waited with some anxiety for this display to begin. It began over the trees behind Serpa. Blue fire flickered low down, and was quickly doused. Then a crack of light sprang across the inverted black bowl from east to west in three quick movements. Its instant ramifications fractured all the roof in a network of dazzling blue lines. The reticulations of light were fleeting, but never gone. Night contracted and expanded, and the sharp sounds, which were not like thunder, might have been the tumbling flinders of night's roof. We saw not only the river, and the shapes of the trees and the village, as in wavering daylight, but their colours. One flash sheeted the heavens, and its over-bright glare extinguished everything. It came with an explosion, like the firing of a great gun close to our ears, and for a time we thought the ship was struck. In this effort the storm exhausted itself.

The day before we left for the Madeira we took aboard sixty head of cattle. They were wild things, which had been collected in the campo with great difficulty, and driven into lighters. A rope was dropped over the horns of each beast: this was attached to a crane hook, the winch was started, and up the poor wretch came, all its weight on its horns, bumping inertly against the ship's side in its passage, like a bale, and was then dumped in a heap on deck. This treatment seemed to subdue it. Each quietly submitted to a halter. Several lost horns, and one hurt its leg, and had to be dragged to its place. But, to our great joy—we were watching the scene from the bridge—the Brazilian herdsmen on the lighter shouted an anxious warning to their fellows on our deck as a small black heifer, a pot-bellied lump with a stretched neck, rotated in her unusual efforts to free her horns. She even bellowed. She bumped heavily against the ship's side, and tried desperately to find her feet. She was, and I offered up thanks for this benefit, most plainly an implacable rebel. The cattlemen, as punishment for the trouble she had given them ashore, kept her dangling over the deck, and one got level with her face and mocked her, slapping her nose. She actually defied him, though she was quite helpless, with some minatory sounds. She was no cow. She was insurrection, she was the hate for tyrants incarnated. They dropped her. She was up and away like a cat, straight for the winchman, and tried to get the winch out of her path, bellowing as she worked. She put everybody on that deck in the shrouds or on the forecastle head as she trotted round, with her tail up, looking for brutes to put them to death. None of the cows (of course) helped her. By a trick she was caught, and her horns were lashed down to a ring bolt in a hatch coaming. Then she tried to kick all who passed. If the rest of the cattle had been like her none would have suffered. Alas! They were probably all scientific evolutionists, content to wait for men to become kindly apple-lovers by slow and natural uplift; and gravely deprecated the action of the heifer, from which, as peaceful cows, they disassociated themselves.

The Indian says that if he eats a morsel of tiger he becomes fierce and strong. I have not the faith of the Indian, or I would have begged the heart of that heifer, and of it I would have brewed gallons of precious liquor, and brought it home in jars for incomparable gifts to the meek at heart who always do what the herdsmen tell them. The Doctor and I made a pet of that black cow, to the extent of seeing she got her rations regularly. It was no joke wading through manure among a press of nervous animals on a ship's deck in the tropics, in order to see that a brave creature was justly dealt with; particularly as she swore violently whenever she saw us, looking up from her tightly tethered head with eyes full of unabated fury, and tried to get at us on the hatch above her, bound though she was. What a heart! For her head was fixed immovably, unlike the others; yet, till we arrived at Porto Velho she kept her fierce spirit, often kicking over her water bucket with her forefeet. Curse their charity!

With two new pilots, we up-anchored next morning; and full of cattle, flies, and new odours, and a gang of cattlemen who at least appeared villainous, and carried long knives, the "Capella" continued up stream for the Madeira. The cattle were sheltered, as far as possible, with awnings improvised from spare canvas, and their fodder was bales of American hay. The Skipper did his best to meliorate the harsh native methods with dumb things.

And now it seems time to explain why we are bound for the centre of the American continent, where the unexplored jungle still persists, and disease or death, so the legends tell us, come to all white men who stay there for but a few months. If you will get your map of the Brazils, begin from Para, and cruise along the Amazon to the Madeira River—you turn south just before Manaõs—when you have reached Santo Antonio on the tributary stream you have traversed the ultimate wilderness of a continent, and stand on the threshold of Bolivia, almost under the shadow of the Andes. If you find any pleasure in maps, flying in shoes of that kind when affairs pursue you too urgently (and I suppose you do, or you would not be so far into this narrative), you will hardly thank me when I tell you it is possible for an ocean steamer exceeding 23 feet in draught to make such a journey, and so break the romance of the obscure place at the end of it. But it must be said. Even one who travels for fun should keep to the truth in the matter of a ship's draught. As a reasonable being you would prefer to believe the map; and that clearly shows the only way there (when the chance comes for you to take it) must be by canoe, a long and arduous journey to a seclusion remote, and so the more deeply desired. It certainly hurts our faith in a favourite chart to find that its well-defined seaboard is no barrier to modern traffic, but that, journeying over those pink and yellow inland areas, which should have no traffic with great ships, a large cargo steamer, full of Welsh coal, can come to an anchorage, still with many fathoms under her, at a point where the cartographer, for lack of place-names and other humane symbols, has set the word Forest, with the letters spread widely to the full extent of his ignorance, and so promised us sanctuary in plenty. I suppose that in a few years those remote wilds, somehow cleared of Indians, jungle, and malaria—though I do not see how all this can be done—will have no further interest for us, because it will possess many of the common disadvantages of civilisation's benefits: it will be a point on a regular route of commerce. I am really sorry for you; but in the sad and cruel code of the sailor I can only reply as Jack did when he got the sole rag of beef in the hash, "Blow you, Bill. I'm all right." I had the fortune to go when the route was still much as it was in the first chapter of Genesis. "But after all," you question me, hopeful yet, "nothing can be done with 5000 tons of Welsh cargo in a jungle."

People with the nose for dollars can do wonders. It would be unwise to back such a doughty opponent as the pristine jungle with its malaria against people who smell money there. In the early 'seventies there was a man with one idea, Colonel George Church. His idea was to give to Bolivia, which the Andes shuts out from the Pacific, and two thousand miles of virgin forest from the Atlantic, a door communicating with the outside world. He said, for he was an enthusiast, that Bolivia is the richest country in the world. The mines of Potosi are in Bolivia. Its mountains rise from fertile tropical plains to Arctic altitudes. The rubber tree grows below, and a climate for barley is found in a few days' journey towards the sky. But the riches of Bolivia are locked up. Small parcels of precious goods may be got out over the Andean barrier, on mule back; or they may dribble in a thin stream down the Beni, Mamoré, and Madre de Dios rivers—rivers which unite not far from the Brazilian boundary to form the Rio Madeira. The Beni is a very great and deep river which has a course of 1500 miles before it contributes its volume to the Madeira. The Rio Madeira, a broad and deep stream in the rainy season, reaches the Amazon in another 1100 miles. But between Guajara-Merim and San Antonio the Madeira comes down a terrace 250 miles in length of nineteen dangerous cataracts. The Bolivian rubber collectors shoot those rapids in their batelaões, large vessels carrying sometimes ten tons of produce and a crew of a dozen men, when the river is full. Many are overturned, and the produce and the men are lost. The Madeira traverses a country notorious even on the Amazon for its fever, and quite unexplored a mile inland anywhere on its banks; the rubber hunters, too, have to reckon with wandering tribes of hostile Indians.

The country is like that to-day. Then judge its value for a railway route in the early 'seventies. But Colonel Church was a New Englander, and again he was a visionary, so therefore most energetic and compelling; he soon persuaded the practical business folk, who seldom know much, and are at the mercy of every eloquent dreamer, to part with a lot of money to buy his Bolivian dream. We do really find the Colonel, on 1st November 1871, solemnly cutting the first sod of a railway in the presence of a party of Indians, with the wild about him which had persisted from the beginning of things. What the Indians thought of it is not recorded. Anyhow, they seem to have humoured the infatuated man who stopped to cut a square of grass in the land of the Parentintins, the men who go stark naked, and make musical instruments out of the shin bones of their victims.

An English company of engineering contractors was given the job of building the line, and a small schooner, the "Silver Spray," went up to San Antonio with materials in 1872. Her captain, and some of her officers, died on the way.

A year later the contractors confessed utter defeat. The jungle had won. They declared that "the country was a charnel-house, their men dying like flies, that the road ran through an inhospitable wilderness of alternating swamp and porphyry ridges, and that, with the command of all the capital in the world, and half its population, it would be impossible to build the road." (There is a quality of bitterness in their vehement hate which I recognise. I heard the same emotional chord expressed concerning that land, though not because of failure there, only two years ago.)

But the Bank of England held a large sum in trust for the pursuance of this enterprise, and after the lawyers had attended to the trust money in long debate in Chancery, there was yet enough of it left to justify the indefatigable colonel in beginning the railway again. That was in 1876. Messrs Collins, of Philadelphia, obtained the contract. The road, of metre gauge, was to be built in three years. The matter excited the United States into a wonderful attention. The press there went slightly delirious, and the excited Eagle was advised that "two Philadelphians are to overcome the Madeira rapids, and to open up to the world a land as fair as the Garden of the Lord." The little steamer "Mercedita," of 856 tons, with 54 engineers and material, was dispatched to San Antonio on 2nd January 1878. Her departure was made an important national occasion, and it is an historic fact, which may be confirmed by a reference to the files of Philadelphian papers of that date, that strong men, as well as women and children, sobbed aloud on the departure of the steamer. The vessel arrived at San Antonio on the 16th February. They had barely started operations when, so they said, a Brazilian official told them, betraying some feeling, "when the English came here they did nothing but smoke and drink for two days, but Americans work like the devil." Yet, by all accounts, the English method was right. I prefer it, on the Amazon. The preface to work there should be extended to three or even more days of drinking and smoking.

Yet it must be said that if ever men should have honour for holding to a duty when it was far more easy, and even more reasonable, to leave it, then I submit the claim of those American engineers. Having lived in the place where many of them died, and knowing their story, I feel a certain kinship. There is no monument to them. No epic has been written of their tragedy. But their story is, I should think, one of the saddest in the annals of commerce. Of the 941 who left for San Antonio at different times, 221 lost their lives, mostly of disease, though 80 perished in the wreck of a transport ship. That is far higher a mortality rate than that of, say, the South African or the American Civil War.

Few of those men appeared to know the tropics. They thought "the tropics" meant only prodigal largess of fruits and sun and a wide latitude of life—a common mistake. The enterprise became a lingering disaster. Their state was already bad when a supply ship was lost; and they hopefully waited, ill and starving, but with a gallant mockery of their lot, as their letters and diaries attest, for food and medicine which were not to reach them. The doctors continued the daily round of the host of the fever-stricken, giving them quinine, which was a deceit made of flour. The wages of all ceased for legal reasons, and they were in a place where little is cultivated, and so most food has to be imported in spite of a tariff which usually doubles the price of every necessary of life. Some of the survivors, despairing and heroic souls, attempted to escape on rafts down the river; they might as well have tried to cut their way through the thousand miles of forest between them and Manaós. The railway undertaking collapsed again, and the clearing, the huts, and the workshops, and the short line that was actually laid, were left for the vines and weeds to bury. But now again the conquering forest is being attacked. The Madeira-Mamoré Railway has been recommenced, and our steamer, the "Capella," is taking up supplies for the establishment at Porto Velho, from which the new railway begins, three miles this side of San Antonio.

III

O N the morning of the 23rd January, while we were still considering, seeing what the sun was like, and the languid air, and that we were reduced to tinned beans, fat bacon, and butter which was oil and flies, whether it was worth while to note our breakfast bell—the steward stood swinging it, with the gravity of a priest, under the break of the poop—a shout came from the bridge that the Rio Madeira was in view.

As far back as Swansea we had heard legends of this stream, and they were sufficiently disturbing. When we arrived at Para we heard more, and worse. The pilot we engaged there called the Madeira the "long cemetery." At Serpa, for the first time, we saw what happened to frail humanity when it ventured far on the Madeira. One day a river steamer came to Serpa, with a cargo of men from San Antonio. The river steamers of the Amazon are vessels of broad beam and shallow draft, painted the dingy hue of the river itself, and they have two tiers of decks, open-air shelves, between the supports of which the passengers sling their hammocks. The passengers do not sleep in bunks. This paddle-boat came throbbing towards where we were at anchor. It was night, and she was unseen, a palpitation in the dark accompanied somehow by a fountain of sparks. Such boats burn wood in their furnaces. When her noise had ceased, and her lights imperceptibly enlarged as the current dropped her down abeam of us, a breath of her, a draught of air, passed our way. I am more familiar now with the odour malaria causes, but then I though she must have a freight of the dead. She anchored. We could see her loaded hammocks in the light of the few lamps she carried. Through the binoculars next morning I inspected with peculiar interest the row of cadaverous heads, with black tousled hair, lemon-coloured skins, open mouths and vacant eyes, which stared at us over her rails. Each looked as though once it had peered into the eyes of doom, and then was but waiting, caring nothing.

There, ahead, was the Madeira now for us. We were then nearly a thousand miles from the sea, well within South America. But that meeting-place of the Amazon and its chief tributary was an expanse of water surprising in its immensity. As much light was reflected from the floor as at sea. The water was oceanic in amplitude. The forest boundaries were so far away that one could not realise, even when the time we had been on the river was remembered as a prolonged monotony, that this was the centre of a continent. The forest on our port side was near enough for us to see its limbs and its vines; but to the south-west, where we were heading for Bolivia, and to the north, the way to the Guianas, and the east, out of which we had come, and to the west, where was Peru, the land was but a low violet barrier, varying in altitude with distance, and with silver sections in it, marking the river roads. In the north-west there was a broad silver path through the wall, the way to the Rio Negro, Manaõs, and the Orinoco. In the south the near forest, being flooded, was a puzzle of islands. As we progressed they opened out as a line of green headlands. The Madeira appeared to have three widely separated mouths, with a complexity of intermediate and connective minor ditches. Indeed, the gate of the river was a region of inundated jungle. One began to understand why travellers here sometimes find themselves on the wrong river.

Our bows turned in to the forest wall, and for a few minutes I could not see any way for us there. The jungle parted, and we were on a narrow turgid flood, the colour of the main river, but swifter; a majestic forest was near to either beam. We were enclosed. And after we entered the Madeira, my dark thoughts of our future at once left me. If they returned, it was only to be joked about, in the dry way one does refer to a dread that has been long in the distance, and then one day takes shape, becomes material, and settles down with us. Its form, as you know, nearly always allays your alarms. Your simple mind has expected something with the lowering face of evil. Lo! evil has even bright eyes. Its nature, its dark craft which you have dreaded, is not seen, and your mind grows light with surprise. What, only this, then?

I never saw earth look more resplendent and chromatic than on the day when we entered that river with a bad name. Presently, I thought—here was a brief resurgence of the old gloom which had shrouded my conjectural Madeira—I might be called upon to pay the price for this surprising gift of intense colour, light, and luscious heat, for the quickening of the blood, as though the tropic air were a stimulant as well as a narcotic. Well, it does seem but fair, if chance, being happy, gives you a place in the tropics, to expect to have less time there than is given for the job of eking out a meagre existence in the north. It would not be right to look for gain both ways. (You will have noticed already, I suppose, that I have not been on the Madeira fifteen minutes.) This, I thought, as I walked to and fro on the "Capella," is different from that endurance, bitter and prolonged, in the land where there is no sun worth mentioning, where the north-east wind blows, where the poor rate is so and so in the pound (and you are one of the fortunate if you pay it), and Lord Rosebery lectures on Thrift. I mentioned this to the Doctor. He did not remove his pipe from his mouth.

Because (the idea dawned on me as I sank into a deck chair beside the surgeon under the poop awning, and borrowed his silver tobacco-box), because, as to thrift and parching winds, abstinence and prudence, and lectures by the solemn on how to thin out your life in cold climates where all that is worth having is annexed, why praise a man who is willing to deprave his life to sand and frost? There in merry England the poor wretch is, where the riches of earth are not broadcast largess as I see they are here, but are stacked on each side of the road, and guarded by police, leaving to him but the inclement highway, with nothing but Lord Rosebery's advice and benediction to help him keep the wind out of the holes in his trousers; that benefit, and the bleak consideration that he may swink all day for a handful of beans, or go without. What is prudence in that man? It is his goodwill for the police. To be blue nosed and meek at heart, and to hoard half the crust of your stinted bread, is to blaspheme the King of Glory. Some men will touch their crowns to Carnegie in heaven.

Thrift and abstinence! They began to look the most snivelling of sins as I watched, with spacious leisure, the near procession of gigantic trees, that superb wild which did not arise from such niggard and flinty maxims. Frugality and prudence! That is to regard the means to death in life, the pallor and projecting bones of a warped existence, as good men dwell on courage, motherhood, rebellion, and May time, and the other proofs of vitality and growth. Now, I thought, I see what to do. All those improving lectures, reform leagues, university settlements, labour exchanges, and other props for crippled humanity, are idle. It is a generative idea that is wanted, a revelation, a vision. It would be easier and quicker to take regiments of folk out of Ancoats, Hanley, Bethnal Green, and the cottages of the countryside, for one long glance at the kind of earth I see now. The world would expand as they looked. They would get the dynamic suggestion. In vain, afterwards, would the monopolists and the superior persons chant patriotic verse to drown the noise of chain forging at the Westminster foundry. Not the least good, that. The folk would not hear. Their minds would be absent and outward, not locked within to huddle with cramped and respectful thoughts. They would not start instinctively at the word of command. They would begin with dignity and assurance to compass their own affairs, and in an enormous way; and they would make hardly a sound as they moved forward, and they would have uplifted and shining eyes. ("Then you think more of 'em than I do," said the surgeon.)

It would be no use, I saw clearly, sending the folk to Algeria, Egypt, or New York. Such places never betray to the traveller that our world is not a shapeless parcel of fields and buildings, tied up with bylaws, and sealed by the Grand Lama as his last act in the stupendous work of creation. There it is, and angular package in the sky, which the sun reads, and directs on its way to heaven in advance of its limited syndicate of proprietors.

Here on the Madeira I had a vision instead of the earth as a great and shining sphere. There were no fences and private bounds. I saw for the first time an horizon as an arc suggesting how wide is our ambit. That bare shoulder of the world effaced regions and constellations in the sky. Our earth had celestial magnitude. It was warm, a living body. The abundant rain was vital, and the forest I saw, nobler in stature and with an aspect of intensity beyond what the Amazon forests showed, rose like a sign of life triumphant.

You see what that tropical wilderness did for me, and with but a single glance. Whatever comes after, I shall never be the same again. The complacent length of the ship was before us. Amidships were some of the fellows staring overside, absorbed. Now and then, when his beat brought him to the port side. I could see the head of the little pilot on the bridge. His colleague was sleeping in one of the hammocks slung between the stanchions of the poop awning. The Doctor was scrutinising a pair of motuca flies which hovered about his ankles, waiting for him to go to sleep. He wanted them for specimens. The Skipper, looking a little anxious, came slowly up the poop ladder, crossed over, and stood by our chairs. "The river is full of big timber," he said. He went to stare overside, and then came back to us. "The current is about five knots, and those trees adrift are as big as barges. I hope they keep clear of the propeller." The Skipper's eye was uneasy. He was glum with suspicion; he spoke of the way his fools might meet the wiles of fortune at a time when he was below and his ship was without its acute protective intelligence. He stood, a spare figure in white, in a limp grass hat with flapping eaves, gazing forward to the bridge mistrustfully. He had brought us in a valuable vessel to a place unknown, and now he had to go on, and afterwards get us all out again. I began to feel a large respect for this elderly master mariner (who did not give the beard of an onion for any man's sympathy) who had skilfully contrived to put us where we were, and now was unaware what mischance would send us to rot under the forest wall, the bottom to fall out of our adventure just when we were in its narrowest passage and achievement was almost within view. "This is no place for a ship," the captain mumbled. "It isn't right. We're disturbing the mud all the time; and look at those butterflies now, dodging about us!" He was continuing this monologue as a dirty cap appeared at the head of the ladder, and a long and ragged length of sorrowful sailor mounted there, and doffed the cap. The Skipper brusquely signed to him to approach. He was a youngster in an advanced stage of some trouble, and he had no English. I think he was a Swede. He demonstrated his sickness, baring his arm, muttering unintelligibly. The limb, like his hand, was distorted with large blisters. There was his face, too. I mistrusted my equanimity for some moments, but braced my eyes, compelling them to be scientific and impersonal. By signs we gathered he had been sleeping on deck, such was the heat of the forecastle, and the mosquitoes, the Doctor said, had poisoned a body already tainted from the stews of Rotterdam. The corroding spirit of the jungle was beginning to permeate through our flaws.

The Doctor went to his surgery. The pilot sat up in his hammock, glanced indifferently at the sick sailor, yawning and stretching his arms, his dainty little brown feet dangling just clear of the deck. He began to roll a cigarette of something which looked like tea. Then he dropped out, and went forward to release his mate on the bridge, and the senior pilot came up as the Doctor had finished his job. The junior pilot, a fragile, girlish fellow, rather taciturn, greets us always with a faintly supercilious smile. His chief is a round, jolly little man, hearty, and lavish with ornamental gestures. We both smiled involuntarily as he marched across to us, with his uniform cap, bearing our ships' badge, stuck on the back of his head with a bias to the right ear. There is not enough of Portuguese in our ship's company to serve one conversation adequately, but we get on well with this pilot, and he with us. He sits in a hammock, making pantomime explanatory of Brazil to us strangers, and we pick him up with alacrity, after but brief pauses. While the Doctor beguiled him into dramatic moments, I lay back and watched him, searching for Brazilian characteristics, to report here.

You know that, when you have returned from a far country, you are asked unanswerable questions about its people, and especially about its women. We are easily flattered by the suggestion that we are authoritative, with opinions got from uncommon experience, especially where women with strange eyes and dark skins are concerned. So, once upon a time, I caught myself—or rather, I caught that cold, critical, and impartial part of me, which is a solemn fake—when answering a question of this kind, explaining in a comprehensive way the character of the Brazilian people, as though I were telling of the objective phenomena of one simple soul. Presently the wise and ribald part of me woke, caught the note of that inhuman voice, and raised a derisive cry, heard by me with grave deprecation, but not heard at all by my listener. I stopped. For what do I know of the Brazilian character? Very little. Is there such a thing? I suppose the true Brazilian is like the true Englishman, or the typical bird which is known by its bones, but may be anything from a crow to a nightingale, but is more likely a lark. You can imagine the foreigner taking his knowledge of the British pickpocket who met him at the landing-stage, the pen-portraits of Bernard Shaw, the Rev. Jeremiah Hardshell, Father O'Flynn, You, Me, the cabman who swore at him, his landlady and her daughter, Lloyd-George, Piccadilly by night, and Tom Bowling, carefully adjusting all that valuable British data, just as Professor Karl Pearson does his physical statistics, and explaining the result as the modern English; adding, in the usual footnote, what decadent tendencies are to be deduced, in addition, from the facts which could not be worked into the major premises.

Now, there was the handsome Brazilian customs officer, tall, august, with dark eyes haughty and slow with thought, the waves of his romantic black hair faintly traced in silver, who might have been a poet, or a philosophic revolutionist; but who was the man, as the first mate told us (after we had searched everywhere for the articles) who "pinched your bloomin' field-glasses and my meerschaum."

Take, if you like, the ultra-fashionable ladies at the Para hotel, who looked at us with sleepy eyes, and who, I suspect, were not Brazilians at all. Supposing they were, there must be counted the wife of the official at Serpa. She came aboard there with her husband to see an English ship; she reminded me of that picture of the Madonna by Sassoferrato in the National Gallery; I am unable to come nearer to justice to her than that. Again, there was a certain vain native apothecary, and he had the idea that I was bottle-washer to the "Capella's" surgeon, much to that fellow's secret delight. The chemist treated me with a studied difference in consequence; and though our surgeon could have undeceived the mistaken man, having some Portuguese, he refused to do so. I remember the pilot who, when he left us at Serpa, and I bade him farewell, did, before all our ship's company, embrace me heartily, rest his cheek against mine, and make loving noises in his throat. And there is our present chief guide, now swinging in his hammock, and looking down upon us waggishly.

He had not been a pilot always. Once he was a clown in a circus; that little fact is a clue to much which otherwise would have been obscure in him. When he boarded us at Serpa to take the place of the man who shrank from the thought of the Madeira, the chart-room under the bridge was given to him, and as the mate put it, "he moved in." He had bundles, boxes, bags, baskets, a tin trunk, a chair, a parrot, a hammock, and some pictures. He was going to be with us for two months, but his affair had the conclusive character of a migration, a final severance from his old life. His friends came to see him depart, and they wound themselves in each others arms, heads laid in resignation on shoulders. "Looks as if we're bound for the Golden Shore," commented the boatswain.

This little rounded man, the pilot, with his unctuous olive skin, tiny moustache of black silk, and impudent eyes, looked ripe in middle age, though actually he was but thirty. He wore a suit of azure cotton, ironed faultlessly, and his tunic fitted with hooks and eyes across his throat. His boots were sulphur coloured and Parisian. A massive gold ring,

which carried a carbonado nearly as large as the stopper of a
beer bottle, was embedded in a fat finger of his right hand. In
the front of his cap he had sewn the badge of our line, and he
was curiously proud of that gaudy symbol. He would wear
the cap on one ear, and walk up and down in display, with a
lofty smile, and a carriage supposed to appertain to a British
officer in a grand moment. He had a great admiration for all
that was British, except our food. If you were up at sunrise
you could see him at his toilet, and the spectacle was worth
the effort. His array of toilet vesicles reminded me of the
shelves in a barber's shop. Oiled and fragrant, he took his
seat for breakfast with much formal politeness. He shook
our saloon company into a sense of its responsibilities, for
we had grown indifferent as to dress, and sometimes we had
three-day beards. His handkerchiefs and linen were scented,
and dainty with floral designs. And ours—oh, ours—! He
took wine at breakfast, and after idling a little with our
foreign dishes he would wipe his mouth on our tablecloth,
and then leave for the bridge. As he passed across the poop
we would hear him hawk violently, and spit on the deck.
Then the Skipper would glare, and drive his chair backwards
in a dark passion.

Gazing at the foliage as it unfolded, our pilot named the
paranas, tributaries, and islands, when they drew abeam. He
told us what the trees were; and then with head shakes and
uplifted hands and eyes, indicated what grave things were
behind that screen of leaves. (Though I don't suppose he
knew.) His mimicry was so spontaneous and exact that it
was more entertaining and just as instructive as speech. He
taught us how the Indians kill you, and what some villagers
did to a naughty padre, and how the sucuruju swallows a
deer, and how to make love to a Brazilian girl. He kicked the
slippers from his little feet, and smuggled into the hammock
mesh for a snooze, waving a hand coyly to us over the edge
of his nest.

The dinner bell rang. Because the saloon is now hot
beyond endurance, the steward has fixed a table on deck, and
so, as we eat, we can see the jungle pass. That keeps some of

our mind from dwelling over much on the dreary menu. The potatoes have begun to ferment. The meat is out of tins; sometimes it is served as fritters, sometimes we recognise it in a hash, and sometimes, shameless, it appears without dress, a naked and shiny lump straight from its metal bed. Often the bread is sour. The butter, too, is out of tins. Feeding is not a joy, but a duty. But it is soon over. Although everybody now complains of indigestion, we have far to go yet, and the cheerfulness which faces all circumstances brazenly must be our manna. Our table, some deal planks on trestles, is mellowed by a white tablecloth. We sit round on boxes. Over head the sun flames on the awning, making it golden and translucent. I let the soup pass. The next dish is a hot pot of tinned mutton and preserved vegetables. Something must be done, and I do it then. There is some pickled beef and pickled onions. I watch the forest pass. Then, for desert, the steward, the hot beads touring about the mounts of his large pale face, brings along oleaginous fritters of plum duff. The Doctor leaves. I follow him to the chairs again, and we exchange tobacco-boxes and fill our pipes. This may seem to you unendurable for long. I did not think so, though of habits so regular and engrained that my chances of survival, when viewed comparatively, for my ship mates were hardened and usually were more robust, seemed poor enough. But I enjoyed it. There was nourishment, a tonic stay, in our desire to greet every onset of the miseries, which now were camped about us, besieging our souls, with sans-culotte insolence. We called to the Eumenides with mockery. Like Thoreau, I believe I could live on a tenpenny nail, if it comes to that.

There is no doubt the forest influences our moods in a way you at home could not understand. Our minds take its light and shade, and just as our little company, gathered in the Chief's room at a time when the seas were running high, recalled sombre legends which told of foredoom, so this forest, an intrusive presence which is with us morning, noon, and night, voiceless, or making such sounds as we know are not for our ears, now shadows us, the prescience of destiny, as though an eyeless mask sat at table with us, a being which could tell us what we would know, but though it stays, makes no sign.

This forest, since we entered the Para River, now a thousand miles away, has not ceased. There have been the clearings of the settlements from Para inwards; but as Spruce says in his Journal, those clearings and campos alter the forest of the Amazon no more than would the culling of a few weeds alter the aspect of an English cornfield. The few openings I have seen in the forest do not derange my clear consciousness of a limitless ocean of leaves, its deep billows of foliage rolling down to the only paths there are in this country, the rivers, and there overhanging, arrested in collapse. There is no land. One must travel by boat from one settlement to another. The settlements are but islands, narrow footholds, widely sundered by vast gulfs of jungle.

The forest of the Amazons is not merely trees and shrubs. It is not land. It is another element. Its inhabitants are arborean; they have been fashioned for life in that medium as fishes to the sea and birds to the air. Its green apparition is persistent, as the sky is and the ocean. In months of travel it is the horizon which the traveller cannot reach, and its unchanging surface, merged through distance into a mere reflector of the day, a brightness or a gloom, in his immediate vicinity breaks into a complexity of green surges; then one day the voyager sees land at last and is released from it. But we have not seen land since Serpa. There are men whose lives are spent in the chasms of light where the rivers are sunk in the dominant element, but who never venture within its green surface, just as one would not go beneath the waves to walk in the twilight of the sea bottom.

Now I have been watching it for so long I see the outer aspect of the jungle does vary. When I saw it first on the Para River it appeared to my wondering eyes but featureless green cliffs. Then in the Narrows beyond Para I remember an impression of elegance and placidity, for there, the waters still being tidal and saline, the palms were conspicuous and in profuse abundance. The great palms are the chief feature of that forest elevation, with their graceful columns, and their generous and symmetrical fronds which sometimes are like gigantic green feathers, and again are like fans. A tall palm, whatever its species, being a definite expression of life—not an agglomeration of leaves, but body and crown, a regal personality—the forest of the Narrows, populous with such exquisite beings, had marges of straight ascending lines and flourishing and geometrical crests.

Beyond the river Xingu, on the main stream, the forest, persistent as a presence, again changed its aspect. It was ragged and shapeless, an impenetrable tangle, its front strewn with fallen trees, the vision of outer desolation. By Obydos it was more aerial and shapely again, but not of that light and soaring grace of the Narrows. It was contained, yet mounted not in straight lines, as in the country of the palms, but in convex masses. Here on the lower Madeira the forest seems of a nature intermediate between the rolling structure of the growth by Obydos, and the grace of the palm groves in the estuarine region of the Narrows. It is barbaric and splendid, easily prodigal with illimitable riches, sinking the river beneath a wealth of forms.

On the Madeira, as elsewhere in the world of the Amazons, some of the forest is on "terra-firma," as that land is called which is not flooded when the waters rise. There the trees reach their greatest altitude and diameter; it is the region of the caa-apoam, the "great woods" of the Indians. A stretch of *terra firma* shows as a low, vertical bank of clay, a narrow ribbon of yellow earth dividing the water from the jungle. More rarely the river cuts a section through some undulating heights of red conglomerate—heights I call these cliffs, as heights they are in this flat country, though at home they would attract no more attention than would the side of a gravel-pit—and again the bank may be that cherry and saffron clay which gives a name to Ita-coatiara. On such land the forest of the Madeira is immense, three of four species among the greater trees lording it in the green tumult expansively, always conspicuous where they stand, their huge boles showing in the verdant façade of the jungle as grey and brown pilasters, their crowns rising above the level roof of the forest in definite cupolas. There is one, having a neat and compact dome and a grey, smooth, and rounded trunk, and dense foliage as dark as that of the holm oak; and another, resembling it, but with a flattened and somewhat disrupted dome. I guessed these two giants to be silk-cottons. Another, which I supposed to be of the leguminous order, had a silvery bole, and a texture of pale green leafage open and light, which at a distance resembled that of the birch. These three trees, when assembled and well grown, made most stately riverside groups. The trunks were smooth and bare till somewhere near ninety feet from the ground. Palms were intermediate, filling the spaces between them, but the palms stood under the exogens, growing in alcoves of the mass, rising no higher than the beginning of the branches and foliage of their lords. The whole overhanging superstructure of the forest—not a window, an inlet, anywhere there—was rolling clouds of leaves from the lower rims of which vines were catenary, looping from one green cloud to another, or pendent, like the sundered cordage of a ship's rigging. Two other trees were frequent, the pao mulatto, with limbs so dark as to look black, and the castanheiro, the Brazil nut tree.

The roof of the woods lowered when we were steaming past the igapo. The igapo, or aqueous jungle, through which the waters go deeply for some months of the year, is of a different character, and perhaps of a lesser height—it seems less; but then it grows on lower ground. I was told to note that its foliage is of a lighter green, but I cannot say I saw that. It is in the igapo that the Hevea Braziliensis flourishes, its pale bole, suggestive of the white poplar, deep in water for much of the year, and its crown sheltered by its greater neighbours, so that it grows in a still, heated, and humid twilight. This low ground is always marked by growths of small cecropia trees. These, with their white stems, their habit of free and regular branching, and their long leaves, digital in the manner of the horse-chestnut, have the appearance of great candelabra. Sometimes the igapo is prefaced by an area of cane. The numberless islands, being of recent formation, have a forest of a different nature, and they seldom carry the larger trees. The upper ends of many of the islands terminate in sandy pits, where dwarf willows grow.

So foreign was the rest of the vegetation, that notwithstanding its volume and intricacy I detected those humble little willows at once, as one would start surprised at an English word heard in the meaningless uproar of an alien multitude.

The forest absorbed us; as one's attention would be challenged and drawn by the casual regard, never noticeably direct, but never withdrawn, of a being superior and mysterious, so I was drawn to watch the still and intent stature of the jungle, waiting for it to become vocal, for some relaxing of its static form. Nothing ever happened. I never discovered it. Rigid, watchful, enigmatic, its presence was constant, but without so much as one blossom in all its green vacuity to show the least friendly familiarity to one who had found flowers and woodlands kind. It had nothing that I knew. It remained securely aloof and indifferent, till I thought hostility was implied, as the sea implies its impartial hostility, in a constant presence which experience could not fathom, nor interest soften, nor courage intimidate. We sank gradually deeper inwards towards its central fastnesses.

By noon on our first day on the Madeira we reached the village of Rozarinho, which is on the left bank, with the tributary of the same name a little more up stream, but entering from the other side. Here, as we followed a loop of the stream, the Madeira seemed circumscribed, a tranquil lake. The yellow water, though swift, had so polished a surface that the reflections of the forest were hardly disturbed, sinking below the tops of the inverted trees to the ultimate clouds, giving an illusion of profundity to the apparent lake. The village was but a handful of leaf huts grouped about the nucleus of one or two larger buildings with white walls. There was the usual jetty of a few planks to which some canoes were tied. The forest was high background to those diminished huts; the latter, as we came upon them, suddenly increased the height of the trees.

In another place the shelter of a family of Indians was at the top of a bank, secretive within the base of the woods. A row of chocolate babies stood outside that nest, with four jabiru storks among them. Each bird, so much taller than the babies, stood resting meditatively on one leg, as though waiting the order to take up an infant and deliver it somewhere. None of them, storks or infants, took the least notice of us. Perhaps the time had not yet come for them to be aware of mundane things. Certainly I had a feeling myself, so strange was the place, and quiet and tranquil the day, that we had passed world's end, and that what we saw beyond our steamer was the coloured stuff of dreams which, if a wind blew, would wreathe and clear; vanish, and leave a shining void. The sunset deepened this apprehension. There came a wonderful sky of orange and mauve. It was over us and came down and under the ship. We moved with glowing clouds beneath our keel. There was no river; the forest girdled the radiant interior of a hollow sphere.

The pilots could not proceed at night. Shortly after sundown we anchored, in nine fathoms. The trees were not many yards from the steamer. When the ship was at rest a canoe with two Indians came alongside, with a basket of guavas. They were shy fellows, and each carried in his hand a bright machete, for they did not seem quite sure of our company. After tea we sat about the poop, trying to smoke, and, in the case of the Doctor and the Purser, wearing at the same time veils of butterfly nets, as protection from the mosquito swarms. The netting was put over the helmet, and tucked into the neck of the tunic. Yet, when I poked the stem of the pipe, which carried the gauze with it, into my mouth, the veil was drawn tight on the face. A mosquito jumped to the opportunity, and arrived. Alongside, the frogs were making the deafening clangour of an iron foundry, and through that sound shrilled the cicadas. I listened for the first time to the din of a tropical night in the forest. There is no word strong enough to convey this uproar to ears which have not listened to it.

Jan. 24. A bright still sunrise, promising heat; and before breakfast the ship's ironwork was too hot to touch. The novelty of this Madeira is already beginning to merge into the yellow of the river, the blue of the sky, and the green of the jungle, with but the occasional variation of low roseous cliffs. The average width of the river may be less than a quarter of a mile. It is loaded with floating timber, launched upon it by "terras-cahidas," landslides, caused by the rains, which carry away sections of the forest each large enough to furnish an English park with trees. Sometimes we see a bight in the bank where such a collapse has only recently occurred, the wreckage of trees being still fresh. Many of the trees which charge down on the current are of great bulk, with half their table-like base high out of the water. Occasionally rafts of them appear, locked with creepers, and bearing flourishing gardens of weeds. This characteristic gives the river its Portuguese name, "river of wood." The Indians know the Madeira as the Cayary, "white river."

Its course to-day serpentines so freely that at times we steer almost east, and then again go west. Our general direction is south-west. At eight this morning, after some anxious moments when the river was dangerous with reefs, we passed the village of Borba, 140 miles from Serpa. Here there is a considerable clearing, with kine browsing over a hummocky sward that is well above the river on an occurrence of the red clay. This release of the eyes was a smooth and grateful experience after the enclosing walls. Some steps dug in the face of the low cliff led to the white houses, all roofed with red tiles. The village faced the river. From each house ascended the leisurely smoke of early morning. The church was in the midst of the houses, its bell conspicuous with verdigris. Two men stood to watch us pass. It was a pleasant assurance to have, those roofs and the steeple rising actually into the light of the sky. The dominant forest, in which we were sunk, was here definitely put down by our fellow-men.

We were beyond Borba, and its parana and island just above it, before the pilot had finished telling us, where we watched from the "Capella's" bridge, that Borba was a settlement which had suffered much from attacks of the Araras Indians. The river took a sharp turn to the east, and again went west. Islands were numerous. These islands are lancet-shaped, and lie along the banks, separated by side channels, their paranas, from the land. The smaller river craft often take a parana instead of the main stream, to avoid the rush of the current. The whole region seems lifeless. There is never a flower to be seen, and rarely a bird. Sometimes, though, we disturb the snowy heron. On one sandy island, passed during the afternoon, and called appropriately, Ilho do Jacaré, we saw two alligators. Otherwise we have the silent river to ourselves; though I am forgetting the butterflies, and the constant arrival aboard of new winged shapes which are sometimes so large and grotesque that one is uncertain about their aggressive qualities. As we idle on the poop we keep by us two insect nets, and a killing-bottle. The Doctor is making a collection, and I am supposed to assist.

When I came on deck on the morning of our arrival in the Brazils it was not the orange sunrise behind a forest which was topped by a black design of palm fronds, nor the warm odour of the place, nor the height and intensity of the vegetation, which was most remarkable to me, a new-comer from the restricted north. It was a butterfly which flickered across our steamer like a coloured flame. No other experience put England so remote.

A superb butterfly, too bright and quick to be anything but an escape from Paradise, will stay its dancing flight, as though with intelligent surprise at our presence, hover as if puzzled, and swoop to inspect us, alighting on some such incongruous piece of our furniture as a coil of rope, or the cook's refuse pail, pulsing its wings there, plainly nothing to do with us, the prismatic image of joy. Out always rush some of our men at it, as though the sight of it had maddened them, as would a revelation of accessible riches. It moves only at the last moment, abruptly and insolently. They are left to gape at its mocking retreat. It goes in erratic flashes to the wall of trees and then soars over the parapet, hope at large.

Then there are the other things which, so far as most of us know, have no names, though a sailor, wringing his hands in anguish, is usually ready with a name. To-day we had such a visitor. He looked a fellow the Doctor might require, so I marked him down when he settled near a hatch on the after-deck. He was a bee the size of a walnut, and habited in dark blue velvet. In this land it is wise to assume that everything bites or stings, and that when a creature looks dead it is only carefully watching you. I clapped the net over that fellow and instantly he appeared most dead. Knowing he was but shamming, and that he would give me no assistance, I stood wondering what I could do next; then the cook came along. The cook saw the situation, laughed at my timidity with tropical forms, went down on his knees, and caught my prisoner. The cook raised a piercing cry.

On the bridge I saw them levelling their glasses at us; and some engineers came to their cabin doors to see us where we stood on the lonely deck, the cook and the Purser, in a tableau of poignant tragedy. The cook walked round and round, nursing his suffering member, and I did not catch all he said, for I know very little Dutch; but the spirit of it was familiar, and his thumb was bleeding badly. The bee had resumed death again. The state of the cook's thumb was a surprise till the surgeon exhibited the bee's weapons, when it became clear that thumbs, especially when Dutch and rosy, like our cook's, afforded the right medium for an artist who worked with such mandibles, and a tail that was a stiletto.

In England the forms of insect life soon become familiar. There is the housefly, the lesser cabbage white butterfly, and one or two other little things. In the Brazils, though the great host of forms is surprising enough, it is the variety in that host which is more surprising still. Any bright day on the "Capella" you may walk the length of the ship, carrying a net and a collecting-bottle, and fill the bottle (butterflies, cockroaches, and bugs not admitted), and perhaps have not three of a species. The men frequently bring us something buzzing in a hat; though accidents do happen half-way to where the Doctor is sitting, and the specimen is mangled in a frenzy. A hornet came to us that way. He was in violet armour, as hard as a crab, was still stabbing the air with his long needle, and working on a fragment of hat he held in his jaws. But such knights in mail are really harmless, for after all they need not be interfered with. It is the insignificant little fellows whose object in life it is to interfere with us which really make the difference.

So far on the river we have not met the famous pium fly. But the motuca fly is a nuisance during the afternoon sleep. It is nearly of the size and appearance of a "blue-bottle" fly, but its wings, having black tips, look as though their ends were cut off. The motucas, while we slept, would alight on the wrists and ankles, and where each had fed there would be a wound from which the blood steadily trickled.

The mosquitoes do not trouble us till sundown. But one morning in my cabin I was interested in the hovering of what I thought was a small, leggy spider which, because of its colouration of black and grey bands, was evasive to the sight as it drifted about on its invisible thread. At last I caught it, and found it was a new mosquito. In pursuing it I found a number of them in the cabin. When I exhibited the insect to the surgeon he did not well disguise his concern. "Say nothing about it," he said, "but this is the yellow-fever brute." So our interest in our new life is kept alert and bright. The solid teak doors of our cabins are now permanently fixed back. Shutting them would mean suffocation; but as the cabins must be closed before sundown to keep out the clouds of gnats, the carpenter has made wooden frames, covered with copper gauze, to fit the door openings at night, and rounds of gauze to cap the open ports; and with a damp cloth, and some careful hunting each morning, one is able to keep down the mosquitos which have managed to find entry during the night and have retired at sunrise to rest in dark corners. For our care notwithstanding the insects do find their way in to assault our lighted lamps. The Chief, partly because as an old sailor he is a fatalist, and partly because he thinks his massive body must be invulnerable, and partly because he has a contempt, anyway, for protecting himself, each morning has a new collection of curios, alive and dead, littered about his room. (I do not wonder Bates remained in this land so long; it is Elysium for the entomologist.) One of the live creatures found in his room the Chief retains and cherishes, and hopes to tame, though the object does not yet answer to his name of Edwin. This creature is a green mantis or praying insect, about four inches long, which the Chief came upon where it rested on the copper gauze of his door-cover, holding a fly in its hands, and eating it as one would an apple. This mantis is an entertaining freak, and can easily keep an audience watching it for an hour, if the day is dull. Edwin, in colour and form, is as fresh, fragile, and translucent as a leaf in spring. He has a long thin neck—the stalk to his wings, as it were—which is quite a third of his length. He has a calm, human face with a pointed chin at the end of his neck; he turns his face to gaze at you without moving his body, just as a man looks backwards over his shoulder. This uncanny mimicry makes the Chief shake with mirth. Then, if you alarm Edwin, he springs round to face you, frilling his wings abroad, standing up and sparring with his long arms, which have hooks at their ends. At other times he will remain still, with his hands clasped up before his face, as though in earnest devotion, for a trying period. If a fly alights near him he turns his face that way and regards it attentively. Then sluggishly he approaches it for closer scrutiny. Having satisfied himself it is a good fly, without warning his arms shoot out and that fly is hopelessly caught in the hooked hands. He eats it, I repeat, as you do apples, and the authentic mouthfuls of fly can be seen passing down his glassy neck. Edwin is fragile as a new leaf in form, has the same delicate colour, and has fascinating ways; but somehow he gives an observer the uncomfortable thought that the means to existence on this earth, though intricately and wonderfully devised, might have been managed differently. Edwin, who seems but a pretty fragment of vegetation, is what we call a lie. His very existence rests on the fact that he is a diabolical lie.

Gossamers in the rigging to-day led the captain to prophesy a storm before night. Clouds of an indigo darkness, of immense bulk, and motionless, reduced the sunset to mere runnels of opaline light about the bases of dark mountains inverted in the heavens. There was a rapid fall of temperature, but no rain. Our world, and we in its centre on the "Capella," waited for the storm in an expectant hush. Night fell while we waited. The smooth river again deepened into the nadir of the last of day, and the forest about us changed to material ramparts of cobalt. The pilot made preparations to anchor. The engine bell rang to stand-by, a summons of familiar urgency, but with a new and alarming note when heard in a place like that. The forest made no response. A little later the bell clanged rapidly again, and the pulse of our steamer slowed, ceased. We could hear the water uncoiling along our plates. The forest itself approached us, came perilously near. The Skipper's voice cried abruptly, "Let go!" and at once the virgin silence was demolished by the uproar of our cable. The "Capella" throbbed violently; she literally undulated in the drag of the current. We still drifted slowly down stream. The second anchor was dropped, and held us. The silence closed in on us instantly. Far in the forest somewhere, while we were whispering to each other in the quiet, a tree fell with a deep, significant boom.

Jan. 25. We had been under way for more than an hour when my eyes opened on the illuminated panorama of leaves and boles unfolding past the door of my cabin. The cicadas were grinding their scissors loudly in the trees alongside. I spent much of this day on the bridge, where I liked to be, watching the pilot at work. The Skipper was there, and in a cantankerous mood. The pilot wants us to make a chart of the river. He has given the captain and me a long list of islands, paranas, tributaries, villages, and sitios. Every map and reference to the river we have on board is valueless. A map of the river indicates many settlements with beautiful names; and at each point, when we arrive, nothing but the forest shows. How the cartographers arrived at such results is a mystery. This river, which their generous imaginings have seen as a tortuous bough of the Amazon, laden with villages which they indicate on their maps with marks like little round fruits, is almost barren. Every day we pass small sitios or clearings; maybe the map-makers mean such places as those. Yet each clearing is but a brief security, a raft of land—the size of the garden of an English villa— lonely in an ocean of deep leaves, where a rubber man has built himself a timber house, and some huts for his serfs. It will have a jetty and a huddle of canoes, and usually a few children on the bank watching us. We salute that place with

our syren as we pass, and sometimes the kiddies spring for
home then as though we were shooting at them. Or we see
a little embowered shack with a pile of fuel logs beside it,
and a crude name-board, where the river boats replenish
when traversing this stream, during the season, for rubber.
Our pilots have much to say of these stations, and of all the
rubber men on the river and their wealth. But away with
their rubber! I am tired of it, and will keep it out of this book
if I can. For it is blasphemous that in such a potentially
opulent land the juice of one of its wild trees should be dwelt
upon—as it is in the states of Amazonas and Para—as
though it were the sole act of Providence. The Brazilians can
see nothing here but rubber. The generative qualities of this
land through fierce sun and warm showers—for rarely a day
passes without rain, whatever the season—a land of constant
high summer with a free fecundity which has buried the
earth everywhere under a wild growth nearly two hundred
feet deep, is insignificant to them. They see nothing in it at
all but the damnable commodity which is its ruin. Para is
mainly rubber, and Manaõs. The Amazon is rubber, and
most of its tributaries. The Madeira particularly is rubber.
The whole system of communication, which covers 34,000
miles of navigable waters, waters nourishing a humus which
literally stirs beneath your feet with the movements of
spores and seeds, that system would collapse but for the
rubber. The passengers on the river boats are rubber men,
and the cargoes are rubber. All the talk is of rubber. There
are no manufactures, no agriculture, no fisheries, and no
saw-mills, in a region which could feed, clothe, and shelter
the population of a continent. There was a book by a Brazilian I saw at Para, recently published, and called the "Green
Hell" (Inferno Verde). On its cover was the picture of a nude
Indian woman, symbolical of Amazonas, and from wounds
in her body her blood was draining into the little tin cups
which the rubber collector uses against the incisions on the
rubber tree. From what I heard of the subject, and I heard
much, that picture was little overdrawn. I begin to think the
usual commercial mind is the most dull, wasteful, and
ignorant of all the sad wonders in the pageant of humanity.

It is only on the "Capella's" bridge that you feel the stagnant air which is upset by the steamer's progress. There it spills over us, heavy with the scent of the lairage on the fore deck. The bridge is a narrow, elevated outlook, full in the sun's eye, where I can get a view of the complete ship as she serpentines in her narrow way. On the port side of it the Skipper has a seat, and there now he sits all day, gazing moodily ahead. The dapper little pilot stands centrally, throwing brief commands over his shoulder into the open window of the wheel-house, where a sailor, gravely chewing tobacco, his hands on the wheel, is as rapt as though in a trance. I think the pilot finds his way by divination. The depth of the river is most variable. In the dry season I hear the stream becomes but a chain of pools connected by threads which may be no more than eighteen inches deep, the rest of its bed being dry mud cross-hatched by sun cracks. The rains in far Bolivia, overflowing the swamps there, during some months of the year increase the depth of the Madeira by forty-five feet. The local rainy season would make hardly any difference to it. The river is fed from reservoirs which stretch beneath the Andes.

There is rarely anything to show why, for a spell, the pilot should take us straight ahead in mid-stream, and then again tack to and fro across, sometimes brushing the foliage with our shrouds. I have plucked a bunch of leaves in an unexpected swoop inshore. And the big timber comes down afloat to meet us in a never-ending procession; there are the propellor blades to be thought of. I see, now and then, the swirls which betray rocks in hiding, and when dodging those dangerous places the screw disturbs the mud and the stinks. But the pilot takes us round and about, we with our 300 feet of length and 23 feet draught, as a man would steer a motor car. To aid it our rudder has had fixed to it a false wooden length. The "Capella" is a very good girl, as responsive to the pilot's word as though she knew that he alone can save her. She stems this powerful current at but four knots, and sometimes we come to places where, if she hesitated for but two seconds, we should be put athwart stream to close the channel. And what would happen to us with nothing but unexplored malarial forest each side of us is not useful to brood on. Occasionally the pilot, grasping the top of the "dodger," stares beyond us fixedly to where the refracted sunshine is blinding between the green cliffs, and gives quick and numerous orders to the wheelhouse without turning his head. The Skipper gets up to watch. The "Capella" makes surprising swerves, the pilot nervously taps the boards with his foot. . . . Then he says something quietly, relaxes, and comes to us blithely, the funny dog with a nonsense story, and the Skipper sinks couchant again. Once more I watch the front of the jungle for what may show there. Seldom there is anything new which shows. It is rare, even when close alongside, that one can trace the shape of a leaf. There are but the conspicuous grey nests of the ants and wasps. Yet several times to-day I saw trees in blossom; domes of lilac in the green forest roof. Again, to-day we put up a flight of hundreds of ducks; and another incident was a black-water stream, the Rio Mataua, the line of demarcation between the Madeira's yellow flood and its dark tributary being distinct.

Jan. 26. The forest is lower and more open, and the pao mulatto is more numerous. We saw the important village of Manicoré to-day, and Oncas, a little place within a portico of the woods which was veiled in grey smoke, for they were coagulating rubber there. For awhile before sunset the sky was scenic with great clouds, and glowing with the usual bright colours. The wilderness was transformed. Each evening we seem to anchor in a region different, in nature and appearance, under these extraordinary sunset skies, from the country we have been travelling since daylight. Transfiguration at eventime we know in England. Yet sunset there but exalts our homeland till it seems more intimately ours than ever, as though then came a luminous revelation of its rare intrinsic goodness. We see, for some brief moments, its aura. But this tropical jungle, at day-fall, is not the earth we know. It is a celestial vision, beyond physical attaining, beyond knowledge. It is ulterior, glorious, transient, fading before our surprise and wonder fade. We of the "Capella" are its only witnesses, except those pale ghosts, the egrets about the dim aqueous base of the forest.

Darkness comes quickly, the swoop and overspread of black wings. The stopping of the ship's heart, because the pulsations of her body have had unconscious response in yours, as by an incorporeal ligament, is the cessation of your own life. At a moment there is a strange quiet, in which you begin to hear the whisper of inanimate things. A log glides past making faint labial sounds. You are suddenly released from prison, and float lightly in an ether impalpable to the coarse sounds and movements of earth, but which is yet sensitive to the most delicate contact of your thoughts and emotions. The whispering of your fellows is but the rustling of their thoughts in an illimitable and inviolate silence.

Then, almost imperceptibly, the frogs begin their night-long din. The crickets and cicadas join. Between the varying pitch of their voices come other nocturnes in monotones from creatures unknown to complete the gamut. There are notes so profound, but constant, that they are a mere impression of obscurity to the hearing, as when one peers listening into an abysm in which no bottom is seen, and others are stridulations so attenuated that they shrill beyond reach.

A few frogs begin it. There are ululations, wells of mellow sound bubbling to overflow in the dark, and they multiply and unite till the quality of the sound, subdued and pleasant at first, is quite changed. It becomes monstrous. The night trembles in the powerful beat of a rhythmic clangour. One cannot think of frogs, hearing that metallic din. At one time, soon after it begins, the chorus seems the far hubbub, mingled and levelled by distance, of a multitude of people running and disputing in a place where we who are listening know that no people are. The noise comes nearer and louder till it is palpitating around us. It might be the life of the forest, immobile and silent all day, now released and beating upwards in deafening paroxysms.

Alongside the engine room casing amidships the engineers have fixed an open-air mess-table, with a hurricane lamp in its midst, having but a brief halo of light which hardly distinguishes the pickle jar from the marmalade pot. A haze of mosquitoes quivers round the light. The air is hot and lazy, and the engineers sit about limply in trousers and shirts, the latter open and showing bosoms as various as faces. The men cheer themselves with comical plaints about the heat, the food, the Brazils, and make sudden dabs at bare flesh when the insects bite them. The Chief rallies his boys as would a cheery dad—Sandy, though, is nearly his own age, but still much of a lad, quietly despondent—and the Chief heartily insists on food, like it or lump it. I go forward to the captain's tea table on the poop deck, where we have two hurricane lamps, and where the figures of us round the table, in that dismal glim, are the thin phantoms of men. The lamps have been lighted only that moment, and as we take our seats, the insects come. Just as sharply as though something derisive and invisible were throwing them at us, big mole crickets bounce into our plates. A cicada, though I was then unaware of his identity, a monstrous fly which looked as large as a rat, and with a head like a lantern, alighted before me on the cloth, and remained still. Picking it up tentatively it sprang a startling police rattle between my finger and thumb, and the other chaps shouted their merriment. The steward places a cup of tea before each of us, and in an interval of the talk the Skipper announces a smell of paraffin in his cup. We experiment with ours, and gravely confirm. The surgeon, bending close to a light with his cup, the deep characteristics of his face strongly accentuated—he seems but a bodiless head in the dark—says he detects globules of fat. The Skipper crudely outlines this horror to the steward, who makes an inaudible reply in German, and disappears down the companion. We get a new and innocent brew.

There is hash for us. There is our familiar the pickled beef. There are saucers of brown onions. There are saucers of jam and of butter. To-night the steward has baked some cakes, and their grateful smell and crisp brown rugged surface, studded with plums, determine in my mind a resolution to eat four of them, if I can get them without open shame. I assert that our Skipper has a counting eye for the special dishes; though you may eat all the hash you want. Damn his hash! The bread is sour. I want cakes.

After tea the pilots get into their hammocks and under their curtains, out of the way of the mosquitoes. We know where they are because of the red ends of their cigarettes. We sit around anywhere, the Skipper, the Chief, the Doctor and the Purser. There is little to be said. We talk of the mosquitoes, in ejaculations, for the little wretches quite easily penetrate linen, and can manage even worsted socks. Occasionally flying insects bump into the tin lamp placed above us on the ice chest. (No; there is no ice.) Thin divergent arrows of light, the fireflies, lace the gloom, and the trees alongside are gemmed with them. We find still less to say to each other, but fear to retire to our heated berths, for as it is just possible to breathe in the open we continue to defy the mosquitoes. The first mate serenades us on his accordion. At last there is no help for it. The steward comes to tell the master that his cot is ready. The "old man" sleeps in a cot draped with netting, and slung from the awning beams on the starboard side. Nightly he turns in there, and unfailingly a rain cloud bursts in the very early morning, pounding on the awning till the cool spray compels him, and he retreats in his pyjamas for shelter, taking his pillow with him. It is for that reason I do not use the cot he made for me, which hangs on the port side; though it is delightful for the afternoon nap.

The Skipper disappears. The Doctor and I go below to the surgery, and from the settee there he removes books, tobacco tins, fishing tackle, phials, india rubber tubing, and small leather cases, making room for us both, and first we have some out of his bottle, and then we try some out of mine. The stuff is always tepid, for the water in the carafe has a temperature of 80 degrees. The perspiration begins a steady permeation as we talk, for now we can talk, and talk, being together, and talking is better than sleep, which at its best is but a fitful doze in the tropics. We fall, as it were, on each other's necks. Though the Doctor's breast—I say nothing of mine—is not one which appears to invite the weak tear of a fellow mortal who is harassed by solitude. You might judge

it too cold, too hard and unresponsive a support, for that;
and I have seen his eye even repellent. He is not elderly, but
he is grey, and pallid through too much tropics. The lines
descending his face show he has been observing things for
long, and does not think much of them. When disputing
with him, he does not always reply to you; he smiles to
himself; a habit which is an annoyance to some people,
whose simple minds are suspicious, and who are unaware
that the surgeon is sometimes forgetful that his weaker
brethren, when they are most heated and disputative with
him, then most lack confidence in their case, and need the
confirmation of the wit they know is superior. That is no
time when one should look at the wall, and smile quietly.
The "Capella's" company feel that the surgeon stands where
he overlooks them, and they see, where he stands unassum-
ingly superior, that he looks upon them politely. They do
not know he is really sad and forgetful; they think he is
amused, but that he prefers to pretend he is well bred. I must
confess it is known he has prescience having a certain
devilish quality of penetration. There was one of our stokers,
and one night he was drunk on stolen gin, and latitudinous,
and so attempted a curious answer to the second engineer,
who sought him out in the forecastle concerning work. Now
the second engineer is a young man who has a number of
photographs of himself which display him, clad but in
vanity and shorts, back, front, and profile, arms folded
tightly to swell his very large muscles. He has really a model
figure, and he knows it. The cut over the stoker's nose was
a bad one.

To the surgeon the stoker went, early next morning,
actually for a hair of the dog, but with a story that he was
then to go on duty, and so would miss his ration of quinine,
which is not served till eleven o'clock. The quinine, as you
know, is given in gin. The surgeon complimented the man
on such proper attention to his health, and willingly gave
him the quinine—in water. He also stood at the door of the
alleyway to watch the man retained the quinine as far as the
engine room entrance.

Eight bells! Presently I also must go and pretend to sleep.

The surgeon's last cheery comment on the cosmic scheme remains but as a wry smile on our faces. We grope in our minds desperately for a topic to keep the talk afloat. There goes one bell!

I arrive at my haunt of cockroaches, where the second mate is already asleep on the upper shelf. The brown light of the oil lamp has its familiar flavour, and the cabin is like an oven. What a prospect for sleep! Raising the mosquito curtain carefully I slip through the opening like an acrobat, hoping to be ahead of the insidious little malaria carriers. A drove of cockroaches scuttles wildly over my warm mattress as I arrive. Striking matches within what the sailor overhead calls my meat safe, I examine my enclosure carefully for mosquitoes, but none seems to be there, though I know very well I shall find at least a dozen, gorged with blood, in the morning. The iron bulkhead which separates my bed from the engine room is, of course, hot to the touch. The air is a passive weight. The old insect bites begin to irritate and burn. I kick the miserable sheet to the foot, and lie on my back without a movement, for I fear I may suffocate in that shut box. My chest seems in bonds, and for long there is no relief, though the body presently grows indifferent to the misery, and the anxiety goes. It is remarkable to what brutality the body will submit, when it knows it must. Yet nothing but a continuous effort of will kept the panic suppressed, and me in that box, till the feeling of anxiety had passed. Thenceforward the sleepless mind, like a petty balloon giddy on a thin but unbreakable thread of thought, would tug at my consciousness, revolving and dodging about, in spite of my resolution to keep it still. If I could only break that thread, I said to myself, turning over again, away it would fly out of sight, and I should forget all this . . . all this . . . And presently it broke loose, and dwindled into oblivion.

Then I knew nothing more till I saw, fixed where I was in hopeless horror, the baby face of one I dwell much upon, in moments of solitude, and it had fallen wan and thin, and was full of woe unutterable, and its appealing eyes were blind. I woke with a cry, sitting up suddenly, the heart going like a rapid hammer. There was the curtained box about me. The clothes were on the hooks. I could see the black shape of the cabin doorway. By my watch it was four o'clock. The air had cooled, and as I sat waiting for the next thing in the silence the mate snored profoundly overhead. Ah! So that was all right.

Jan. 27. This has been a day of anxious navigation, for the river has had frequent reefs. We remain in a stagnant chasm of trees. The surgeon and I, accompanied by a swarm of flies, went forward into the cattle stew this morning to see how the beasts fare. The patient brutes were suffering badly, and some, quite plainly were dying. The change form the lush green stuff of the Itacoatiara swamps to compressed American hay put under their noses on an iron deck, and the stifling heat under partial awnings, had ruined them. Some stood, heads down, legs straddled, too indifferent to disperse the loathly clouds of parasites. Most were plagued by ticks, which had the tenacity and appearance of iron bolt heads. But the little black cow, the rebel, blared at us, bound and suffering as she was. Vive la revolution! We drove the flies from her hide, and she tried to kick us, the darling. We found a steer with his shoulder out of joint, lying inert in the sun, indifferent to further outrage. That had to be seen to, and we told the Skipper, who ordered it to be killed. We wanted some fresh meat badly, he added. The boatswain explained that he knew the business, and he brought a long knife, and quite calmly thrust it into the front of the prone creature, and seemed to be trying to find its heart. Nothing happened, except a little blood and some convulsing movements. Another sailor produced a short knife and a hammer, and tapped away behind the horns as though he were a mason and this were stone. The frowning surgeon supposed the fellow was trying to sever the vertebrae. I don't know. Yet another fellow jumped on its abdomen. At last it died. I put down merely what happened. No two voyages are alike, and as this episode came into mine, here it is, to be worked in with the sunsets and things. There was some cheerful talk at the prospect of the first fresh meat since England, and later, passing the cook's galley, I saw an iron bin, and lifted its cover to see what was there. And there was, as I judged there would be, liver for tea that evening. But I learned that though I am a carnivore yet I have not the pluck to be a vulture.

The next day we passed the Cidada de Humayta, the chief town on the Madeira. Actually it was of the size of an unimportant home village. There was nothing there to support the pilot's sonorous title of cidada. For some reason we were visited to-day by an extraordinary number of butterflies. One large specimen was of an olive green, barred with black. Another had wings of a bluish grey, striped with vermilion. Helicons came, and once a morpho, the latter a great rarity away from the interior of the woods. At four in the afternoon the sky grew ominous. We had just time to notice the trees astern suddenly convulsed, writhing where they stood, and the storm sprang at us, roaring, ripping away awnings and loose gear. The noise in the forest round us was that of cataclysm. The rain was an obscurity of falling water, and the trees turned to shadows in a grey fog. The ship became full of waterspouts, large streams and jets curving away from every prominence. This lasted for but twenty minutes; but the impending clouds remained to hasten night when we were in a place which, more than anything I have seen, was the world before the coming of man. The river had broadened and shallowed. The forest enclosed us. There were islands, and the rank growth of swamps. We could see, through breaks in the igapo, extensive lagoons beyond, with the high jungle brooding over empty silver areas. Herons, storks, and egrets were white and still about the tangle of aqueous roots. It was all as silent and other world as a picture.

Jan. 29. When shouting awakened me this morning I saw the chief hurry by my cabin, half-dressed, and looking very anxious. By the almost stationary foliage I could see the ship had merely way on her. Out I jumped. On the forecastle head a crowd was gathered, peering overside. A large tree was balanced accurately athwart our stem, and refused to move.

What worried the staff was that it would, when free, sidle along our plate till it fouled the propeller. The propeller had to be kept moving, for the river was narrow and its current unusually rapid. There the log obstinately remained for the most of an hour, but suddenly made up its mind, and went, clearing the stern by inches. After that the engines were driven full, for the pilot hoped to get us to Porto Velho by nightfall. In the late afternoon, when passing the Rio Jamary, the clouds again banked astern, bringing night before its time, and another violent storm compelled an early anchorage. The forest was remarkably quiet after the tumult of the squall, and the "Capella" had been put over to the left bank, when close to us on the opposite shore there was a landslip. We saw a section of the jungle wall sway, as thought that part was taken by a local tempest, and then the green cliff and its supports fell bodily into the river, raising thunderous submarine explosions. Such landslides, terras cahidas, can be rarely foreseen, and are a grave danger to craft when they come close in to rest at night. To-day we passed a small raft drifting down. A hut was erected in its middle, and we saw two men within.

Jan. 30. Talk enough there has been of a place called Porto Velho, a name I heard first when I signed the articles of the "Capella" at Swansea, and of what would happen to us when we arrived. But I am looking upon it all as a strange myth. There has been time to prove those superstitions of Porto Velho. And what has happened? There was a month we had of the vacant sea, and one day we came upon a low coast where palms grew. There has been a month which has striped the vacant mind in three colours, constant in relative position, but without form, yellow floor, green walls, and a blue ceiling. Plainly we have got beyond all the works of man now. We have intrigued an ocean steamer thousands of miles along the devious waterways of a uninhabited continental jungle, and now she must be near the middle of the puzzle, with voiceless regions of unexplored forest reeking under the equatorial sun at every point of the compass. The more we advance up the Amazon and Madeira rivers the less the likelihood, it seems to me, of getting to any place where our ship and cargo could be required. We shall steam and steam till the river shallows, the forest closes in, and we are trapped. Yet the Madeira looks now much the same as when we entered it, still as broad and deep. I was thinking this morning we might go on so for ever; that this adventure was all of the casual improbabilities of a dream was in my mind when, smoking the after breakfast pipe on the bridge, we turned a corner sharply, and there was the end of the passage within a mile of us, Porto Velho at last.

The forest on the port side ahead was uplifted on an unusually high cliff of the red rock. Beyond that cliff was a considerable clearing, with many buildings of a character different from any we had seen in the country. At the end of the clearing the forest began again, unconquered still, standing across our course as a high barrier; for, leaving Porto Velho, the river turned west almost at a right angle, and vanished; as though now it were done with us. We had arrived. A rough pier was being thrown out on palm boles to receive us, but it was not ready. We anchored in five fathoms, about thirty yards from the shore, and in the quiet which came with the stop of the ship's life we waited for the next thing, all hands lining the "Capella's" side surveying this place of which we had heard so much.

Plainly this was not the usual village. Many acres of trees had been newly cleared, leaving a great bay in the woods. The earth was still raw from a recent attack on what had been inviolate from time's beginning. Trenches, new red gashes, scored it, and holes were gouged in the hill side. You could think man had attacked the forest here in a fury, but had spent his force on one small spot, as though he had struck one wound again and again. The fight was over. The footing had been won, a base perhaps for further campaigns because wooden emergency houses, sheds and barracks, had been built. The assailant evidently had made up his mind to settle on his advantage, though he was tolerating a little quickly rebellious scrub. Just then he was resting, as if the whole affair had been over but five minutes before we came, and now the conqueror was sleeping on his first success. Completely round the conquered space the jungle stood indifferently regarding the trifle of ground it had lost. The jungle on the near opposite shore rose straight and uninterrupted from the river, the front rank, lost each way in distance, of an innumerable army. At the upper end of the clearing the jungle began again on our side, and turned to run across our bows, the complement of the host across the water, and both ranks continued up stream, dark and indeterminate lines converging, till, three miles away, a delicate flickering of light, a mere dimmer, faint but constant, bridged the two walls. No doubt that delicate light would be the San Antonio cataracts, the first of the nineteen rapids of the Madeira.

Porto Velho behaved as though we were not there. A pitiless sun flamed over that deep red wound in the forest, and they who had made it were in their shelters, resting out of sight after such a recent riot of exertion. Nothing was being done then. Two or three white men stood on the dismantled foreshore, placidly regarding us. We might have been something they were not quite sure was there, a possibility not sufficiently interesting for them to verify. There was a hint of mockery, after all our anxiety and travail, in this quiet disregard. Had we arrived too late to help, and were not wanted? I confess I should not have been surprised to have heard suppressed laughter, some light hilarity from the unseen, at us innocently puzzling as to what was to happen next. There was a violent scream in the forest near our bows, and we turned wondering to that green wall. A locomotive ran out from the base of the trees, still screaming.

In a little while a man left a house, striding down over the debris to the foreshore, and some half-breeds brought him in a canoe to the "Capella." He was a tall youngster, an American, and his slow body itself was but a thin sallow drawl; only his eyes were alert, and they darted at ours in quick scrutiny. His solemn occupying assurance and accent precipitated reality. He was a doctor and he ordered us to be mustered on the after deck for inspection for yellow fever. We were passed; and then this doctor went below to the saloon, distributing his long limbs and body over several chairs and part of the table, and began with lazy words and gestures to give us a place in the scene. We learned we should stay as we were till the pier was finished and that the railway was actually in being for a short distance. He said something about Porto Velho being hell.

He left us. We sat about on deck furniture, and waited on the unknown gods of the land to see what they would send us. All day in the clearing figures moved about on some mysterious business, but seldom looked at us. We had nothing to do but to watch the raft of timber and flotsam expand about our hawsers, a matter of some concern to us, for the current ran at six knots. Our brief sense of contact got from the medical inspection had gone by night. Reality contracted, closing in upon the "Capella" with rapidly diminishing radii as the light went, till we had lost everything but our steamer.

Into the saloon, where some of us sat listening in sympathy to the Skipper's growls that night, burst our cook, disrespectful and tousled, saying he had seen a canoe, which bore a light, overturn in the river. There was a stampede. We each seized a lantern and leaned overside with it, with that fatuous eagerness to help which makes a man strike matches when looking for one who is lost on a moor. Ghostly logs came floating noiselessly out of darkness into the brief domain of our lanterns, and faded into night again. From somewhere in the collection of driftwood beyond our bows we thought we heard an occasional cry, though that might have been the noise of water sucking through the rubbish, or the creaking of timbers. Our chief mate got out a small boat, and vanished; and we were already growing anxious for him when his luminous grin appeared below in the range of my lantern, and with him came the ponderous figure of a man. The latter, deft and agile, came up the rope ladder, and stepped aboard with innocent inconsequence, shocking my sense of the gravity of the affair; for this streaming object, lifted from the grip of the boney one just in time, was chuckling. "Say," said this big ruddy man to our gaping crowd, "I met a nigger ashore with a letter for the captain of this packet. Said he didn't know how to get. So I brought it, but a tree overturned the canoe. I came up under the timber jam all right, all right, but it took me quite a piece to get my head through." In the saloon, with a pool of water spreading round him, while we got him some dry clothes, he produced this pulpy letter. "Dear Captain (it ran) I'm dry as hell, have you brought drinks in the ship?"

The bland indifference of Porto Velho to the "Capella," which had done so much to get there; the locomotive which ran screaming out of those woods where, till then, was the same unbroken front which from Para inwards had surrendered nothing; the inconsequential doctor who carefully examined us for what we had not got; the ruddy man who rose to us streaming out of the deeps, as though that were his usual approach, bearing another stranger's unreasonable letter complaining of thirst, were most puzzling. I even felt some anxiety and suspicion. What, then, were all the other incidents of our difficult six thousand mile voyage? What was this place to which we had come on urgent business long and carefully deliberated, where men merely looked at the whites of our eyes, or changed wet clothes in the saloon, or lightly referred to hell—they all did that—as if hell were an unremarkable feature of their day? Were all these unrelated shadows and movements but part of a long and witless jest? The point of it I could not see. Was there any point to it or did casual episodes appear at unexpected places till they came, just as unexpectedly, to an empty end? The man the mate had rescued sat at the saloon table opposite me, leaning a yard wide chest, which was almost bare, on the red baize, his bulging arms resting before him, and his hairy paws easily clasped. I thought that perhaps this imperturbable being, who could come with easy assurance, his bright friendly eyes merely amused, his large firm mouth merely mocking, and his face heated, from a desperate affair in which his life nearly went, to announce to strangers, "Boys, I'm old man Jim," must have had the point of the joke revealed to him long since, and so now had no respect for its setting, and could have no care and understanding of my anxious innocence. He sat there for hours in quiet discourse. I listened to him with my ears only, his words jostling my thoughts, as one would puzzle over and listen to a superior being which had unbent to be intimate, but was outside our experience. I heard he had been at this place since 1907. He began the work here. Porto Velho did not then exist. Off where we were anchored, the jungle rose. He had his young son with him, a cousin, and two negroes, and he began the railway. Inside the trees, he said they could not see three yards, but down it all had to come. There is a small stingless bee here, which "old man Jim" called the sweat bee. It alights in swarms on the face and hands, and prefers death to being dislodged from its enjoyment. The heat, these bees, the ants, the pium flies, the mosquitoes, made the existence of Jim and his mates a misery. Jim merely drawled about in a comic way. Fever came, and mistrust of natives compelled him to dress a dummy, put that in his hammock at night, while he slept in a corner of the hut one eye open, nursing a gun. I could not see "old man Jim" ever having faith that trains would run, or needed to run, where Indians lurked in the bush, and jaguars nosed round the hut at night. Why these sufferings then? But we learned the line now penetrated into the forest for sixty miles, and that beyond it there were camps, where surveyors were seeing that further way was made, and beyond them again, among the trees of the interior, the surveyors were still, planning the way the line should run when it had got so far.

Though we could not get ashore, there was enough to watch, if it were only the men leisurely driving palm boles into the river, making a pier for us. While at breakfast to-day a canoe of half-breeds came flying towards us in pursuit of an object which kept a little ahead of them in the river. It passed close under our stern, and we saw it was a peccary. The canoe ran level with it then, and a man leaned over, catching the wild pig by a hind leg, keeping its snout under the water while another secured its feet with a rope. It was brought aboard in bonds as a present for the Skipper, who begged the natives to convey it below to the bunkers and there release it. He said he would tame it. I saw the eye of the beast as it lay on the deck champing its tusks viciously, and guessed we should have some interesting moments while kindness tried to reduce that light in its eye. The peccary disappeared for a few days.

There being nothing to do this fine morning, we watched the cattle put ashore. This was not so difficult a business as shipping them, for the beasts now submitted quietly to the noose which was put on their horns. The steam tackle hoisted them, they were pushed overside, and dropped into the river. Some natives in a canoe cleared the horns, and the brute, swimming desperately in the strong current, was guided to the bank. Some of the beasts being already near death they were merely jettisoned. The current bore them down stream, making feeble efforts to swim—food for the alligators. We waited for the turn of the black heifer. She was one of the last. She was not led to the ship's side. The tackle was attached to her horns, and made taut before her head was loosed. She made a furious lunge at the men when her nose was free, but the winch rattled, and she was brought up on her hind legs, blaring at us all. In that ugly manner she was walked on two legs across the deck, a heroine in shameful guise, while the men laughed. She was hoisted, and lowered into the river. She fought at the waiting canoe with her feet, but at last the man released her horns from the tackle. With only her face above water she heaved herself, open mouthed, at the canoe, trying to bite it, and then made some almost successful efforts to climb into it. The canoe men were so panic-stricken that they did nothing but muddle one another's efforts. The canoe rocked dangerously. This wicked animal had no care for its own safety like the other cattle. It surprised its tormentors because it showed its only wish was to kill them. Just in time the men paddled off for their lives, the cow after them. Seeing she could not catch them, she swam ashore, climbed the bank, looking round then for a sight of the enemy—but they were all in hiding—and then began browsing in the scrub.

As leisurely as though life were without end, the work on the pier proceeded; and we on the "Capella," who could not get ashore, with each of our days a week long, looked round upon this remote place of the American tropics till it seemed we had never looked upon anything else. The days were candent and vaporous, the heat by breakfast-time being such as we know at home in an early afternoon of the dog-days. The forest across the river, about three hundred yards away, from sunrise till eight o'clock, often was veiled in a white fog. There would be a clear river, and a sky that was full day, but not the least suspicion of a forest. We saw what seemed a limitless expanse of bright water, which merged into the opalescent sky walls. Such an invisible fog melted from below, and then the revelation of the dark base of the forest, in mid-distance, was as if our eyes were playing tricks. The forest appeared in the way one magic-lantern picture grows through another. The last of the vapour would roll upwards from the tree-tops for some time, and you could believe the woods were smouldering heavily. Thenceforward the quiet day would be uninterrupted, except for the plunge of a heavy fish, the passing of a canoe, a visit from an adventurous visitor from the shore, or the growing of a cloud in the sky. We tried fishing, though never got anything but some grey scaleless creatures with feelers hanging about their gills. It was not till the evening when the visitors usually came that the day began really to move. The new voices gave our saloon and cabins vivacity, and the stories we heard carried us far and swiftly towards the next breakfast-time. They were strange characters, those visitors, usually Americans, but sometimes we got an Englishman or a Frenchman. They took possession of the ship.

There was an elderly man, Neil O'Brien, who was often with us. At first I thought he was a very exceptional character. He was one of the first to visit our ship. I even felt a little timidity when alone with him, for he had a habit of sitting limply, looking at nothing in particular, and dumb, and plainly he was a man whose thoughts ran in ways I could not even surmise. His pale blue eyes would turn upon me with that searching openness which may mean childish innocence or madness, and I could not forget the whispers I had heard of his dangerously inflammable nature. I could not find common footing with him for some time. My trouble was that I had come out direct from a country where few men are free, and so most of us live in doubt of what would happen to us if we were to act as though we were free men. Where, if a self-reliant man contemptuously dares to a bleak and perilous extremity, he makes all his lawful fellows in-draw their timid breaths; that land where even a reward has been instituted, as for merit, for uncomplaining endurance under life-long hardships, and called an old-age pension. You cannot live much of your life with natural servants, the judicious and impartial, the light shy, and those who look twice carefully, but never leap, without betraying some reflected pallor of their anæmia. O'Brien, the quiet master of his own time, with his eyes I could not read, and his gun, betrayed obliquely in our casual talks together such an ingenuous indifference to accepted things and authority, that I had nothing to work with when gauging him. He was his own standard of conduct. I judged his bearing towards the authority of officials would be tolerant, and even tender, as men use with wilful children. He was not a rebel, as we understand it, one who at last grows impatient and angry, and so votes for the other party. I suppose he was not opposed to authority, unless it were opposed to him. He was outside any authority but his own. He lived without State aid. He himself carried the gun, always the symbol of authority, whether of a man or of a State, and if any man had attempted to rob him of his substance, certainly O'Brien would have shot that man according to his own law and his own prophesy, and would then have cooked his supper. He surprised me for a day or two. I puzzled much over this phenomenon of a free man, who took his freedom so quietly and naturally that he never even discussed the subject, as we do, with enthusiasm, in England. What else? It was long since he was separated from his mother. Soon I found he was but a type. I met others like him in this country. Their innocence of the limitations of a careful man like myself was disconcerting. Once O'Brien casually proposed that I should "beat it," cut the ship, and make a traverse of that wild place to distant Colombia, to some unknown spot by the approximate source of a certain Amazon tributary, where he knew there was gold. First I laughed, and then found, from his glance of resentful candour, that he was quite serious. He generously meant this honour for me; and I think it was an honour for an elderly, quiet, and seasoned privateer like O'Brien, to invite me to be his only companion in a region where you must travel with alert courage and wide experience, or perish. I have learned since he has gone to that far place alone. But what a time he will have. He will have all of it to himself. Well—I was thinking, when I refused him, of my old-age pension. I should like to get it.

Men like O'Brien are called here, quite respectfully, "bad men," and "land sailors." The lawless lands of the South American republics—lawless in this sense, that their laws need be little reckoned by the daring, the strong, and the unscrupulous—seem particularly attractive to men of the O'Brien type. I got to like them. I found them, when once used to their feral minds, always entertaining, and often instructive, for their naive opinions cut our conventions across the middle, showing the surprising insides. They dwell without bounds. As I have read somewhere, we do not think of the buffalo, which treats a continent as pasturage, as we do of the cow which kicks over the pail at milking time and jumps the yard fence. These men regard priest, magistrate and soldier with an indifference which is not even contemptible indifference. They are merely callous to the calculated effect of uniforms. When in luck, they are to be found in the cities, shy and a little miserable, having a good time. Their money gone, they set out on lonely journeys across this continent which show our fuss over authentic explorers to be a little overdone. O'Brien was such a man. He told me he had not slept under a roof for years. He had no home, he confessed to me once. Any place on the map was the same to him. He had spent his life drifting alone between Patagonia and Canada, looking for what he never found, if he knew what he was looking for. His travels were insignificant to him. He might have been a tramp talking of English highways. As he droned on one evening I began to doubt he was unaware that his was an extraordinary narrative. I guessed his unconcern must be an air. It would have been, in my case. I looked straight over at him, and he hesitated nervously, and stopped. Was he wasting my time, he asked? Prospecting for his illusion, his last journey was over the Peruvian Andes into Colombia. He broke an arm in a fall on the mountains, set it himself, and continued. On the Rio Yapura an Indian shot an arrow through his leg, and O'Brien dropped in the long grass, breaking the arrow short each side of the limb, and in an ensuing long watchful duel presently shot the Indian through the throat. And then, coming out on the Amazon, his canoe overturned, and the pickle jar full of gold dust was lost. He put no emphasis on any particular, not even on the loss of his gold.

He was pointed out to me first as a singular fellow who kept doves; a tall, gaunt man, with a deliberate gait, perhaps fifty years of age, in old garments, long boots laced to the knees, and a battered pith helmet. He strolled along with his eyes cast down. If you met him abroad, and stopped him, he answered you with a few mumbles while looking away over your shoulder. His big mouth drew down a grizzled moustache cynically, and one of his front teeth was gold plated. Before he passed on he looked at you with the haughty but doubtful stare of an animal. He seemed too slow and dull to be combustible. I ceased to credit those tales of his berserker rage. He always moved in that deliberate way, as if he were careful, but bored. Or he stood before his doves, and made bubbling noises in his loose, stringy throat. He embarrassed me with a present of many of the trophies he had secured in years of travel in the wilds. One day a negro and O'Brien were in mild dispute on the jetty, and the negro called the white a Yankee. The river was twenty feet below swiftly carrying its logs. O'Brien took the big black, and with vicious ease threw him into the water. The negro missed the floating rubbish, and struck out for the bank. No one could help him. By good luck he managed to get to the water-side; yet O'Brien meanwhile had hurried his long legs over the ties of the skeleton structure, his face transfigured, and was waiting for the negro to emerge, a spade in his hand. But under other circumstances I have not the least doubt he would have fought the Brazilian army single-handed, and so finished, in defence of that same negro.

IV

NIGHT brought one of these men to each of our cabins, and put a party of them drinking in the saloon. After my habit of thinking of people in crowds, as an Anglican Church, or an ethical society, a labour movement, a federation of proprietors, or suffragists, or Jews, or stockbrokers' clerks, crowds moving with massed exactitude by the thousand at least, when prompted, this man O'Brien standing on his two legs by himself, old man Jim, and the rest, each of them defending and running his own particular kingdom, and governing that, ill or well—for I saw them fairly drunk now and then—and never waiting for a word from any master or delegate, made me wonder whether till then I had met a living man, or had heard merely of a population of bundles of newspapers. These men had no leaders. They attended to all that. Each had to find his own way. They were unrelated to anything I knew, and beyond the help of even a candidate for Parliament. I suppose they had never heard of a Defence League. They could have found no use for it, because a challenge to defend themselves would never catch them unwilling or unable. Each man soldiered himself, and perhaps was rather too ready to deal with a show of insolence, or an assumption of power in another. Yet they were not the violent and headstrong fellows of romantic tales. They were simple and kind, submitting with a sick smile to the prickly ridicule of their fellows round the board. They regarded meat, drink, and tobacco as common; they were ready to leap into the dark for a friend.

There was one young bearded Englishman among them who was more than a friendly figure to me. All were friendly; but the Americans bore themselves with the easy assurance of the favoured heirs of Adam; though their successful work in that tropical swamp perhaps justified them. The Englishman had less of that assurance of a unique favour which was so completely bestowed that irresolution never shook the aplomb of its lucky inheritors. He came into my cabin one night, hoping he was not disturbing me, and bringing as a present a sheaf of native arrows tipped with red and blue macaw feathers, as he had promised.

"They come from Bolivia—forest Indians—three hundred miles from here." He explained he had reached our point in the Brazilian forest from the Pacific side. He had crossed the mountains, descended to the level jungle at the base of the Andean wall, and followed the rivers eastward, alone in a canoe till he chanced upon our steamer unloading Welsh fuel into a forest clearing. To a new-comer in a mysterious land, this was a clear invitation to listen, and I looked at the man expectantly. He was lighting his pipe. The country through which he must have passed was unknown, as our maps showed. But he simply indicated that manner of his advent, as though it were the same as any other, and sat looking through the door of my cabin, smoking, absently gazing at the night scene on the after-deck.

The hombres were working at the hold immediately below us, their labours made obscurely bright by a roaring flame of volatilised oil. The light pulsed on the face of the Englishman, and chequered my cabin in black and luminous gold. Of all the region of forest about us nothing showed but a cloud of leaves, which leaned towards us out of the night, supported on two pale, tremulous columns. The hold of the ship was a black rectangle, and the almost naked negroes and brown men moving about it, or peering into the chasm, were like sinister figures on an inscrutable business about the verge of the pit. They were not men, but the debris of men, moving with awful volition, merely a bright cadaverous mask hovering in a void, or two arms upheld, or a black headless trunk. For the roaring illuminant on deck dismembered the ship and its occupants, bursting into the weight of surrounding night as a fixed explosion, beams rigid and glowing, and shadows in long solid bars radiating from its incandescent heart.

"I'm glad you're here," said my companion. He never gave

me his name, and I do not know it now. "I hav'n't heard home talk for a year. Hav'n't heard much of anything. A little Spanish coming along; and here some American."

We continued looking at the puzzling, disrupted scene outside for some time without speaking, secure in a chance and lucky sympathy. Then a basket of coal tipped against a hatch coaming and whirled away, scattering the men. We rose to see if any were hurt.

"Curious, this desperate haste, isn't it?" said the English-man. "At every point of the compass from here there's at least a thousand miles of wilderness. Excepting at this place it wouldn't matter to anybody whether a thing were done to-night, or next week, or not at all. But look at those fellows—you'd think this was a London wharf, and a tide had to be caught. Here they are on piece-work and overtime, where there's nothing but trees, alligators, tigers, and sav-ages. An unknown Somebody in Wall Street or Park Lane has an idea, and this is what it does. The potent impulse! It moves men who don't know the language of New York and London down to this desolation. It begins to ferment the place. The fructifying thought! Have you seen the graveyard here? We've got a fine cemetery, and it grows well. Still, this railway will get done. Yes, people who don't know what it's for, they'll make a little of it, and die, and more who don't know what it's for, and won't use it when it's made, they'll finish it. This line will get its freights of precious rubber moving down to replenish the motor tyres of civilisation, and the chap who had the bright idea, but never saw this place, and couldn't live here a week, or shovel dirt, or lay a track, and wouldn't know raw rubber if he saw it, he'll score again. Progress, progress! The wilderness blossoms as the rose. It's wonderful, isn't it?"

I was just a little annoyed. After all, I was part of the job. I'd made my sacrifices, too. But I admitted what he said. Why not? It was something, that fancy, that every rattle of the winch outside, bringing up another load, moved abruptly under the impulse of another thought from London Town— six thousand miles away; two months' travel. Great London Town! It was true. If London shut off its good will that winch would stop, and the locomotives would come to a stand to rot under the trees, and the lianas would lock their wheels; and in a month the forest would have foundered the track under a green flood. Where the American accent was dominant, the jaguars would moan at night. That long wound in the forest would be annealed and invisible in a year. While it persisted, the idea could conquer and maintain.

"Yes, but it's all chance," said the Englishman. "That uncertain and impersonal will controls us. Have you ever worked desperately, the fever in your bones, at a link in a job the rest of which was already abandoned, though you didn't know it? Yet perhaps even so there is something gained, the knowledge that all you do is fugitive, that there is nothing but an idea, which may be withdrawn without warning at any moment, under the most complicated and inspiring structure. Having that foreknowledge you can work with a light heart, secure against betrayal, ready with your own laugh when the mockery comes. A community finds it must have a bridge; Wall Street hears of it, and finances a contractor, who finds an architect to design it. An army builds it. And then this blessed old planet moves in its sleep, and the obstructing river flows another way. Well for us we can rarely see the beginning and the end of the work we are doing. Most of the men on this job have not been here three months. They come and shovel a little dirt, and die. Or they get frightened, and go. But that idea, that remains here, using up men and forests, using up all that comes within its invisible influence, drawing in material and pressing it into its unseen mould, so that out of the invisible sprouts a railway, projecting length by length, transmuted men and timber. A courtier once gave his cloak to Queen Elizabeth to save her feet; but what is that when these men give their bodies to make an easier road for the commerce of their fellows? They say every sleeper on a tropical line represents a man. The conquering human, who lives by dying!

"The unseen idea remains—some stranger's idea—of gain; profit out of a necessity not his, filled by other men unknown to him. You can't escape it. First and last, it uses you. It uses you up. You may twist and double, but 'when me you fly, I am the wings,' as Emerson says. Once, once, I deliberately tried to escape from it, to get out of its range. I thought it was local, that idea, a mean and local urge. I believed I had escaped it too. I was young, though, then. But we all try when we're young. There is but one way of escape—you may use up others; but that isn't an easy way of escape, for some of us.

"No alternative but that, and a man cannot take it. There you are; use, or be used. Once I thought I had escaped. Once upon a time, every morning at eight o'clock, I went to an office in Leadenhall Street. Know that place? My first job. I was one in a crowd of fifty clerks. We sat on high stools, facing each other across double desks. There were brass rails above each desk, where we rested ledgers and letter baskets. Each of us marked his stool somewhere with a personal symbol. My own, my sole point of vantage there, my support in life, that high stool; and I would have been prepared to maintain it upright—following our office code of honour, I as firm as may be upon it—even if, treacherously blabbing, I had had to deprive all my fellow-clerks of their supports in life. We were not a community, working out a common ideal. An idea used us. And that was a job I got as a favour, mark you. Someone had known my dead father.

"I knew the name of my boss, but that was all. I never spoke to him. I used to see him, a middle-aged man with sad eyes and a petulant mouth, clean shaved, and bald headed. He came in a carriage every morning, and went straight to a room kept from us by opaque glass. I used to wonder what he did in there. He rarely came into the office. When he did come into it, his was the only voice which ever spoke there above a whisper; a sharp, startling, and minatory voice. But we rarely saw him there. A bell would ring, a sinister summons on the ceiling over the desk of a principal clerk, and that chap would drop anything he was doing, anything, and go. I've seen my senior clerk, an elderly man in spectacles, jump as if he'd been struck when his bell whirred. It was such an awfully solemn place. Nobody ever thought of calling across that room, but would go round to another desk, and whisper. You felt you were part of a grave and secret plot, scribbling away to bring it to a completion, and that all your fellow-conspirators were possible traitors.

"But the plot was never complete. It went on and on, day after day, in an everlasting, suffocating sanctity, with the opaque shining glass front of the private room overlooking us, a luminous face entirely blank, though you knew the brain behind it saw everything, and was aware of all. It even knew old Beckwith, my senior, had got deeply into debt through his wife's doctor's bills, and had been fool enough to go to the moneylenders. His bell sprang a summons one morning; in Beckwith went; came out again, looking grey, poor old perisher, went straight to the hat rack, passed awkwardly through the swing doors, letting in a burst of traffic noise from the street, while we watched him furtively, and that was the last of Beckwith. I have heard our boss was a rigid moralist. He said a man who drank, gambled, or got into debt, not being able to control his own life, was no good for the business of another man. A system should have no bowels. Out the incompetent had to go. It was Spartan, but it paid twenty per cent., I've heard. Once we had a rebellious interruption of our sacred quiet, but only once. I never knew exactly why it was. We had a huge factory somewhere in the East End—Cubitt Town way—and one afternoon a woman came to the counter, and asked for the cashier. She was so obviously East End, in a shawl, that the counter clerk was shocked at the bare idea of it. She kept demanding the cashier. The clerk politely, but nervously, because of her rising, emotional voice, resisted her. She began to shout. We all stopped to see what would happen. Shouting there! She was still crying out—she wanted justice for a daughter whose body had got into a machine, I think—and the cashier was forced to appear. I was surprised that he was so quiet with her. She was weeping hysterically at our polished mahogany counter, with its immaculate blotters, and flat, crystal ink-pots, where there were men in silk hats, looking at the unusual scene sideways and smiling. She could not be pacified; and suddenly she picked up an ink-pot, and hurled it through that frozen glass face of the private room. A devastating crash. The shocking, raucous horror of blasphemy. The silence following was unendurable. We looked to the private door for outraged power to appear. Nothing happened. A policeman came and removed the woman, the cashier smiling indulgently at the officer, and shaking his head. The system, after a momentary halt, moved on again, broad, serene, and irresistible.

"I never catch the smell of an open Bible now but it conjures a picture of that arid office, angular, polished, and hard, where the ledgers before the disciplined men exude a dusty, leathery smell. But there I stayed for years, smelling it, and making out bills of lading and invoices. It was my lot. There was a junior who assisted me, a chap with flat, shiny hair parted in the middle. He had a habit of whispering about girls, when he was not whispering about the music hall last night, or the football next Saturday. When the cashier, a young man, and a relative of the boss, came walking down the avenue of desks, his sharp eyes narrowed to slits, and his mouth a little open, it was funny to see my junior put on speed, and get an intent and earnest look in his face.

"When I was done for the day, I'd get my book out of my bag, and wonder, going home, whether I'd ever see those places I read about, Java, India, and the Congo, where you went about in a white helmet and a white uniform, and did things in a large, directive way, helping Indians and niggers to make something of their country. Not this niggling, selfish, petty chandlery written large in stone, mahogany, and glass, disguised in magnitude and gravity. Cocoanut palms and forests with untold tales. But like the boys who found fun with the girls, with music halls and football, but were afraid of the sack, I did nothing. I was even afraid of girls.

"One day as usual I went with some of the other fellows to lunch, at an A.B.C. shop. We always went there. The girls knew us and would smile at our jokes. Small coffee and a scone and butter. My life! I found a *Telegraph* some one had left on a chair, and I read it more because I didn't want to listen to that virulent abuse of our mean cashier—he certainly was mean—than because I wanted to read. In it, by chance, I noticed an advertisement for a book-keeper who would go to the tropics. That I noted. Of course, I stood no chance. But I could try.

"That night at home I wrote an application. I wrote it, I think, a dozen times, till the letter was impeccable, a thing of beauty and precision. I felt this was a most momentous affair. Whether it was the excitement of doing something in the veritable direction of romance, or whether it was through reading 'Waterman's Wanderings' I don't know, but I remember a curious dream I had that night. I was alone in a forest which made me afraid and expectant. It was still and secretive. You know the empty stage in an unnatural, rosy light, with a glorified distance in which you expect a devil or a fairy queen to appear. There was a hammock hanging motionless from a branch. Something was in it, but I could not see what. That hammock was as still as the leaves hanging over it. Then the hammock shook, and a girl rose in it and smiled at me. She was tiny, but adult, and her eyes were shining in the dusk of her hair, which fell thickly over her little coffee-coloured breasts.

"A telegram came for me, just as I was leaving for the office one morning. It required me to call on Mr Utah R. Brewster at the Hotel Palace, that very day, but at a time when I should have been industriously at work for another. The question was, should I catch that morning 'bus I had never missed—or take all the possibilities beyond this door which promised to open on romance? I made up my mind, which went drunk with rebellion. I got into my seventh-day clothes. Utah R. Brewster and freedom! The Blackwell 'bus—do you remember those old hearses, with a straight companion-ladder to the upper deck where the outside passengers sat, knees up, back to back along the middle?— well, it had to go by the office, and I was actually in doubt whether, aware of my unprecedented revolt, it would stop outside the familiar glum office and lawfully refuse to budge till I alighted. It went on, blundering past the place, all strangely unconscious of what it was doing, bearing me with my courage screwed down to bursting-point. The driver even said what a lovely May morning it was.

"The Hotel Palace! I had often seen that ornate building when Saturday afternoon release took me west. Red carpeting on the steps, a glimpse of ferns, women all as strange as exotics going in and out, and between me and it a chasm which cut clear to the very centre of the earth. I carried my attack beyond the portals. It was nothing, after all. A flunkey put me in a chair too full of cushions to be easy, and I watched men and women who, at that time of the day, when all the folk I knew were making desperate and cunning efforts to keep their places here safe—I watched those men and women behaving as though all eternity were theirs, and it was the angels' business to bear them up. It was as great a mystery to me, whose every week-day morning was the inviolate possession of another, as Joshua's solar miracle. I was called, led along a silent corridor full of shut doors, and after a long walk found myself beyond all the noise of London, far in solitude with a man in a dressing-gown, who stood before a fire, working a cigar with strong, mobile lips. He put up a monocle, and looked at me shyly. Then began to walk up and down the hearth-rug, talking.

" 'Well,' he said. 'All right. I guess you'll do. Say, you look pretty fit. You don't drink, eh? Don't get nervous when you see the dead, huh? All right.' He put his monocle back into his eye, and grinned at me. I told him, in a rush, how much I wanted to see the tropics. He said nothing. He got a large blue map, intricate with white lines, and told me of The Company. The Job."

"I did not fully comprehend it then. I don't now. He left out too much. There was no beginning and no ending. There was hardly a middle. He merely indicated unrelated points; but at any rate the points were so widely sundered and so different that the bare indication of them conveyed a sense of an enormous undertaking, difficult, important, and necessary. Work for an army. I should be but an insignificant sutler in that army. But at least I should be one in it, one of those putting this important affair through for future generations. The communal idea, this. The very size of it gave me a sense of security. It was too broad-based to collapse. Success was inherent in its impersonal nature. A state affair.

Brewster briefly mentioned some showy names, names of great financiers. They were my generals, and I should never see them. But their reputations were partly in my keeping.

"Hallelujah! I had escaped. I never went back to the office. I never replied to its curt inquiry. In a week I sailed from Liverpool. Much I heard, on the mail boat, of The Company, this new enterprise which was going to make a tropical region one of the richest countries in the world; develop it, fling its riches to all. In four weeks more I arrived at a small tropical island, at which I had to wait for The Company's tug to take me to the mainland and my business.

"There was a club-house ashore, where I stayed for a few days. There I met some men who had been working for the Company, but for incomprehensible reasons were leaving this work to which I had come so eagerly; they were returning home. They were strangely pallid and limp as though the dark of some hot damp underground had turned their blood white. Their talk was drawled out, the weary utterance of the disillusioned who yet showed fate no resentment. They might have been the dead speaking, long untouched by any warm human vanity. I was really glad to get away from them. A tug conveyed me to the mouth of the river, up which I was to proceed to my station. I joined a shallow-draught river steamer.

"The river, that gateway to my dream come true, was a narrow place, a cleft in universal trees, every tree the same. Mangroves, I suppose. Soon the forest changed, often rising on each bank to meet overhead. Those were uncertain places of leaves and dead timber, and as quiet and still as church-yard yews at midnight. The thumps of our paddle-wheels did not sound pleasant. Deeper and deeper we went, making turns so often that I wondered how we could ever be got out again. Sometimes in an open space we saw a flock of birds. I saw no other sign of life. There were no men. All my fellow-passengers—there were ten of us—were newcomers; some from the States, some from Germany, and a Frenchman. I was the only Englishman. Each of us knew what was expected of himself; none of us knew what that was which all would be doing. There were clerks with us, miners, civil engineers, timber men, and a metallurgist. We speculated much, were perhaps a trifle anxious, but reposed generally on the great idea.

"In two hundred miles we reached a clearing. Why it should have been at that particular place did not show. But there it was, the tangible link in an invisible, encompassing scheme. It was my place. I landed with my box. There was a white man on the river bank, sitting on a sea-chest, his head in his hands. He looked up. 'You the victim?' he said. 'Well, there you are'—sweeping a lazy arm round the small enclosed ground—'that's your job. There's your store. There's your house. That's where the niggers live.'

" 'Pedro!' he called. A copper-coloured native, in shorts and a wide grass hat, loafed over to us. 'This is your servant,' he said. 'He's a bit mad, but he's not a fool. He's all right. Keep your eye on the niggers though. They are fools, and they're not mad. You'll find the inventory and the accounts in the desk in your hut. The quinine's there too. Take these keys. Oh, the mosquito curtain's got holes in it. See you mend it. I couldn't. Had the shakes too bad. Cheer up!'

"He went aboard. The steamer saluted me with its whistle, turned a corner, and the sound of its paddles diminished, died. I seemed to concentrate, as though I had never known myself till that instant when the sound of the steamer failed, when the last connection with busy outer life was gone. I could smell something like stephanotis. In that dead silence my hearing was so acute that I caught a faint rustling, which I thought might be the sound of things growing. I turned and went to my hut, sad Pedro following with my box. The cheap American clock in the hut made a terrific noise, filling the afternoon with its rapid and ridiculous beat, trying to recall to me that time still was moving quickly, when it was quite evident that time had now come for me to an absolute stand in a broad-glowing noon. I sat surveying things from a chair. Then leisurely took my envelope and read my instructions—how I was to receive and take charge of shovels, lanterns, machinery parts, railway metals, soap, cooking utensils, axes, pumps, and so on, which consignments I must divide and parcel according to directions to come, marking each consignment for its own destination. The names of a hundred destinations I should hear about in my future work were given. They were names meaning nothing to me. Then followed some brief rules for a novice in the governing of men. Through all the rules ran an incongruous note for such a place as that, a reminiscence of Leadenhall Street and its miserable whine. Yet it hardly disturbed me. I sat and thought over this expansion of my life. A melancholy bird called in two notes at intervals. The leaves which formed the thatch of my hut hung a long coarse black fringe at the door. My walls were of leaves, and the floor a raft of small logs, still with the bark on, just clear of the ground. The sunlight came through one dark wall, studding it with sparks. No. That dubious and familiar note in the instructions was nothing. I was clear beyond all that now—all those occasions for carking anxiety which deprave the worker, and make him hate the task to which whipping necessity drives him. The domineering manner of my instructions, the fretfulness of the old correspondence I found carelessly scattered about, addressed to my predecessor, was the illusion. The forest behind the hut, the black river, the quiet, the insects, the foreign smell, the puzzling men, my men to command, who kept passing without in the violent light, they were not from books any more, they made evidence direct to my own senses now. I was authority and providence, moulding and protecting as I thought right. This place should be kept reasonable, four square, my plot of earth to be clean and unashamed, frankly open to the eye of the sky. I would see what I could do; and I would start now. I laughed at authority—all I could see of it—reflected in a fragment of mirror kept to a door tree by nail heads; the funny hat and the shirt which did not matter, bad as it was, for I was authority there by very reason of that white shirt; and the beard which was coming. Latitude, my boy, latitude! I strolled out to survey my little world.

"Of the weeks that followed, nothing comes back so strongly as some quite irrelevant incidents. A tiger I saw one morning, swimming the river. Pedro, insensible for two days with fever; and death, which came to over-rule my viceroy authority. The first blow! There was a flock of parrots which visited us one day, and it surprised me that the men should regard them merely as food. But there was work to be done, and in a definite way; but why we did it—and I know we did it well—and how it joined up with the Job, I could not see. That was not my affair. There was the inventory to be checked, for one thing, and before I was through with it the work had fairly imprisoned me, and the new romantic circumstances became burred and over written. That inventory was so extravagantly wrong that in a week I was going about heated and swearing at the least provocation. It was fraudulent. There was a sporadic disorder of goods irreconcilable with their neat records, though each record bore the signs and counter-signs of Heaven knows how many departments of the Company. All an inextricable welter of calm errors, neatly initialled by unknown fools.

"Every few days a steamer of the Company would call, loaded with more goods, or would come down river to me to take goods away. The confusion grew and interpenetrated, till I felt that nothing but dumping all that was there into the river, and beginning again with a virgin station, would ever clear the muddle. The place grew maddening through ridiculous blundering from outside. I had six men to attend to, all with temperatures and all useless. The arrears of accounts, my work on sweltering nights while the very niggers slept, the arrears grew. A steam-shovel came, without its shovel, and not all my written protests to headquarters could complete that irrational creature lying in sections rotting in sun and rain, minus the very reason for its existence, an impediment to us and an irritation. Constant urgent orders came to me from up country to ship there this abortion. I declined, in the name of sanity. There followed peremptory demands for a complete steam-shovel, violent with animosity for me, the unknown idiot who obstinately refused to let a steam-shovel go, just as though I was in love with the damned thing, and could not part with it. But I understood those letters. They were from chaps, irritated, like myself, by all this awful tomfoolery. And from headquarters came other letters, shot with a curt note of innocent insolence, asking whether I was asleep there, or dead, and adding, once, that if I could not keep up communications better I had better make way for one who could. There were plenty who could do it. Pleasant, wasn't it? They complained querulously of my accounts, almost insinuating that I debited more wages to the Company than I credited to the men. I had too many sick men, they said. Did I pamper them? And again, I had too many who died; I must take care; they did not want the local government to get alarmed.

"The time came when I got amusement out of those letters from headquarters; for their faults were so plain that I conceived the headquarters staff having much time to spend, and a sort of instruction at large to administer ginger to men, like myself, on the spot, on general principles, so to keep us not only alive, but brisk and anxious; and doing it with the inconsequential abandon of little children playing with sharp knives. I got comfort from that view; and when I looked round my placid domain where my men, with whom I was on good terms, laboured easily and rightly under the still woods, I told myself I was still fretting because the business was new, that things would come easier soon. But at night I felt I was anxious exactly because it was all so old and familiar to me.

"One day, having given a group of men at work in a distant corner of the clearing some advice, I noticed a little path enter the wood beside a big tree. I had never been into the forest. To tell the truth, I had had no time. The trees stood round us, keeping us from—what? I had always felt a little doubt of what was there and could not be seen. I turned inwards. I found myself at once in a cool gloom. I went on curiously, peering each side into those shadows, where nothing moved, and in an hour came to another clearing, smaller than my own, and with no river in view. By the sun, which now I saw again, this place was north of our station. The opening was being rapidly choked by a new growth. I was turning for home again, for the afternoon was late, when I saw a hammock slung between two saplings beside a dismantled hut. I could just see the hammock and hut through the scrub. I went over there, and was so carefully

looking for snakes and beastly things in the bush that I had
arrived before I knew it. The hut had been long abandoned.
The hammock had something in it, and I was turning
something in my mind as I went up to it. There were some
ragged clothes in the bottom of it, partly covering bones, and
among the rags was a globe of black hair.

"Next morning I woke late, feeling I had gone wrong. My
hands were yellow and my finger nails blue, and I was
shaking with cold. But the tootling of an up-coming steamer
forced me to business. The steamer was towing six lighters,
filled with labourers. They were Poles, I think. Afterwards,
I learned, some hundreds of these men had been collected for
us somewhere by a clever, business-like, recruiting agent,
who promised each poor wretch a profitable time in the
Garden of Eden. My responsibility, thirty of them, was
landed. They stood by the river, gaping about them, wondering, some alarmed, more of them angry, most clad in
stuffy woollens, poor souls. Having the fever, I was not very
interested. I told my foreman negro to find them shelter and
to put them to work. We were making our clearing larger,
and were building more store-houses.

"Something like the pale morning light which wakens
you, weary from a fitful sleep, to the clear apprehension
again of an urgent trouble which has filled the night with
dreams, I came through each bout of fever to know there was
really trouble outside with the new men. Daily I had to
crawl about, shivering, my head dizzy with quinine, till the
fever came near its height, when I got into my hammock,
and would lie there, waiting, burning and dry, tremulous
with an anxiety I could not shape. Sometimes then I saw my
big negro foreman come to the door, look at me, as though
wishing to say something, but leave, reluctantly, when I
motioned him away.

"One morning I was better, but hardly able to walk, when
shouts and a running fight, which I could see through the
door, showed me the Poles had mutinied. There was a
hustling gang of them outside my door, filling it with
haggard, furious faces. I could not understand them, but one
presently began to shout in French. They refused to work.

The food was bad. They wanted meat. They wanted their contracts fulfilled. They wanted bread, clothes, money, passages out of the country. They had been fooled and swindled. They were dying. I argued plaintively with that man, but it made him shout and gesticulate. At that the voices of all rose in a passionate tumult, knives and axes flourishing in the sunlight. In a sudden cold ferocity, not knowing what I was doing, I picked up my empty gun—I had no ammunition—and moved down on them. They held for a moment, then broke ground, and walked away quickly, looking back with fear and malice. Next day they had gone. Yes, actually. The poor devils. They had gone, with the exception of a few with the fever. They had taken to that darkness around us, to find a way to the coast. Talk of the babes in the wood! The men had no food, no guide, and had they known the right direction they could not have followed it. If the Company did not take you out of that land, you stayed there; and if the Company did not feed you there, you died. No creature could leave that clearing, and survive, unless I willed it. The forest and the river kept my men together as effectively as though they were marooned without a boat on a deep-sea island. Those men were never heard of again. Nobody was to blame. Whom could you blame? The Company did not desire their death. Simply, not knowing what they were doing, those poor fellows walked into the invisibly moving machinery of the Job, not knowing it was there, and were mutilated.

"We had news of the same trouble with the Poles up river. Some of the mutineers tried to get to the sea on rafts. Such amazing courage was but desperation and a complete ignorance of the place they were in. One such raft did pass our place. Some of them were prone on it, others squatting; one man got on his feet as the raft swung by our clearing, and emptied his revolver into us. A few days later another raft floated by, close in, with six men lying upon it. They were headless. Somewhere, the savages had caught them asleep.

"No. I was not affected as much as you might think. I began to look upon it all with insensitive serenity. I was getting like the men I met on the island, months before. I saw us all caught by something huge and hungry, a viewless, impartial appetite which swallowed us all without examination; which was slowly eating me. I began to feel I should never leave that place, and did not care. Why should others want to leave it, then? Often, through weakness, the trees around us seemed to me to sway, to be veiled in a thin mist. The heat did not weigh on my skin, but on my dry bones. I was parched body and mind, and when the men came with their grievances I felt I could shoot any of them, for very weariness, to escape argument. The insolence from headquarters I filed for reference no longer, but lit my pipe with it. But the correspondence ceased at length, and because now I was callous to it, I failed to notice it had stopped.

"Some vessels passed down river, coming suddenly to view, a rush of paddles, and were gone, tootling their whistles. The work went on, mechanically. The clearing grew. The sheds spread one by one. The inventory was kept, the accounts were dealt with. There came a time when I was forced to remember that the steamer had not called for ten days. We were running short of food. I had a number of sick, but no quinine. The men, those quick, faithful fellows with the dog-like, patient eyes, they looked to me, and I was going to fail them. I made pills of flour to look like quinine, for the fever patients, trying to cure them by faith. I wrote a report to headquarters, which I knew would get me my discharge; I was not polite. There was no meat. We tried dough fried in lard. When I think of the dumb patience of those black fellows in their endurance for an idea of which they knew nothing, I am amazed at the docility and kindness inherent in common men. They will give their lives for nothing, if you don't tell them to do it, but only let them trust you to take them to the sacrifice they know nothing about.

"That went on for a month. We were in rags. We were starved. We were scarecrows. No steamer had been by the place, from either direction, for a month. Then a vessel came. I did not know the chap in charge. He seemed surprised to see us there. He opened his eyes at our gaunt crew of survivors, shocked. Then he spoke.

" 'Don't you know?' he asked.

"Even that ridiculous question had no effect on me. I merely eyed him. I was reduced to an impotent, dumb query. I suppose I was like Jack the foreman, a gaping, silent, pathetic interrogation. At last I spoke, and my voice sounded miles away. 'Well, what do you want here?'

" 'I've come for that steam-shovel. I've bought it.'

"The man was mad. My sick men wanted physic. We all wanted food. But this stranger had come to us just to take away our useless steam-shovel. 'I thought you knew,' he said. 'The Company's bought out. Some syndicate's bought 'em out. A month ago. Thought the Company would be too successful. Spoil some other place. There's no Company now. They're selling off. What about that steam-shovel?' "

V

W E had 5200 tons of cargo, and nearly all of it was patent fuel. This was to be put into baskets, hauled up, and emptied into railway trucks run out on the jetty alongside. We watched the men at work for a few days and nights, and judged we should be at Porto Velho for a month. I saw for myself long rambles in the forest during that time of golden leisure, but saw them no more after the first attempt. The clearing on its north side rose steeply to about a hundred feet on the hard red conglomerate; to the south, on the San Antonio side, it ended in a creek and a swamp. But at whatever point the Doctor and I attempted to leave the clearing we soon found ourselves stopped by a dense undergrowth. At a few places there were narrow footpaths, subterranean in the quality of their light, made by timbermen when searching for suitable trees for the saw-mill. These tracks never penetrated more than a few hundred yards, and always ended in a well of sunshine in the forest where some big trees would be prone in a tangle of splintered branches, and a deep litter of leaves and broken fronds. And that was as far as man had got inwards from the east bank of the Madeira river. Beyond it was the undiscovered, and the Araras Indians. On the other side of the river the difficulty was the same. The Rio Purus, the next tributary of the Amazon westward from the Madeira, had its course, it was guessed, perhaps not more than fifty miles across country from the river bank opposite Porto Velho; but no one yet has made a traverse of the land between the two streams. The dark secrecy of the region was even oppressive. Sometimes when venturing alone a little beyond a footpath, out of hearing of the settlement, surrounded by the dim tangle in which there was not a movement or a sound, I have become suspicious that the shapes about me in the half light were all

that was real there, and Porto Velho and its men an illusion,
and there has been a touch of panic in my haste to find the
trail again, and to prove that it could take me to an open
prospect of sunny things with the solid "Capella" in their
midst.

We carried our butterfly nets ashore and went of a
morning across the settlement, choosing one of the paths
which ended in a small forest opening, where there was
sunlight as well as shadow. Few butterflies came to such
places. You could really think the forest was untenanted. A
tanager would dart a ray of metallic sheen in the wreckage of
timber and dead branches about us, or some creature would
call briefly, melancholy wise, in the woods. Very rarely an
animal would go with an explosive rush through the leaves.
But movements and sounds, except the sound of our own
voices, were surprises; and a sight of one of the larger
inhabitants of the jungle is such a rarity that we knew we
might be there for years and never get it. Yet life about its
various business in the woods kept us interested till the
declining sun said it was time to get aboard again. Every foot
of earth, the rotting wood, the bark of the standing trees,
every pool, and the litter of dead leaves and husks, were
populous when closely regarded. Most of the trees had
smooth barks. A corrugated trunk, like that of our elm, was
exceptional. But when a bole had a rough surface it would be
masked by the grey tenacious webbing of spiders; on one
such tree we found a small mantis, which so mimicked the
spiders that we were long in discovering what it really was.
Many of the smooth tree trunks were striated laterally with
lines of dry mud. These lines were actually tunnels, covered
ways for certain ants. The corridors of this limitless mansion
had many such surprises. There were the sauba ants; they
might engross all a man's hours, for in watching them he
could easily forget there were other things in the world.
They would move over the ground in an interminable
procession. Looked at quickly, that column of fluid life
seemed a narrow brook, its surface smothered with green
leaves, which it carried, not round or under obstructions,
but upwards and over them. Nearly every tiny creature in

that stream of life held upright in its jaws a banner, much larger than itself, cut from a fresh leaf. It bore its banner along hurriedly and resolutely. All the ants carrying leaves moved in one direction. The flickering and forward movement of so many leaves gave the procession of ants the wavering appearance of shallow water running unevenly. On both sides of the column other ants hurried in the reverse direction, often stopping to communicate something, with their antennæ, to their burdened fellows. Two ants would stop momentarily, and there would be a swift intimation, and then away they would go again on their urgent affairs. We would see rapid conversations of that kind everywhere in the host. Other ants, with larger heads, kept moving hither and thither about the main body; having an eye on matters generally, I suppose, policing or superintending them. There was no doubt all those little fellows had a common purpose. There was no doubt they had made up their minds about it long since, had come to a decision communally, and that each of them knew his job and meant to get it done. There did not appear to be any ant favoured by the god of the ants. You have to cut your own leaf and get along with it, if you are a sauba.

There they were, flowing at our feet. I see it now, one of those restricted forest openings to which we often went, the wall of the jungle all round, and some small attalea palms left standing, the green of their long plumes as hard and bright as though varnished. Nothing else is there that is green, except the weeds which came when the sunlight was let in by the axe. The spindly forest columns rise about, pallid in a wall of gloom, draped with withered stuff and dead cordage. Their far foliage is black and undistinguishable against the irregular path of overhead blue. It never ceased to be remarkable that so little that was green was there. The few pothos plants, their shapely parasitic foliage sitting like decorative nests in some boughs half-way to the sky, would be strangely conspicuous and bright. The only leaves of the forest near us were on the ground, brown parchments all of one simple shape, that of the leaf of the laurel. I remember a stagnant pool there, and over it suspended some enamelled dragon-flies, their wings vibrating so rapidly that the flies were like rubies shining in obscure nebulæ. When we moved, the nymphs vanished, just as if a light flashed out. We sat down again on our felled tree to watch, and magically they reappeared in the same place, as though their apparition depended on the angle and distance of the eye. When a bird called one started involuntarily, for the air was so muffled and heavy that it was strange to find it open instantly to let free the delicate sibilation.

In the low ground beyond Porto Velho up stream there was another place in the forest where sometimes we would go, the approach to it being through a deep cutting made by the railwaymen in the clay. This clay, a stiff homogeneous mass mottled rose and white, was saturated with moisture, and the helicon butterflies frequented it, probably because is was damp; and a sight of their black and yellow, or black and crimson wings, spread on the clean plane of the beautifully tinted rock, was far better than putting them in the collecting box. The helicons are bold insects, and did not seem to mind our close inspecting eyes. Beyond the cutting was a long narrow clearing, with a giant silk-cotton tree, a province in itself, on the edge of the forest. Looking straight upward we could see its foliage, but so far away was the spreading canopy of leaves that it was only a black cloud, the outermost sprays mere wisps of dark vapour melting in the intense brightness of the sky. The smooth grey trunk was heavily buttressed, the "sapeomas" (literally, flat roots) ascending the bole for more than fifty feet, and radiating in walls about the base of the tree; the compartments were so large that they could have been used as stabling for four or five horses. From its upper limbs a wreckage of lianas hung to the ground. Beyond this giant the path rose to a place where the clearing was already waist high with scrub. Then it descended again to the woods. But the woods there were flooded. That was my first near view of the igapo. We had approached the trees, for they seemed free of the usual undergrowth, and passed into the sombre colonnades. The way appeared clear enough, and we thought we could move ahead freely at last, but found in a few steps the bare floor

was really black water. The base of the forest was submerged, the columns which supported the unseen roof,
through which came little light, diminished down soundless
distance into night. After the flaming day from which we
had just come this darkness was repellent. The forest, that
austere, stately and regarding Presence draped interminably
in verdant folds, while we gazed upon it suspecting no new
thing of it, as by a stealthy movement had withdrawn its
green robe, and our sight had fallen into the cavernous
gloom of its dank and hollow heart.

It was about the little wooden town itself, where the
scarified earth was already sparsely mantled with shrubs,
flowering vines, and weeds, and where the burnt tree
stumps, and even the door posts in some cases, were freshly
budding—life insurgent, beaten down by fire and sword, but
never to its source and copious springs—that most of the
butterflies were to be found. In a land where blossoms were
few, these were the winged flowers. About the squalid
wooden barracks of the negro and native labourers, which
were built off the ground to allow of ventilation, and had a
trench round them foul with drainage and evil with smells,
a Colœnis, a scarlet butterfly with narrow, swallow-like
wings, used to flash, and frequently would settle there. Over
the flowering weeds on the waste ground there would be, in
the morning hours, or when the sky was overcast, glittering
clouds of the smaller and duller species, though among them
now and then would stoop a very emperor of butterflies, a
being quick and unbelievably beautiful to temperate eyes.
After midday, when the sun was intense, the butterflies
became scarce. When out of the shade of the woods, and
stranded, at that time, in the hopeless heat of the bare
settlement, we could turn into one of the houses of the
officials of the company for shelter. These also were of
timber, cool, with a verandah that was a cage of fine copper
gauze to keep out the insects. All the doors were self-
closing. The fewest chances were offered to the mosquitoes.
There was no glass, for the window openings also were
covered with copper mesh. Here we could sit in shaded
security, in lazy chairs, and look out over the clearing to the

river below, and to the level line of forest across the river, while listening to stories which had come down to Porto Velho from the interior, brought by the returning pioneers.

Porto Velho had a population of about three hundred. There were Americans, Germans, English, Brazilians, a few Frenchmen, Portuguese, some Spaniards, and a crowd of negroes and negresses. There was but one white woman in the settlement. I was told the climate seemed to poison them. The white girl, who persisted in staying in spite of warnings from the doctors, was herself a Brazilian, the wife of one of the labourers. She refused to leave, and sometimes I saw her about, petite, frail, looking very sad. But her husband was earning good money. It was a busy place, most of it being workshops, stores, and offices, with an engine and trucks jangling inconsequentially on the track by the shore. The line crossed a creek by a trestle bridge, and disappeared in the forest in the direction of San Antonio. The hospital for the men was nearly two miles up the track.

It was along the railway track towards the hospital, with the woods to the left, and a short margin of scrub and forest, and then the river, on the right hand, that I saw one morning in sauntering a few miles as many butterflies as there are flowers in an English garden in June. They were the blossoms of the place. The track was bright with them. They settled on the hot metals and ties, clustered thickly round muddy pools, a plantation there as vivid and alive, in the quick movements of their wings, as though a wind shook the petals of a bed of flowers. They flashed by like birds. One would soar slowly, wings outspread and stable, a living plane of metallic green and black. There was a large and insolent beauty—he did not move from his drink at a puddle though my boot almost touched him—his wings a velvety black with crimson eyes on the underwings, and I caught him; but I was so astonished by the strength of his convulsive body in the net that I let him go. Near the hospital some bushes were covered with minute flowers, and seen from a distance the countless insects moving about those bushes were a glistening and puzzling haze.

All that morning I had felt the power of the torrid sun,

which clung to the body like invisible bonds, and made
one's movements slow, was a luscious benefit, a golden
bath, a softening and generative balm; a mother heat and
light whose ardent virtues stained pinions crimson and
cobalt, and made bodies strong and convulsive, and caused
the earth to burst with rushing sap, to send up green
fountains; for so the palms, which showed everywhere in
the woods, looked to me. You could hear the incessant low
murmur of multitudinous wings. And I had been warned to
beware of all this. I felt instead that I could live and grow for
ever in such a land.

Presently, becoming a little weary of so much strong light,
I found it was midday, and looking back, there was the ship
across a curve of the river. It was two good miles away; two
intense, shadeless, silent afternoon miles. I began the return
journey. An increasing rumbling sound ahead made me look
up, as I stepped from tie to tie, and there came at me a trolley
car, pumped along slowly, four brown bodies rising and
falling rhythmically over its handle. A man in a white suit
was its passenger. As it passed me I saw it bore also
something under a white cloth; the cloth moulded a childish
figure, of which only the hem of a skirt and the neat little
booted feet showed beyond the cloth, and the feet swayed
limply with the jolts of the car in a way curiously appealing
and woeful. The car stopped, and the white man, a cheerful
young doctor chewing an extinct cigar, came to me for a
light. He stood to gossip for a few minutes, giving his men a
rest. "That's the Brazilian girl," he said; "she wouldn't go
home when told, poor thing."

This Madeira river had the look of very adventurous
fishing, and the doctor had brought with him an assortment
of tackle. The water was opaque, and it was deep. Its
prospects, though the forest closed round us, were spacious.
It flowed silently, with great power, and its surface was
often coiled by profound movements. The coils of the river,
as we were looking over the side one morning, began to
move in our minds also, and the Doctor mentioned his
tackle. There was the forest enclosing us, as mute as the

water, its bare roots clenched in aqueous earth. Nobody could tell us much about the fish in this river, but we heard stories of creatures partly seen. There was one story of a thing taken from the very place in the river where we were anchored, a fish in armour which the natives declared was new to them; a fearful ganoid I guessed it, reconstructing it in vision from fragments of various tales about it, such as is pictured in a book on primeval rocks. There were alligators, too, and there was the sucuruju, which I could call the great water serpent, only the Indian name sounds so much more right and awful; and that fellow is forty feet long in his legend, but spoils a good story through reducing himself by half when he is actually killed. Still, twenty feet of stout snake is enough for trouble. I saw one, just after it was killed, which was twenty-two feet in length, and was three feet round its middle. So to fish in the Madeira was as if one's hook and line were cast into the deeps where forms that are without name stir in the dark of dreams. We got out our tackle, and the cook had an assortment of stuff he did not want, and that we put on the hooks, and waited, our lines carried astern by the current, for signals from the unknown. Yet excepting for a few catfish, nothing interrupted the placid flow of stream and time. The doctor put a bight of the line round his wrist, sat down, and slept. We had fine afternoons, broad with the wealth of our own time.

Old man Jim came aboard and saw our patience with amusement. He suggested dynamite, and no waiting. The river was full of good fish, and he would come next day with a canoe and take us where we could get a load. It was a suggestion which needed slurring, to look attractive to sportsmen. Jim took it for granted that we simply wanted fish to eat, and as many as we could get; and next morning there he was alongside with his big boat and its crew. Jim himself was in the stern, the navigator, and he was sitting on what I was told was a box of dynamite. Now, there were two others of our company who, but the day before, were even eager to see what dynamite would send up from the bottom of that river; but when they saw the craft alongside with its wild-looking crew, and Jim with his rifle sitting on a power which could lift St. Paul's, they considered everything, and decided they could not go that day. I went alone.

I suppose men do plucky things because they are largely thoughtless of the danger of the things they do. As soon as I was sitting on the level of the water in that crazy boat, with Jim and his explosive, and beside him what whisky he had not already consumed, and saw under my nose the eddies and upheavals of the current, I knew I was doing a very plucky thing indeed, and wished I was high and safe on the "Capella." But we had pushed off.

Jim, with his eyes dreamy through barley juice, was the pilot, and there was a measure of confidence to be got from the way he navigated us past the charging trees afloat. There was no drink in the steering paddle, at least. But the shore was a long swim away; yet perhaps it would have been as pleasant to be drowned or blown-up as to be lost in the jungle. We turned into a still creek, where the trees met overhead. Jim continued his course till the inundated forest was about us. The gloom was hollow, the pillars rising from the black floor were spectral, and our voices and paddles sounded like a noisy irruption among the aisles of a temple. The echoes fled from us deeper into the dark. But Jim was all unconscious of this; he but stopped our progress, and opened the box of cartridges.

I had never seen dynamite, but only heard of it. I understood it had unexpected qualities. Jim had a cartridge in his hand, and was digging a knife into it. I repeat, the flooded wilderness was round us, and below was the black deep. Jim fitted a detonator to a length of fuse, and stuck it in the cartridge. He was in no hurry. He stopped now and then for another drink. Having got the cartridge ready, with its potent filament, he tied four more cartridges round it. I put these things down simply, but my hand ached with the way I gripped the gunwale, and I could hear myself breathing.

Then Jim struck a match on his breeches, with all the fumbling deliberation of the fully ripe—brushing the vine leaves from his eyes the better to see what he was doing— and he lit the fuse, after it had twice dodged the match. It fizzed. The splutter worked downwards energetically. Jim did not deign to look at it, though it fascinated me. He slowly scratched his back with his disengaged hand, and gazed absently into the forest.

The spark and its spurts of smoke were now near the bottom. Jim changed the menace into his right hand, in order to reach another part of his back with his leisurely left. His eyes were still on the forest. I kept swallowing.

"Jim," I said eagerly—though I did not know I was going to speak—"don't—don't you think you'd better throw it away now?"

He regarded me steadily, with eyes half shut. The spark spurted, and dropped another inch. He looked at it. He looked round the waters without haste. Then, and I could have cried aloud, he threw the shocking handful away from us.

It sank. There were a few bubbles, and we sat regarding each other in the quiet of a time which had been long dead, waiting for something to happen in a time to come. At the end of two weeks the bottom of the river fell out, with the noise of the collapse of an iron foundry on a Sunday. Our boat tried to leap upwards but failed. The water did not burst asunder. It vibrated, and was then convulsed.

Dead fish appeared everywhere, patches of white all round; but we hardly saw them. There was a great head which emerged from the floor, looking upwards sleepily, and two hands moved slowly. These quietly sank again. The tail of the saurean appeared, slowly described a half circle, and went. The big alligator then lifted itself, and performed some grotesque antics with deliberation and gravity. Then it gathered speed. It rotated, thrashed, and drummed. It did all that a ten-horse-power maniac might. I think the natives shrieked. I think Jim kept saying "hell"; for I was conscious only with my eyes. When the dizzy reptile recovered, it shot away among the trees like a torpedo.

We went home. That night I understand the second mate was kept awake listening to me, as I slept, bursting into spasms of dreadful merriment.

When you are lost in the map of a country that is beyond the worn routes, trying to discover therein the place name which is the most secluded and inaccessible, if the map should happen to be that of South America, then your thought would naturally wander to the neighbourhood of San Antonio of the Rio Madeira. There you stay, to wonder what strange people and rocks and trees are to be found at San Antonio. It looks remote, even on the map. The sign which stands for the village is caught in a central loop of the mesh which is the river system of the Amazon forest. San Antonio must be beyond all, and a great journey. It is far outside the radius. And that would be enough, to be beyond the last ripple of the traffic and at peace, where that dark disquiet, that sombre emanation which rises from the soured earth where myriads have their chimneys, their troubles and their strife, staining even the morning and the morning thought, is no more. A place where the light has the clarity of the first dawn, and one might hear, while sure of absolute solitude, the winding of a strange horn, and suspect, when coming to an opening in the woods, the flight of a shining one; for somewhere the ancient gods must have sanctuary. A land where the rocks have the moss of unvisited fastnesses, and you can snuff the scents of original day.

Where we were anchored, San Antonio was in view, about five miles up stream. Where at the end of that reach of river a line of tremulous light, which we thought was the cataracts, bridged the converging palisades of the jungle, in the trees of the right bank it was sometimes easy to believe there was a glint of white buildings. But looking again, to reassure your sight, the apparition of dwellings vanished. At night, in the quiet, sometimes the ears could detect the shudder of the weighty rapids by San Antonio; but it was merely a tremor felt; there was no sound. The village remained to us for some time just that uncertain gleam by day, and the rapids but a minute reduction of a turmoil that was far. For in that languorous heat we counted miles differently, and it was pleasanter to suspect than to go and prove, and much easier.

One day I went. When in a small boat the jungle towered. The river, too, had a different character. From the shore, or from the big "Capella," the river was an expanse of light, an impression of shining peace. Whenever you got close to its surface it became alive and menacingly intimate. Our little boat seemed to roll in the powerful folds of a monster which wallowed ponderously and without ceasing. The trees afloat, charging down swiftly and in what one felt was an ominous quiet, stood well above our tiny craft.

We steered close in-shore to avoid the drifting wood and the set of the current. The jungle's sheer height, confusion, and intensity were more awesome than when seen from the steamer. Not many of the trees were of great beam, but their consistent height, with the lianas in a wreck from the far overhanging cornice, dwarfed our boat to an unimportant straw. At times the forest had a selvage of cane, and growths of arrow grass, bearing long white plumes twelve feet above us, and a pair of fan-shaped leaves resembling palm leaves.

The sound of the cataracts increased, and a barrier grew in height athwart the Madeira. Mounting high right ahead of us at last was a mass of granite boulders, with broad smooth surfaces, having the structure of gigantic masonry in ruin which weathered plutonic rock so often assumes. Beyond the barrier the river was plainly above our level. It was seen, resplendent as quicksilver, through the crenellations of the black rocks. One central mass of rock, higher than the rest, had a crown of dark and individual palms, standing paramount in the upper light. Yet, with that gleam of wide river behind, no great rush of water broke there. A few fountains spurted, apparently without source, and collapsed, and pulsed again. The white runnels of foam which laced the contours of the piled boulders gave the barrier the appearance of being miraculously uplifted, as though one saw thin daylight through its interstices. Not till the village was in view did we see where the main river avoided the barrier. The course here was looped. Above the barrier the river turned from the right bank, and heaped itself in a smooth steep glide through a narrow pass against the opposite shore, the roaring welter then running obliquely across the foot of the rocks to the front of San Antonio on the right bank again. The forest beside the falls seemed to be tremulous with continuous and profound underground thunder.

The little huddle of San Antonio's white houses is on slightly rising ground, and the lambent green of the jungle is beside them and over them. The foliage presses the village down to the river. Like every Amazonian town and village, it appears, set in that forest, as rare a human foothold as a ship in mid-ocean; a few lights and a few voices in the dark and interminable wastes. So I landed from our little craft elated with a sense of luckily acquired security.

The white embowered village, the leaping fountains and the rocks, the air in a flutter with the shock of ponderous water collapsing, the surmounting island in mid-stream with its coronet of palms, the half-naked Indians idling among the Bolivian rubber boats hauled up to the foreshore below, the unexplored jungle which closed in and framed the scene, the fierce sun set in the rounded amplitude of the clouds of the rains, made the tropical picture which was the right reward for a great journey. I had come down long weeks of empty leisure, in which the mind got farther and farther away from the cities where time is so carefully measured and highly valued. The centre of the ultimate wilderness was more than a matter of fact. It was now a personal conviction which needed no verification.

The village had but one street. There were two rows of houses of a single storey, built of clay and plaster, dilapidated, the whitewash stained and peeling, every house open and cavernous below, without doors, in the way of Brazilian dwellings, to give coolness. The street was almost deserted when we entered it. A few children played in the shadows, and outside one house a merchant in a white cotton suit stood overlooking the scales while the half-breeds weighed balls of rubber; for this town is in the midst of the richest rubber country of the world, and all the wealth of the rivers Mamoré, Beni, and Madre de Dios comes this way. And that was why as we idled through its single thoroughfare, some dark girls came to stand at the house openings, dressed in odorous muslin, red flowers in their shiny black hair, and their smiling eyes full of interest in us. The rough road between the dwellings was overgrown with grass, and in the centre of it, partly hidden by the grass, was the line laid long ago by the railway enterprise which ended so tragically. To-day the rubber men use it as a portage for their boats. There were several inns, half-obliterated names painted on their outer walls. They had crude interior walls of mud, and floors of bare earth. In such an inn would be a few iron tables and chairs, and there a visitor might drink from bottles which at least bore European labels, though the contents and cost were past all European understanding. I forgot to say that by the foreshore of this little village is the head depôt of a great rubber house, a building apparently out of all proportion to the size of San Antonio. But I looked on that place with the less interest, though from what my native companion told me the head of the house is a monarch more absolute and undisputed in this wild country than most eastern kings are to-day.

I was more interested in the huge boulders of smooth granite which rose strangely from the street in places, and broke its regularity. These rounded and noble rocks often topped the houses. What man had built looked mean and transitory beside the poise and fine contours of the rocks. The colony of giant rocks had a look of settled and tranquil solidity, a friendly and hospitable aspect. They might have been old friends which time had proved; the houses beside them were alien by contrast. I felt that San Antonio had merely imposed itself on them, that they tolerated the village because it was but an incident; that they could afford to wait. When I saw them there I recognised the village of my map. I climbed to the summit of one, over its weather-worn shelves. It had a skin of lichen, warm in the sun and harshly familiar. The curious hieroglyphics of the lichen were intelligible enough, and more easily read than the signs on the walls of the inns. I learned where I was; and knew that when the day of the great rubber house had long passed, my village would still be there, and prospering.

Below my rock, on the land side—to which I had turned my back—was a monstrous cesspool. It was in the centre of the village. It was the capital of all flies, and the source and origin of all smells, varying smells which reposed, as I had found when below in the hot and stagnant street, in strata, each layer of smell invisible but well-defined. Among the weeds in the roads were many derelict cans. Over the empty tins, and the garbage, pulsed and darted hundreds of Brazil's wonderful insects.

But I was above all that, on my high rock. Its height released me to a wide and splendid liberty. I cannot tell you all that my vantage surveyed. But chiefly I was assured by what I saw that I was more central even than my eyes showed; they merely found for me the intimation. Here was all the proof I wanted; for faith is not blind, but critical, yet instantly transcends to knowledge at the faintest glimmer of authentic light, as when an exile who is beset by inexplicable and puissant circumstance among strangers whose tongue is barbarous, is surprised at a secret sign passed there of fellowship, and is at once content. Yet I can report but a broad river flowing smooth and bright out of indefinite distance between dark forests to the wooded islands below; and by the islands suddenly accelerated and divided, in a slight descent, pouring to a lower level in taut floods as smooth, noiseless, and polished as mercury. Lower still was the gleaming turmoil of the falls, pulsing, and ever on the point of vanishing, but constant, its shouting riot baffled by the green cliffs everywhere. But I could escape, for once, over the parapets of the jungle to the upper rolling ocean of leaves; to the distance, dim and blue, the region where man has never been.

There was a man who looked like a sensational ruffian who boarded us one morning at Porto Velho, and said he had come to find me. He was going up into the forest, beyond the track, and would I go with him? That made me look at him again, and with some anxiety; for I had tried before to get away, but the crowd on the "Capella" disliked the idea. The Doctor talked dysentery and things. He said it was safer to keep to the ship during the month we had still to spend at Porto Velho. I felt, overborne by their arguments, a rather thin sort of adventurer. That mysterious railway would have drawn the mind of any man who had not lost his curiosity, and who valued being alive more than his chance of old age.

The track went from Porto Velho into outer darkness. It left
the clearing and the village of mushroom buildings, the
place where the inhuman had been moderately subdued,
where a modicum of industry was established in a continent
of primitive wild, crossed a creek by a trestle bridge in view
of our steamer, and vanished; that was the end of it, so far as
we knew. Men came back to the settlement through that
hole of the forest, and boarded the "Capella" to tell us, in
long hot nights, something of what the forest of the Madeira
was hiding; and they were bearded like Crusoe, pallid as
anæmic women, and speckled with insect bits. These men
said that where they had been working the sun never shone,
for his light was stopped on the unbroken green which,
except where the big rivers flowed, roofed the whole land. I
liked the look of the stranger who had come to persuade me
to this rare holiday. He said his name was Marion Hill, of
Texas. He wore muddy riding breeches, and a black shirt
open at the throat, and boots of intricately embossed leather
which came well up his thighs, spurs that would have
ravelled a pachyderm, and the insolent hat of a bandit. He
had a waistbelt heavy with guns and ammunition. I saw his
face, and divined instantly that this was a man, and that the
memory of a time with him would serve me as a refuge in
the grey and barren years, and as a solace. I told him I would
get my things together. The Skipper called after me that if I
returned too late I should have to walk home.

There was a commissary train next morning, taking men
and supplies to the camps. It had a number of open waggons,
loaded with material, about which the labourers going up to
replenish the gangs made themselves as comfortable as they
could. I had an india rubber bag for all my belongings, being
told that it was best for strapping to a mule, and a valuable
lifebuoy when a canoe overturned. I accepted it with perfect
faith, for I knew nothing of mules or canoes. The train
moved off, a bell on the engine ringing sepulchrally. Hill and
I were packed into a box car, which had a door open on either
side for light and air. Two American engineers were in
charge, there was an Austrian to superintend the distribution at each camp of the provisions, the Austrian had an

Italian assistant, and a few Barbadian blacks were there to move about the packages. I sat on a case of tinned fruit. Hill reposed on one of the shelves where we should stow fever victims, when we collected them. There was no more room in the car, and another degree of heat would have meant complete ruin.

When Porto Velho is left for the place where the line is to end, when completed, though it is but 250 miles away, two months at least is required for the return journey. That way goes the paymaster, with his armed escort, and every bundle of shovels and tin of provisions. When I went, too, the train helped for sixty miles. Then most of the material was transported at the Rio Caracoles, a tributary of the Madeira, and taken by boats in stages up the main stream, cargoes and boats being hauled round each cataract. Travellers could shorten the journey by going overland part of the way, mules being kept on the hither side of the Caracoles river for that purpose.

We delivered some patients at the hospital, went through a cutting of red granite to the back of San Antonio, and then entered the forest. That absorbed us. Thenceforward, and until I reached the ship again, I was dominated by the lofty, silent, confused, and brooding growth. Everywhere it was dramatically passionate in its intensity, an arrested riot of green life, and its muteness kept expectant attention fixed upon it. The right of way through the forest was a hundred feet wide. On each side of us the trees rose like virid cliffs. The trees usually were of slender girth, almost as straight as fir poles, rising perhaps for sixty feet without a branch. Occasionally there was a giant, a silk-cotton tree, or the strange tree with its grey trunk and pale birch-like habit of foliage which I had noticed on the riverside; but they were not common. Palms were numerous. From ground to high parapet the spaces between the columns were filled with lianas, unrelated big leaves, and the characteristic fronds of the endogens. In this older part of the track, though it had been made but little more than a year, the scrub was dense. The undergrowth was often so strong and aggressive as to brush the train as we slowly bumped along. Sometimes we went through deep cuttings in the red clay, close enough for me to notice it was interstratified with waterworn but angular quartz pebbles. But the track usually was over flat country, only rarely crossing a gulley.

At every maintenance camp we stopped to deliver supplies. From out of a small huddle of shanties made of leaves and poles, insignificant beneath the forest wall, a number of languid half-breeds, merely in pants and hats, would loiter through the hot sun to us for their sustenance. The men of those secluded huts must have been glad of our temporary uproar, and our new faces. The bell rang, and we left them to burial in their deep silence again. There were intervening camps, which had been deserted as the work progressed. These were even more interesting to me. The work of the human, when he leaves it to the wild from which he has won it with so much pain, has an appeal of its own, with its abandoned ruin returning to the ground again. There would be a sandy swamp, and standing back from the line some weather-worn shanties with roofs awry. I am sure there were ghosts in those camps. One we passed, and it was called Camp 10½, and resting against its open front where the posts were giving was a butterfly net. I pointed this out. "Oh, that," said Hill. "Old man Biddell. I knew him. He was all right. He was great on bugs and butterflies. Used to wear spectacles. He was a good engineer though. Died of blackwater fever before the line got past this camp. That was his shack." And that was his butterfly net, all of Biddell now, his sole monument and reminder. As we bumped by the huts the helicons and swallow tails rose precipitously from the mangled cans and cast rubbish. I never knew Biddell, the man with spectacles and a butterfly net, but a first rate railway man, who left that net outside his hut one morning, and at evening was buried, but now I am doomed to think of him while I live.

It was near midnight when we reached the last active camp but one on the line, where we alighted. It was wiser, I was told, to run the remaining length of the track by daylight. Here a doctor and a few engineers, bearing hand-lamps against which moths were blundering, met us in a place which seemed to be the bottom of a well, for the black shadows which rose round us shut out all but a few stars. The men raised joyous cries at the sight of Hill; and they took this stranger on trust. We fed in a hut which was four poles and a roof. One pole had a hurricane lamp tied to it. There was an enormous quiet, which the men seemed to delight in breaking with their voices. Four planks nailed unevenly to uprights was our table, and we sat crooked on a similar but lower construction. We ate out of enamelled plates with iron instruments, and it was very good indeed. There were four of us who were white, and we were babes in the wood. One of us pretended he was playing on a Jew's-harp, sang songs riotously, and then began to talk long and earnestly of New York. These men lived in four railway waggons which had doors made of copper gauze, berths with mosquito bars, and portraits of the folk at home; and in the case of the doctor the waggon smelt of iodoform, had one wall full of bottles, and a table with a board and chessmen. In one of those waggons I lay down to sleep under a net; but the blanket felt damp and had a foreign smell. My thoughts crowded me. For long I listened to so much jungle pressing close to my bed, waiting for it to make known its near but unseen presence with a voice; but it did not.

Next morning at sunrise the train moved forward to the construction camp at the Rio Caracoles. I rode on a truck pushed in front of the locomotive, perched there with some engineers who kept a careful eye on the track. I saw at once why the train did not proceed at night. It was too speculative altogether. Behind us the locomotive's smoke stack rolled like a steamer's funnel when a beam sea is running. This part of the line crossed many ravines, where we looked down upon the tree tops; and when on a frail wooden bridge which crossed a vacancy like that such movements of the drunken engine behind us became dazzling. Then, too, there were some high "fills," or embankments. After heavy rains these have a habit of retiring from the metals, which are left looped and twisted in mid-air. An engineer told me that one cannot always tell when an embankment is on the point of retiring. He was carefully watching, however. But we reached the construction camp.

At the construction camp by the side of the Rio Caracoles we stayed two days. There was the end of the line, and the men who were growing the track were so busy that I was left to my own devices. Till the railwaymen came none but the Caripuna Indians knew what was there; so into the woods, of course, I would go, trying every track which led from the camp. A botanist might have seen some difference from the forest at Porto Velho, but I could not discover any. In appearance it was exactly the same. The trees mostly were arborescent laurels I believe, with smooth brown boles which were blotched through their outer cuticle peeling away, much in the manner of that of the plane tree. The brown parchments of their laurel-like leaves covered the floor of the woods. The trees were rarely of great diameter, but their crowns were so distant that nothing could be made of their living foliage. I saw no flowers at all. There were few orchids, but the large shapely emerald coloured leaves of pothos plants were very frequent, sitting in the angles of branches and trunk. Aloft was always the wreckage of vines suspended, as vaguely seen and as motionless as cobwebs and dilapidations in the overhead darkness of high vaults. I rarely heard a sound in that forest, though there was a bird which called. I often heard it in the woods of the upper Madeira. It called thrice, as a boy who whistles shrilly through his fingers; a long call, and then another whistle in the same key followed instantly by a falling note. One delightful walk was along a path which had not been made by the railwaymen, for it was evidently old, as it ran, a cleft in the trees, not through broken timber, but in partial sunshine, with a mesh of vines and freely growing plants on either side. It led downwards to a small stream, which was cumbered with fallen and rotting timber, a cool hollow where ferns were abundant. It was in the woods at the Caracoles that I first saw the great morpho butterfly at home. This species, peculiar to South America, is rarely seen except in the shades of the virgin forest. One day in the twilight aisles near the Caracoles camp, where nothing moved, and all was a grey monotone, it so surprised me with its happy undulating flight—as though it danced along, and were in no hurry—its great size, and its bright blue wings, that I rose mesmerised, stumbling after it through the dank litter, thoughtless of direction, not thinking of the danger of losing my way, thinking of nothing but that joyous resplendent creature dancing aloft ahead of me in the gloom and just beyond my reach. Its polished blue wings flashed like speculae. It might have been a drifting fragment of sunny sky. I had never seen anything alive so beautiful. A fall over a log brought me to sobriety, and when I looked up it was gone. Afterwards I saw many of them; sometimes when walking the forest there would be morphos always in sight.

The construction camp was not more than a month old. Perched on an escarpment by the line was a row of tents, and at the back of the tents some flimsy huts built of forest stuff. They stood about a ruin of felled trees, with a midden and its butterflies in the midst. Probably thirty white men were stationed there. They were then throwing a wooden bridge across the Caracoles. Most of them were young American civil engineers, though some were English; and when I found one of them—and he happened to be a countryman of mine—balancing himself on a narrow beam high over a swift current, and, regardless of the air heavy with vapour and the torrid sun, directing the disposal of awkward weights with a concentration and keenness which made me recall with regret the way I do things at times, I saw his profession with a new regard. I noticed the men of that transient little settlement in the wilds were in constant high spirits. They betrayed nothing of the gravity of their undertaking. They might have been boys employed at some elaborate jest. But it seemed to me to be a pose of heartiness. They repelled reality with a laugh and a hand clapped to your shoulder. At our mess table, over the dishes of toucan and parrot supplied by the camp hunters, they rallied each other boisterously. There was a touch of defiance in the way they referred to the sickness and the shadow; for it was notorious that changes were frequent in their little garrison. They were forced to talk of these changes, and this was the way they chose to do it. As if laughter was their only prophylactic! But such laughter, to a visitor who did not have to wait till fever took him, but could go when he liked, could be answered only with a friendly smile. Some of my cheery friends of the Caracoles were but the ghosts of men.

Hill warned me late one afternoon to be ready to start at sunrise, and then went to play poker. On my way to my hut, at sunset, I stopped to gossip with the young doctor, where he was busy dressing wounds at his surgery. The labourers, half-breeds, Brazilians, and Bolivian Spaniards, work being over, were giving the doctor a full evening with their ailments. Mostly these were skin troubles. The least abrasion in the tropics may spread to a horrid and persistent wound. The legs of the majority of these natives were unpleasant with livid scars. In one case a vampire bat had punctured a man's arm near the elbow while he slept, and that little wound had grown disastrously. We were in a region where the pium flies swarmed, tiny black insects which alight on the hand and face, perhaps a dozen at a time, and gorge themselves, though you may be unconscious of it. Where the pium fly feeds it leaves a dot of extravasated blood which remains for weeks, so that most of us were speckled. Even these minute wounds were liable to become deep and bad. There were larger flies which put their eggs in the human body, where they hatch with dire results. (Do not think the splendid tropics have nothing but verdure, orchids, butterflies, and coral snakes banded orange and black and crimson and black.) So the doctor was a busy man that evening. The floor of his surgery was made of unequal boughs; the walls and roof were of dried fronds. A lamp was slung on a door-post. He was a young American, and he did not grumble at his bumpy floor, the bad light, the appliances and remedies which were all one should expect in the jungle, nor the number of his patients, except comically. He told me he was rather keen on the diseases of the tropics. He liked them. (I should think he must have liked them.) He was merrily insolent with those swarthy and melancholy men, and they smiled back sadly at the clever, handsome, and lively youngster. He was quick in his decisions, deft, insistent, kind, and thorough, working down that file of pitiable humanity, as careful with the last of the long row as with the first; telling me, as he went along, much that I had never heard before, with demonstrations. "Don't go," he cried when I would have left him; for I thought it might be he was as kind with this stranger as he was with the others. "Ah! don't go. Let me hear a true word or two." He said he would give me a treat if I stayed. He finished, put his materials away deliberately, accurately, his back to me, while I saluted him as a fine representative of ours. He turned, free of his task and jolly, and produced that treat of his, two bottles of treasured and precious ginger ale. It was like a miracle performed. We talked till the light went out.

Much later a cry in the woods woke me. It was yet dark, but I could see Hill up, and fumbling with his accoutrements. Out I jumped, though still unreasonably tired; and sleepily dressed. When I turned to Hill, to see if he were ready, he was then under his net, watching me. He explained he had just returned from poker, and was wondering why I was dressing, but did not like to ask, knowing that Englishmen have ways that are not American. So the sun was up long before we were, though presently, in a small canoe, we embarked on the Caracoles. This tributary of the Madeira comes from nobody knows where. It is a river of the kind which explorers in these forests have sometimes mentioned, to our fearful joy. The sunlight hardly reached the water. The river was merely a drain burrowing under the jungle. The forest on its banks met overhead. There was little foliage below; we saw but the base of the forest, grey columns that might have been of stone upholding a darkness from which dead stuff suspended. The canoe had to dodge the lianas, which dropped to the water. The noise of our paddles convoyed us down stream, a rout of panic echoes trying to escape. We came to an opening and full daylight presently, and landed by a mule corral; and I began a lonely ride with Hill through the forest. The mule was such a docile little brown creature that I was left in the silence to my thoughts, which were interrupted now and then by the wandering blue flame of a morpho. My mule followed Hill's mule along a winding trail, and our leader was nearly always out of sight. I do not remember much of my first ride in the forest. I had an impression of being at a viewless distance from the sun. We were on the abysmal floor of a growth which was not trees, but the hoary pediments of a structure which was too high and vast for human sight. We rode in the basal gloom of it, no more than lost ants there, at an immeasurable depth in the atmosphere. The roof of the world was far away. Somewhere was the sun, for occasionally there was a well which its light had filled, and a grove of green palms, complete and personal, standing at the bottom of the well, living and reasonable shapes. Or one of the morphos would flicker among those spectral bastions, aerial and bright as a fairy in Hades. The sombre mind caught it at once, an unexpected gleam of hope, a bright blue thought to set among one's shapeless fears. We descended into hollows, going down into darker fathoms of the shades; mounted again through brighter suffusions of day, and in a while came out upon the open lane in the woods, the long cut in the jungle made for the railway, when it should get so far.

Now I could see my companion. He was from Texas, and it was easy to guess that. In the long rides which followed in the land where we looked upon what was there for the first time since genesis, where we might have been in the hush of the seventh day, so new, strange, and quiet was all, the figure ahead of me, with its long boots, negligent black shirt, the guns about the waist, and the hat with its extravagant size nobly raked, made me stop at times to assure myself that I was not pursuing a day-dream of boyhood, too much Mayne Reid in my head, especially when my wild and improbable companion paused under a group of statuesque palms and looked back at me—I suppose to make sure that I was still there, and that the silence had not absorbed me utterly, a faint rustle of intruding sound in a virgin and absorbent world. And again I remember the sparkle and lift of early morning there. The air was new, it was stimulative, it recharged me with buoyant youth. To breathe that air in the fresh of the morning was exaltation, and to see the young sunlight on

the ardent foliage was to know the springs of life were full.
That was at the breakfast hour, when the camp fires
crackled and were aromatic, the smoke going straight to
the tree tops. Then quickly the narrow track through the
forest filled with day, increased in heat till I felt I could
bear no more of it, and so gazed vacantly at the mules's
ears, merely enduring and numbed. The vitality of the
morning went, and in the fierce pour of light I looked no
more to the strange leaves and vines, the curious fronds,
the anthills by the way, the butterflies and birds, but had
only a dull dread that the avenue through which we were
riding was straight and interminable. There was no escape
from this heat. There were no openings through which we
could retreat under the trees. The air was immobile; the air
itself was the incumbent heat. The only shadows were
under the mules' bellies. Cruel and relentless noons! How
the surveyors endured it, standing for long eyeing their
exacting instruments in such a defeating glare, I do not
know. At the end of each day my pigskin leggings were like
wet brown paper with sweat, and my hands crinkled and
bleached as though they had been in a soda bath.

We reached another and greater tributary of the Madeira,
the Rio Jaci-Parana. Here there was a very extensive clearing
as great as the one at Porto Velho. The bridging of the Jaci
would be a considerable undertaking, consequently there
were numerous huts dotted about the rough open ground;
but I think the original intention in cutting back the jungle
to such an extent was that in the days to come a town would
grow there. I imagine it will not, and that the project is
abandoned. In one of my early walks in the woods I came by
chance upon the new cemetery; it was already large. The
Jaci country has proved to be more than usually unhealthy.
The ground was cleared down to a coarse herbage, round
which stood shadowing trees. Little crucifixes, made by
splitting a stick and putting another stick crosswise in the
slit, were planted at all sorts of drunken angles in the
ground. One large cross in the centre stood for all the dead.
There were no names given. A Brazil nut-tree grew alongside
this graveyard in the jungle, so tall that the flock of

screaming parrots about its foliage were but drifting black specks.

Because Hill had a touch of the fever we stayed for some days by the Jaci. I had a hut given to me, typical of the rest; but I was so much alone in it that that hut on the Jaci, where our remoteness from human things tested and known, the aloofness and quiet of the forest, the deadly nature of the romantic and beautiful river bank where we were marooned, and the sickness of my friend Hill, threw me upon my centre, until I began even to talk to myself, and received such an impress of the minute details of my little habitation that, ephemeral as it was and now long since gone, it endures, of coloured and indestructible stuff, with a sunny portal I still can enter whenever my mind turns that way. It was of four palm trunks, lapped round and over with mats of leaves. The floor was of untrimmed branches, two feet from the earth, and their unexpected inequalities, never remembered, were always jolting my thoughts as I walked across. They were crooked, and I could see the dusty earth two feet beneath where brown and green lizards ran. At one end was a verandah with a narrow floor made of the lids of soap and dynamite boxes, and laid without any idea that some curious tenant might wish to read the manufacturers' full names and see their complete trade marks. It was a puzzle. There was nothing to do, and I searched long on my verandah floor for the clue to one embarrassing fragment of a stencilled word. Hill sometimes huddled in a hammock on one side of the verandah, a leg hanging limply over, his thin sallow face drawn and resting on his breast, and his eyes shut; and I sat near him on the rail, silent, alone with any thought I met, and gazing blankly down the steep slope, past two tall Brazil nut-trees, to the half-hidden Rio Jaci below, and the roof of the forest opposite, over which the sun set each day in uplifted splendour. I remember but one conversation during that wait. An elderly white man came up to the verandah one evening, and murmured something to Hill, who opened his eyes, and looked at his visitor under weary lids. This man was one of Hill's subordinates. He had something to say of the work; but one would hardly call it speech. The flow of his life was so weak that he could do no more than lift a few small words from his gaping mouth between his breaths. He held on to the verandah. His loose clothes hung straight down from his bones. The veins were in blue knots on his forehead. "Say," said Hill, rousing himself, "I want you to ride to the Caracoles, go down to Porto Velho, and take this note to the hospital." The man said nothing, but nodded. Hill scrawled his note, and the man left. "He'll be dead in a month," said Hill, five minutes after the man had gone. "But he would not go to the hospital for his health. I have to pretend that he must go for mine. He may as well die in a comfortable bed. . . . I wish those damned parrots would cease!" They were somewhere down by the river, unseen, but all the sound there was, their voices long, keen and distracting flaws in the pellucid and coloured day-fall.

One morning we crossed the Jaci, and on the opposite shore some mules were already geared with Texan saddles, the hombres at their heads, waiting for us. I considered my mule. He was a big, grey, upstanding fellow, with the legs and feet of a race-horse, the head of a hammer, and alert and inquisitive ears. He was very much alive. I had no doubt he could leave anywhere like light, when he had a mind for it. So that I turned to Hill, and said, "Is mine a quiet animal? Is he vicious?" "O say," said my guide, glancing carelessly at my dubious mount, "I guess he's just a mule." When a hombre shouted at my mule he stepped briskly, with more than a hint of the malicious rebel in his gait.

I knew it would happen, and it did. One foot was no sooner buried in a wooden shoe called a stirrup than he was off, like an explosion. A desperate leap got my other leg over my travelling sack, lashed on his rump, and I came down in the saddle, much surprised. Texan saddles are not leather pads for riding domestic creatures, but thrones for ruling devils, and the bit would have broken the mouth of a hippopotamus. The brute stopped, turned back one ear, and his thought was in his swivel eye. "You wait," I saw him say. In the few engrossing moments when his body was expanding and contracting under me I got some idea of the force I was supposed to guide, and it did not make my mind easy, for an office chair had been my most unstable seat till then. Yet off we went quietly, along the track, and Hill was in front, and my mule was as meek as a sheep. There came a swamp, into which he went to the knees, and I dismounted, jumping from hummock to hummock, encouraging him, and showing him the best places. His brown eyes were then like those of a good woman. So leaning forward, when we were through, I patted his sleek neck, and gave him pleasant words. Afterwards, when he showed a certain precious care in difficult places, for the country was very broken, stepping like a tight-rope walker, I was fool enough to think it was because of our understanding. Though I believe he would have deceived anybody.

At noon we left the track and entered the forest by a path so narrow that the trees touched our legs, and sometimes we had just time to duck beneath a noose which a liana dangled in our faces. It was a low and narrow tunnel, and it descended to a bottom where a shallow stream brawled among granite boulders; thence up the trail went through the trees and vines again, and at last we came to a little clearing, where there was a hut, and men who would give us meat and drink. We dismounted. I rubbed my mule's soft nose, and spoke to him playfully, as a familiar; but when entering the hut was rebuked by a man there for making a short cut round the heels of my mule. "Never do it. Don't give him a chance. A mule will be peaches for ten years waiting for the sure chance of getting his heels right on your stomach. They're not horses, them mules. They don't bite, and they don't muzzle you and show friendly. They've got no feelings. That chap of yours, his mother was an ass, and his father was old Solfernio himself. But they've all got one good point—they're barren."

The mule stood deep in thought till I was mounted again; then instantly bolted back along the path which led to the ravine. The idle hombre had mishandled the reins, and I could get no pull. I went across that clearing like (so Hill said afterwards) Todd Sloan up. The beast, his ears back, was in a frenzy, and the convulsions of his powerful body made my thoughts pallid and ghastly. Nothing but disaster could stop him, and the black mouth of that steep tunnel in the forest yawned before us, and grew larger, though not large enough. He took the opening as clean as a lucky shot; but I was laid carefully along his back. Why we missed the tangle of woods and the rocks in that precipitate descent is known only to my lucky stars. I had my feet from the stirrups, my toes hooked on his rump, one arm round the horn of the saddle, and the other stretched along his sawing neck. I saw the roots and stones leap up and by us, close to my face. Several things occurred to me, and one was that some methods of dire fate were fatuous and undignified. I wondered also whether I should be taken back to the ship, or buried there. The impetus of the brute, which I expected would send us somersaulting among the rocks of the bottom, took him partly up the hither slope, and soon he had to gather his haunches for the upward leaps. I slipped off. He swung round at the length of the reins, and eyed me, cocking his ears derisively. A horse's nerves are human-like, and a horse would have been in a muck, but this murderous mule was calm and mocking. I watched him, and listened for an obscene and confident guffaw.

I found afterwards that punishment has no more effect on them than kindness. There is no guidance in this matter, take the mule all round. It is dealing with the uncanny. It is better to cross yourself when you go near a mule. Every morning about a camp we would watch the hombres gear up those pensive and placid creatures. They were sleek, lissom, and beautiful, and it was a pleasure to watch them. But as soon as the business of the day began one of the mules (and there was no prophecy as to which one it would be) became a homicidal maniac. At one camp it was necessary to keep a hundred or more mules in reserve, and there, for their health, a sane old horse was kept also. The horse was a knacker's body, a sorry spectacle, and in that climate he but pottered about waiting for disease to take him. He was smaller than the fine and healthy mules, but the respect the hammer-heads had for him was comical, and a great help to the men. Without the horse, it would have been opening the door of an asylum to have let the mules out of the corral to water at the river. But he led the way, and they bunched round him bashfully, and followed him to the stream. He took no notice of them whatever. He did not flatter them by pretending to be aware of their existence. When he had had his fill, he turned, and ambled through them, scorning to see them, and returned to the corral. Round went all the mules nearest to him, and any of them on the outskirts of the mob that stayed on because they did not see him go lost their heads, when they looked up, and risked their necks in short cuts through the timber. "Ho, mule!" would shout the hombres in alarm; for even mules cost money.

The land through which we were riding shall have a little railway there some day, if the men who are building it keep their hearts of brass, and refuse in working hours to remember London and New York. When it is there, that short line, it will begin and end in places having names which will convey little meaning to people outside Brazil; but to know what endurance of valour, but chiefly what raillery and light-hearted disregard of the gods who put baleful forests guarded by dragons—the dragons of mythology were lambs to what mosquitoes are—in the path of weak men pursuing their purpose, to know what has gone to the building of that track, though it nowhere plainly shows, for the graveyards are casual and obscure, brings you to a stand, surprised into awe of your fellows, as though through a coarse disguise you caught a gleam of divinity. Something shows, a light shows, which is beyond human. Would men be so prodigal of life and time if they were not aware of their great wealth? I don't know. My travels never brought me to that ultimate assurance. But I did see that my fellow-men are indifferent, spend-thrift with their known and scanty store as though they were immortals, the remittance men of Great Jove. I have no doubt now the line will be finished some day; but there were times, riding along the roughly cleared trail where it is to be, and we came upon places where men, in a spasm of pointless and soon expiring energy had scratched and mauled the pristine earth, when I did not think so.

Always the same dumb mystery was about us at noon as at nightfall. I felt we were lost at the back of the world, that we had crossed the boundary beyond which the voice of traffic never goes, and were idly wandering on the confines of oblivion. Sometimes I had that consciousness of futility which comes to us when, in sleep, we are earnest in the absurd activities of a dream, one point of the reason remaining awake to wonder at the antics of the busy but blind mind. Why was I there at all? Was I there? Those forlorn spots in the forest where our fellows had been before us, which we two riders overlooked alone, seemed to show that those men, while in the midst of their feverish labour, had recovered their minds, and had seen the wilderness was too vast, was unconquerable; and they had fled. There before us was what they had done. A deep trench would be in the track, the sand thrown up on either side. Some dead trees would be prone in our path, and we had to ride round them. There would be a few empty huts of leaves, with old ashes at the entrances, and a midden with its usual gorgeous butterflies. There would not be a sign of life, except the butterflies over the refuse, and not a sound or a movement but a clink from our own harness, and the heads of our mules impatient with the flies. Over the evidence of man's far-fetched enterprise and industry, his short and ferocious attack on the wild, brooded the forest. That bent over us, and it might have been solicitous and compassionate, or it might have been merely curious about the behaviour of the surprising creatures who had come there for the first time, and had been so active for a while. Sitting in the pour of the sun, looking upon the scanty work of my fellows, and then upon the near watchful ranks of that continent of trees pressing close to regard the grave-like trench into which man's hope might have been thrown, I had a dread of the easy and enduring dominion of those powers which were before man.

We would ride on then, sometimes up to our saddles in swamps, and every day I lost faith that there was any company of our fellows in that desolation, who would take our mules at nightfall, and show hammocks for our rest. But

always before night caught us we would spy a few huts
diminutive under the cliffs of forest—land ho!—and the
little outpost of two or three engineers and a doctor would
meet us as we came up. Such a camp was like finding
security and fellowship again after the uncertainty and
emptiness of the sea. The voices of new friends disarmed the
forest. It was not curious that we found it so easy to talk and
laugh.

One such camp I remember well. We came upon it late,
and my bones, through a longer ride than usual in the
wooden saddle, had grown into an unjointed frame. This was
the real meaning of fatigue. My body was a comprehensive
ache. Yet my mind was alert and buoyant; and I remembered
that perhaps it was so because I had been well bitten by the
mosquitoes of the Jaci-Parana, a first effect of the inocula-
tion; so I swallowed twenty grains of my store of quinine.

You in settled lands, unless you have been very poor
indeed and know what trouble is and what friends are, have
never seen the face of your brother, nor the serenity of
evening when you have found, without expecting it, shelter
for the night; you don't know what the taste of bread and
meat is, nor the savour of tobacco, nor what comfortable
security is the whispering of a comrade unseen in the
shadows of a resting place, nor what it is to sleep. I found
those gifts are not means to life only, but reasons for living
too; something to live for. With these at nightfall, our frail
little hut, beleaguered in the limitless woods, the shack in
which the ants and spiders swarmed and gross insects rang
on the metal lamp, where we loafed in hammocks, smoking,
and listened to the cries of we knew not what in the
unknown about us, was impregnable to the hosts of darkness.

Perhaps I remember that camp so well because it was a
night of full moon. There were three huts. We were deep in
the trees. The dark walls of that well in the jungle rose sheer
all round us. Nobody knew what was beyond the huts. The
moon appeared just clear of the lofty parapet of the well, and
poured down to us an imponderable rarity of bluish fire.
Wherever this fire lodged it stayed. Half-way up projected

palm fronds, and they were heavy patterns in burnished silver. Nameless shapes grew luminous in the dark about us. The cascade of lustrous fluid metal suddenly congealed. The gloom beneath that shining roof was hollowed by the pale yellow light of a lamp; so I could see, under the eaves, the three hammocks slung from the posts. The quiet talk of my companions was the only sound. I limped with weariness towards the voices, and sat in a shadow listening; and looked beyond to sprays of motionless shining foliage leaning out from inscrutable darkness. I seemed to have escaped from my tired body; my disembodied mind was free and at large. A camp hunter had killed a jaguar there, during the afternoon, they were saying. There were many about, for we were beyond the railway men, the track being but a lane of felled trees. They were saying the country there abounded with wild life. Just as we arrived that evening one of the men brought in a wounded animal, its nature so disguised that I thought it was a kind of sloth. It was about two feet long, and covered with long grizzled hair from its snout to the end of its considerable tail; but when I lifted it, and the poor injured creature shook its hair from its eyes, I saw it was a monkey; that anguished and fearful gaze which met mine was of my own tiny brother. It was a rare and little-known creature, the Hairy Saki, the first of its kind I had seen. The native took it away to eat it. I may say that at every camp we ate what we could get; and being by nature squeamish I never asked what it was that was put before me. Whatever it was, there it was, and it was all they could give me. I only emphatically directed that monkey flesh would be worse to me than hunger.

"There are plenty of tigers about here," called one of our hosts to me; "I'll fix you with a gun tomorrow, and we'll have some fun." But thank you, no. I did not carry arms throughout my journey. The jaguars did me no hurt when I went exploring o' mornings; and as for me, I was not looking for trouble. Quite politely the jaguars retired while I wandered about alone; though I should have been delighted to have sighted one. The whiffs of feral odour I got, especially in the neighbourhood of the mules, about which the jaguars prowled at night, were my only big game trophies. Some-times an indistinguishable object would step across ahead of me, or stir in a bush close by, drawing ear and eye at once in a place where trees and leaves were always as fixtures, like the air. I never met one of the larger natives of the place. I knew the parrots by their voices. I heard and smelt the cats. The monkeys called from a great distance; or a body would slip round a tree so like a shadow moving that when I examined the place, and saw nothing, it was easy to believe the eye was only suspicious.

The men began to talk of the Indians. They said we were in the land of the Caripunas. "You won't see them," said Hill. "I expect they are watching us now though," he added, after a pause. I glanced up with some interest at the spectral foliage, where right before me the pale moonfire on leaves and trunks framed portals in the night. I could see nothing.

"It's odds that some of them have been following us all day," continued Hill. "They watch us. They can't make us out. The rubber men told us the Caripunas would kill and eat us. They kill the rubber men all right, and a good job too. But they only slip through the forest watching us. I saw some once. On the Jaci. I jollied them into putting their canoe ashore. It was only a bark contraption, the roughest thing of its kind I've seen, sharpened fore and aft by lacing the ends together with sinews. They were fine light brown fellows, well made, and stark naked. The black hair of some of them was frizzy. Curious, isn't it? But I've heard that in the slave days runaway niggers got down here, and the forest Indians collared them to improve their own miserable stock. The Brazilians have always had a tradition of a frizzy-haired race on the Madeira; and here they are. They had bows and arrows, those chaps, made entirely of cane and wood. The arrows were tipped with macaw feathers, and were over six feet long. I couldn't bend the bloomin' bow. These fellows keep to the side rivers, and their villages are always hidden in the woods. It's a funny thing, but whenever the surveyors come on a village they find it has been vacated about a week."

We were silent for a time, and then a half-breed crept up

to a hammock and spoke in Spanish to the doctor. The doctor laughed, and the fellow went away. "He's asking for a piece of that onca to eat. He says it will make him strong." They began to talk of that, and the talk went on to what the Indians say of the mai d'aqua, the mother of the waters, who frequents islands in the rivers and is the ruin of young men, and of such dreads as the jurupari, and the curupira, and the maty tapéré.

They admitted it was easy to imagine such things into the forest. It wasn't what was seen there. Only the trees and the shadows were seen. But sometimes there were sounds. One of us, when alone making a traverse in the forest, had heard a scream, as if a woman had been frightened, and then there was no more sound. The camp doctor began to talk. He was an Englishman. He sat upright in the middle of his hammock, swinging it with one foot. "There was a curious yarn I heard about a tiger in Hampshire. Ah! Hampshire! I had a practice there once, you know. It made me so busy and popular that at last I began to wonder whether I wasn't altogether too successful. It was the practice or me. As I wanted to live on and do some useful work I slew the practice. I've got one or two ideas about that beri-beri you chaps die of here. A doctor cannot serve God and a lot of old women with colds. . . . Oh yes, about that tiger. Well, one of those travelling shows came to our village. I could see the steam of its roundabout engines from my surgery windows, and I told the farmer who rented the field to the showmen that if he let a mechanical organ come anywhere near my place again he could take his gallstone somewhere else in future.

"Late one night I got an urgent message to go over to the show. There had been an accident. I was taken into a caravan. There was a fat woman dressed as a pink fairy kneeling over a man stretched on a bunk, shaking him, and crying. The man was dead all right. But I couldn't find a mark on him. Diseased heart, I supposed, but he looked a good 'un. Some of the well-made, powerful chaps have most unreliable hearts. The woman kept crying out something about 'that beast of a tiger.' Curious sort of remark, and I asked the boss afterwards what she meant. He shuffled about a bit, pretending that she was talking silly. 'Nothing to do with the tigress,' he said, 'although the man was found unconscious in her cage.' 'It's such a tame thing,' said the showman. 'Anybody could handle it. Never shows vice. Old Jackson'—that was the dead chap—'he'd been inside tinkering with a partition. When we found him she was lying in a corner as if asleep, and only sat up and yawned when we got him out of her cage. Come and see for yourself.' "

"I went. There was nothing to see, except a slit-eyed tigress sitting up in a corner of her cage, blinking at the lantern, and looking rather spooky. A rather small creature, and prettily marked—one of the melantic variety."

"Well, the chap was buried after an inquest, and that inquest made me ask a lot of questions afterwards. It was a simple affair, the inquest. Death from natural causes. But there was something behind the evidence of the man's wife, and I wanted to find out about that.

"She told me she had a little girl, who got one night into the tent where the big cats were kept. Nobody was there at the time. Next morning she said to her mother, 'Mummie, who was the funny lady in Lucy's cage?'

Lucy was the name of the tigress. The child said that there was only the lady in the cage, and the lady watched her. And that was all they could get out of the kiddie. The funny thing about it is that once before the child had come back with a yarn like that, after straying into the menagerie tent late at night. The wife's idea was her husband had died of fright.

"Don't ask me what I want to make out, boys. I'm only just telling you the yarn. There you are.

"Well, before the show left our village, I heard they'd got a nigger to look after the big cats. He was with the show two days. On the third day he was missing. He went without drawing his money, and he had left open the door of Lucy's cage. She hadn't attempted to get out. The nigger was found some days after, wandering about the country, and a little cracked, by all accounts. And that's all."

The doctor struck a match, and then hoisted his legs into the hammock. Somewhere far in the forest the monkeys were howling.

"That doctor is a good body mender," said Hill to me. "He is the most entertaining liar on this job."

VI

WHEN in the neighbourhood of the Girau Falls we returned to a camp known as 22, which was merely a couple of huts, the station of two English surveyors, who had with them a small party of Bolivians. The Bolivian frontier was then but a little distance to the south-west. We rested for a day there, and planned to make a journey of ten miles across country, to the falls of the Caldeirão do Inferno. By doing so we should save the wearying return ride along the track to the Rio Jaci-Parana, for at the Caldeirão a launch was kept, and in that we could shoot the rapids and reach the camp on the Jaci two days earlier. Some haste was necessary now, for my steamer must be nearing her sailing time. And again, I agreed the more readily to the plan of making a traverse of the forest because it would give me the opportunity of seeing the interior of the virgin jungle away from any track. Though I had been so long in a land which all was forest I had not been within the universal growth except for little journeys on used trails. A journey across country in the Amazon country is never made by the Brazilians. The only roads are the rivers. It is a rare traveller who goes through those forests, guided only by a compass and his lore of the wilderness. That for months I had never been out of sight of the jungle, and yet had rarely ventured to turn aside from a path for more than a few paces, is some indication of its character. At the camp where we were staying I was told that once a man had gone merely within the screen of leaves, and then no doubt had lost, for a few moments, his sense of the direction of the camp, for he was never seen again.

The equatorial forest is popularly pictured as a place of bright and varied colours, with extravagant flowers, an abundance of fruits, and huge trees hung with creepers where lurk many venomous but beautiful snakes with gem-like eyes, and a multitude of birds as bright as the flowers; paradise indeed, though haunted by a peril. Those details are right but the picture is wrong. It is true that some of the birds are decorated in a way which makes the most beautiful of our temperate birds seem dull; but the toucans and macaws of the Madeira forest, though common, are not often seen, and when they are seen they are likely to be but obscure atoms drifting high in a white light. About the villages and in the clearings there are usually many superb butterflies and moths, and a varied wealth off vegetation not to be matched outside the tropics, and there will be the fireflies and odours in evening pathways. But the virgin forest itself soon becomes but a green monotony which, through extent and mystery, dominates and compels to awe and some dread. You will see it daily, but will not often approach it. It has no splendid blossoms; none, that is, which you will see, except by chance, as by luck one day I saw from the steamer's bridge some trees in blossom, domes of lilac surmounting the forest levels. Trees are always in blossom there, for it is a land of continuous high summer, and there are orchids always in flower, and palms and vines that fill acres of forest with fragrance, palms and other trees which give wine and delicious fruits, and somewhere hidden there are the birds of the tropical picture, and dappled jaguars perfect in colouring and form, and brown men and women who have strange gods. But they are lost in the ocean of leaves as are the pearls and wonders in the deep. You will remember the equatorial forest but as a gloom of foliage in which all else that showed was rare and momentary, was foundered and lost to sight instantly, as an unusual ray of coloured light in one mid-ocean wave gleams, and at once goes, and your surprise at its apparition fades too, and again there is but the empty desolation which is for ever but vastness sombrely bright.

One morning, wondering greatly what we should see in the place where we should be the first men to go, Hill and I left camp 22 and returned a little along the track. It was a hot still morning. A vanilla vine was in fragrant flower somewhere, unseen, but unescapable. My little unknown friend in the woods, who calls me at odd times—but I think chiefly when I am near a stream—by whistling thrice, let me know he was about. Hill said he thinks he has seen him, and that my little friend looks like a black-bird. On the track in many places were objects which appeared to be long cups inverted, of unglazed ware. Picking up one I found it was the cap to a mine of ants, the inside of the clay cup being hollowed in a perfect circle, and remarkably smooth. A paca dived into the scrub near us. It was early morning, scented with vanilla, and the intricacy of leaves was radiant. Nowhere in the screen could I see a place through which it was possible to crawl to whatever was behind it. The front of leaves was unbroken. Hill presently bent double and disappeared, and I followed in the break he made. So we went for about ten minutes, my leader cutting obstructions with his machete, and mostly we had to go almost on hands and knees. The undergrowth was green, but in the etiolated way of plants which have little light, though that may have been my fancy. One plant was very common, making light-green feathery barriers. I think it was a climbing bamboo. Its stem was vapid and of no diameter, and its grasslike leaves grew in whorls at the joints. It extended to incredible distances. We got out of that margin of undergrowth, which springs up quickly when light is let into the woods, as it was there through the cutting of the track, and found ourselves on a bare floor where the trunks of arborescent laurels grew so thickly together that our view ahead was restricted to a few yards. We were in the forest. There was a pale tinge of day, but its origin was uncertain, for overhead no foliage could be seen, but only deep shadows from which long ropes were hanging without life. In that obscurity were points of light, as if a high roof had lost some tiles. Hill set a course almost due south, and we went on, presently decending to a deep clear stream over which a tree had fallen. Shafts of daylight came down to us there, making the sandy bottom of the stream luminous, as by a lantern, and betraying crowds of small fishes. As we climbed the tree, to cross upon it, we disturbed several morphos. We had difficulties beyond in a hollow, where the bottom of the forest was lumbered with fallen trees, dry rubbish, and thorns, and once, stepping on what looked timber solid enough, its treacherous shell collapsed, and I went down into a cloud of dust and ants. In clearing this wreckage, which was usually as high as our faces, and doubly confused by the darkness, the involutions of dead thorny creepers, and clouds of dried foliage, Hill got at fault with our direction, but reassured himself, though I don't know how—but I think with the certain knowledge that if we went south for long enough we should strike the Madeira somewhere—and on we went. For hours we continued among the trees, seldom knowing what was ahead of us for any distance, surviving points of noise intruding again after long in the dusk of limbo. So still and nocturnal was the forest that it was real only when its forms were close. All else was phantom and of the shades. There was not a green sign of life, and not a sound. Resting once under a tree I began to think there was a conspiracy implied in that murk and awful stillness, and that we should never come out again into the day and see a living earth. Hill sat looking out, and said, as if in answer to an unspoken thought of mine which had been heard because there was less than no sound there, that men who were lost in those woods soon went mad.

Then he led on again. This forest was nothing like the paradise a tropical wild is supposed to be. It was as uniformly dingy as the old stones of a London street on a November evening. We did not see a movement, except when the morphos started from the uprooted tree. Once I heard the whistler call us from the depths of the forest, urgent and startling; and now when in a London by-way I hear a boy call his mate in a shrill whistle, it puts about me again the spectral aisles, and that unexpectant quiet of the sepulchre which is more than mere absence of sound, for the dead who should have no voice. This central forest was really the vault of the long-forgotten, dank, mouldering, dark, abandoned to the accumulations of eld and decay. The tall pillars rose, upholding night, and they might have been bastions of weathered limestone and basalt, for they were as grim as ancient and ruinous masonry. There was no undergrowth.

The ground was hidden in a ruin of perished stuff, uprooted trees, parchments of leaves, broken boughs, and mummied husks, the iron globes of nuts, and pods. There was no day, but some breaks in the roof were points of remote starlight. The crowded columns mounted straight and far, almost branchless, fading into indistinction. Out of that overhead obscurity hung a wreckage of distorted cables, binding the trees, and often reaching the ground. The trees were seldom of great girth, though occasionally there was a dominant basaltic pillar, its roots meandering over the floor like streams of old lava. The smooth ridges of such a fantastic complexity of roots were sometimes breast high. The walls ran up the trunk, projecting from it as flat buttresses, for great heights. We would crawl round such an occupying structure, diminished groundlings, as one would move about the base of a foreboding, plutonic building whose limits and meaning were ominous and baffling. There were other great trees with compound boles, built literally of bundles of round stems, intricate gothic pillars, some of the props having fused in places. Every tree was the support of a parasitic community, lianas swathing it and binding it. One vine moulded itself to its host, a flat and wide compress, as though it were plastic. We might have been witnessing what had been a riot of manifold and insurgent life. It had been turned to stone when in the extreme pose of striving violence. It was all dead now.

But what if these combatants had only paused as we appeared? It was a thought which came to me. The pause might be but an appearance for our deception. Indeed, they were all fighting as we passed through, those still and fantastic shapes, a war ruthless but slow, in which the battle day was ages long. They seemed but still. We were deceived. If time had been accelerated, if the movements in that war of phantoms had been speeded, we should have seen what really was there, the greater trees running upwards to starve the weak of light and food, and heard the continuous collapse of the failures, and have seen the lianas writhing and constricting, manifestly like serpents, throttling and eating their hosts. We did see the dead everywhere, shells with the worms at them. Yet it was not easy to be sure that we saw anything at all, for these were not trees, but shapes in a region below the day, a world sunk abysmally from the land of living things, to which light but thinly percolated down to two travellers moving over its floor, trying to get out to their own place.

Late in the afternoon we were surprised by a steep hill in our way, where the forest was more open. Palms became conspicuous on the slopes, and the interior of the sombre woods was lighted with bright and graceful foliage. The wild banana was frequent, its long rippling pennants showing everywhere. The hill rose sharply, perhaps for six hundred feet, and over its surface were scattered large stones, and stones are rare indeed in this land of vegetable humus. They were often six inches in diameter, and I should have said they were waterworn but that I had seen them *in situ* at one camp, where they occurred but little below the surface in a friable sandstone, the largest of them easily broken in the hands, for they were but ferrous concretions of quartz grains. After exposure to the air they so hardened that they could be fractured only with difficulty. We kept along the ridge of the hill, finding breaks in the forest through which, as through unexpected windows, we could see, for a wonder, over the roof of the forest, looking out of our prison to a wide world where the sun was declining. In the south-west we caught the gleam of the Madeira, and beyond it saw a continuation of the range of hills on which we stood.

In the low ground between the hill range and the river the forest was lower, and was so tangled a mass that I doubted whether we could make a way through it. We happened upon a deserted Caripuna village, three large sheds, without sides, each but a ragged thatch propped on four legs. The clearing was just large enough to hold them. I could find no relics of the forest folk about. Damp leaves were thick on the floor of each shelter. But it was lucky we found the huts, for thence a trail led us to the river. We emerged suddenly from the forest, just as one goes through a little door into the open street. We were on the bank of the Madeira by the upper falls of the Caldeirão. It was still a great river, with the

wall of the forest opposite, just above which the sunset was
flaming, so far away that its tree trunks were but vertical
lines of silver in dark cliffs. A track used by the Bolivian
rubber boatmen led us down stream to the camp by the
lower falls.

It was night when we got to the three huts of the camp,
and the river could not be seen, but it was heard, a continuous low thundering. Sometimes a greater shock of deep
waters falling, an orgasm of the flood pouring unseen, more
violent than the rest, made the earth tremulous. Men held
up lanterns to our faces, and led us to a hut. It was but the
usual roof of leaves. We rested in hammocks slung between
the posts, and I ached in every limb. But here we were at
last; and there is no more luxurious bed than a hammock,
yielding and resilient, as though you were cradled on air; and
there is no pipe like that smoked in a hammock at night in
the tropics after a day of toil and anxiety in a dissolving heat,
for the heat makes a pipe bitter and impossible; but if a
tropic night is cool and cloudless it comes like a benediction,
and the silence is a peace that is below you and around, and
as high as the stars towards which your face is turned. The
ropes of the hammocks creaked. Sometimes a man spoke
quietly, as though he were at a great distance. The sound of
the waters receded, was heard only as in a sleep, and it might
have been the loud murmur of the spinning globe, heard
because we had left this world and had leisure for trifles in
a securer world apart.

In the morning while they prepared the little steam
launch for its journey down the rapids, I had time to climb
about the smooth granite boulders of the foreshore below
the hut. A rock is so unusual in this country that it is a
luxury when found. The granite was bare, but in its crevices
grew cacti and other plants with fleshy leaves and swollen
stems. Shadowing the hut was a tree bearing trumpet-
shaped flowers, and before the blossoms humming birds
were hovering, glowing and evanescent morsels, remaining
miraculously suspended when inserting their long bills into
the flowers, their little wings beating so rapidly that the air
seemed visible and radiant about them. Another tree here

interested me, for it was Bates Assacu, the only one I saw. It was a large tree, with palmate leaves having seven fingers. Ugly spines studded even its brown trunk.

I looked out on the river dubiously. A rocky island was just off shore, crowned with trees. Between us and the island, and beyond, the water heaved and circled, evidently of great depth, and fearfully disturbed and swift. It looked all its name, the Caldeirão do Inferno—hell's cauldron. There was not much white and broken water. But its surface was always changing, whirlpools forming and revolving, then disappearing in long wrenched strands of water. Sometimes a big tree would leap out of the water, as though it had travelled upwards from the bottom, and then would vanish again.

We set out upon it, with an engineman and two half-breeds, and went off obliquely for mid-stream. The engineman and navigator was a fair-haired German. If the river had been sane and usual I should have had my eyes on the forest which stood along each shore, for few white men had ever looked upon it. But the river took our minds, and never in bad weather in the western ocean have I seen water so full of menace. Yet below the falls it was silent and unbroken. It was its smooth swiftness, its strange checks and mysterious and deep convulsions, as though the river bed itself was insecure, the startling whirlpools which appeared without warning, circling depressions on the surface in which our launch would have been but a straw, which shocked the mind. It was stealthy and noiseless. The water was but an inch of two below our gunwale. We saw trees afloat, greater and heavier than our midget of a craft, shooting down the gently inclined shining expanse just as we were, and express; and then, as if an awful hand had grasped them from below, they were pulled under, and we saw them no more; or, again, and near to us and ahead, a tree bole would shoot from below like an arrow, though no tree had been drifting there. The shores were far away.

The water ahead grew worse. The German crouched by his little throbbing engine, looking anxiously—I could see his fixed stare—over the bows. We were travelling indeed now. The boat, in a rapid tremor, and oscillating violently, was clutched at the keel by something which coiled strongly about us, gripped us, and held us; and the boat, mad and terrified, in an effort to escape, made a circuit, the water lipping at her gunwale and coming over the bows. The river seemed poised a foot above the bows, ready to pour in and swamp us. The German tried to get her head down stream. Hill began tearing at his ammunition belt, and I stooped and tugged at my boot laces. . . .

The boat jumped, as if released. The German turned round on us grinning. "It ees all right," he said. He began to roll a cigarette nervously. "We pull it off all right," said the German, wetting his cigarette paper. The boat was free, dancing lightly along. The little engine was singing quickly and freely.

The Madeira here was as wide as in its lower reaches, with many islands. There were hosts of waterfowl. We landed once at a rubber hunter's sitio on the right bank. Its owner, a Bolivian, and his pretty Indian wife, who had tattoo marks on her forehead, made much of us, and gave us coffee. They had an orchard of guavas, and there, for it was long since I had tasted fruit, I was an immoderate thief, in spite of a pet curassow which followed me through the garden with distracting pecks. The Rio Jaci-Parana, a black-water stream, opened up soon after we left the sitio. The boundary between the clay-coloured flood of the Madeira and the dark water of the tributary was straight and distinct. From a distance the black water seemed like ink, but we found it quite clear and bright. The Jaci is not an important branch river, but it was, at this period of the rains, wider than the Thames at Richmond, and without doubt very much deeper. The appearance of the forest on the Jaci was quite different from the palisades of the parent stream. On the Madeira there is commonly a narrow shelf of bank, above which the jungle rises as would a sheer cliff. The Jaci had no banks. The forest was deeply submerged on either side, and whenever an opening showed in the woods we could see the waters within, but could not see their extent because of the interior gloom. The outer foliage was awash, and mounted, not straight, but in rounded clouds. For the first time I saw many vines and trees in flower, presumably because we were nearer the roof of the woods. One tree was loaded with the pendent pear-shaped nests of those birds called "hang nests," and scores of the beauties in their black and gold plumage were busy about their homes, which resembled monstrous fruits. Another tree was weighted with large racemes of orange-coloured blossoms, but as the launch passed close to it we discovered the blooms were really bundles of caterpillars. The Jaci appeared to be a haunt of the alligators, but all we saw of them was their snouts, which moved over the surface of the water out of our way like rubber balls afloat and mysteriously propelled. I had a sight, too, of that most regal of the eagles, the harpy, for one, well within view, lifted from a tree ahead, and sailed finely over the river and away.

That night I slept again in my old hut at the Jaci camp, and with Hill and another official set off early next morning for the construction camp on Rio Caracoles, which we hoped to reach before the commissary train left for Porto Velho. At Porto Velho the "Capella" was, and I wished, perhaps as much as I have ever wished for anything, that I should not be left behind when she departed. I knew she must be on the point of sailing.

My two companions had reasons of their own for thinking the catching of that train was urgently necessary. In our minds we were already settled and safe in a waggon, comfortable among the empty boxes, going back to the place where the crowd was. But still we had some way to ride; and, I must tell you, I was now possessed of all I desired of the tropical forest, and had but one fixed idea in my dark mind, but one bright star shining there; I had turned about, and was going home, and now must follow hard and unswervingly that star in the east of my mind. The rhythmic movements of the mule under me—only my legs knew he was there—formed in my darkened mind a refrain: get out of it, get out of it.

And at last there were the huts and tents of the Caracoles, still and quiet under the vertical sun. No train was there, nor did it look a place for trains. My steamer was sixty miles away, beyond a track along which further riding was impossible, and where walking, for more than two miles, could not be even considered. The train, the boys told us blithely, went back half an hour before. The audience of trees regarded my consternation with the indifference which I had begun to hate with some passion. The boys naturally expected that we should take it in the right way for hot climates, without fuss, and that now they had some new gossip for the night. But they should have understood Hill better. My tall gaunt leader waved them aside, for he was a man who could do things, when there seemed nothing that one could do. "The terminus or bust!" he cried. "Where's the boss?" He demanded a hand-cart and a crew. I thought he spoke in jest. A hand-cart is a contrivance propelled along railway metals by pumping at a handle. The handle connects with the wheels by a crank and cogs through a slot in the centre of the platform, and you get five miles an hour out of it while the crew continues. For sixty miles, in that heat, it was impossible. Yet Hill persisted; the cart was put on the metals, five half-breeds manned the pump handle, three facing the track ahead, two with their backs to it. We three passengers sat on the sides and front of the trolley. Away we went.

The boys cheered and laughed, calling out to us the probabilities of our journey. We trundled round a corner, and already I had to change my cramped position; fifty-eight miles to go. We sat with our legs held up out of the way of the vines and rocks by the track, and careful to remember that our craniums must be kept clear of the pump handle. The crew went up and down, with fixed looks. The sun was the eye of the last judgment, and my lips were cracked. The trees made no sign. The natives went up and down; and the forest went by tree by tree.

My tired and thoughtless legs dropped, and a thorn fastened its teeth instantly in my boots, and nearly had me down. The trees went by, one by one. There was a large black and yellow butterfly on a stone near us. I was surprised when no sound came as it made a grand movement upwards.

Then, in the heart of nowhere, the trolley slackened, and came to a stand. We had lost a pin. Half a mile back we could hardly credit we really had found that pin, but there it was; and the men began to go up and down again. Hill got a touch of fever, and the natives had changed to the colour of impure tallow, and flung their perspiration on my face and hands as they swung mechanically. The poor wretches! We were done. The sun weighed untold tons.

But the sun declined, some monkeys began to howl, and the sunset tempest sprang down on us its assault, shaking the high screens on either hand, and the rain beat with the roll of kettle-drums. Then we got on an up grade, and two of the spent natives collapsed, their chests heaving. So I and the other chap stood up in the night, looked to the stars, from which no help could be got, took hold of the pump handle like gallant gentlemen, and tried to forget there were twenty miles to go. Away we went, jog, jog, uphill. I thought that gradient would not end till my heart and head had burst; but it did, just in time.

We gathered speed on a down grade. We flew. Presently the man with the fever yelled, "The brake, the brake!" But the brake was broken. The trolley was not running, but leaping in the dark. Every time it came down it found the metals. A light was coming towards us on the line; and the others prepared to jump. I could not even see that light, for my back was turned to our direction, and I could not let go the flying handle, else would all control have gone, and also I should have been smashed. I shut my eyes, pumped swiftly and involuntarily, and waited for doom to hit me in the back. The glow was a long time coming. Then Hill's gentle voice remarked, "All right, boys, it's a firefly."

. . . I became only a piece of machinery, and pumped, and pumped, with no more feeling than a bolster. Shadows undulated by us everlastingly. I think my tongue was hanging out. . . .

Lights were really seen at last. Kind hands lifted us from the engine of torture; and I heard the remembered voice of the Skipper, "Is he there? I thought it was a case."

That night of my return a full moon and a placid river showed me the "Capella" doubled, as in a mirror, and admiring the steamer's deep inverted shape I saw a heartening portent—I saw steam escaping from the funnel which was upside down. A great joy filled me at that, and I turned to the Skipper, as we strode over the ties of the jetty. "Yes. We go home to-morrow," he said. The bunk was superheated again by the engine room, but knowing the glad reason, I endured it with pleasure. To-morrow we turned about.

Yet on the morrow there was still the persistence of the spacious idleness which encompassed us impregnably, beyond which we could not go. The little that was left of the fuel in the holds went out of us with dismal unhaste. The Skipper and the mates fumed, and the Doctor took me round to see the "Capella's" pets, so that we might fill up time. A monkey, an entirely secular creature once with us, had died while I was away. It was well. He had no name; Vice was his name. There were no tears at his death, and Tinker the terrier began to get back some of his full and lively form again after that day when, in a sudden righteous revolution, he slew, and barbarously mangled, the insolent tyrant of the ship. The monkey had feared none but Mack, our red, blue and yellow macaw, a monstrous and resplendent fowl in whose iron bill even Brazil nuts were soft.

But we all respected Mack. He was the wisest thing on the ship. If an idle man felt high-spirited and approached Mack to demonstrate his humour, that great bird gave an inquiring turn to its head, and its deliberate and unwinking eyes hid the rapid play of its prescient mind. The man stopped, and would speak but playfully. Nobody ever dared.

When Mack first boarded the ship, a group of us, gloved, smothered him with a heavy blanket and fastened a chain to his leg. He knew he was overpowered, and did not struggle, but inside the blanket we heard some horrible chuckles. We took off the blanket and stood back expectantly from that dishevelled and puzzling giant of a parrot. He shook his feathers flat again, quite self-contained, looked at us sardonically and murmured "Gur-r-r" very distinctly; then glanced at his foot. There was a little surprise in his eye when he saw the chain there. He lifted up the chain to examine it, tried it, and then quietly and easily bit it through. "Gur-r-r!" he said again, straightening his vest, still regarding us solemnly. Then he moved off to a davit, and climbed the mizzen shrouds to the topmast.

When he saw us at food he came down with nonchalance, and overlooked our table from the cross beam of an awning. Apparently satisfied, he came directly to the mess table, sitting beside me, and took his share with all the assurance of a member, allowing me to idle with his beautiful wings and his tail. He was a beauty. He took my finger in his awful bill and rolled it round like a cigarette. I wondered what he would do to it before he let it go; but he merely let it go. He was a great character, magnanimously minded. I never knew a tamer creature than Mack. That evening he rejoined a flock of his wild brothers in the distant tree-tops. But he was back next morning, and put everlasting fear into the terrier, who was at breakfast, by suddenly appearing before him with wings outspread on the deck, looking like a disrupted and angry rainbow, and making raucous threats. The dog gave one yell and fell over backwards.

We had added a bull-frog to our pets, and he must have weighed at least three pounds. He had neither vice nor virtue, but was merely a squab in a shady corner. Whenever the dog approached him he would rise on his legs, however, and inflate himself till he was globular. This was incomprehensible to Tinker, who was contemptuous, but being a little uncertain, would make a circuit of the frog. Sitting one day in the shadow of the box which enclosed the rudder chain was the frog, and we were near, and up came Tinker a-trot all unthinking, his nose to the deck. The frog hurriedly furnished his pneumatic act when Tinker, who did not know froggie was there, was close beside him, and Tinker snapped sideways in a panic. Poor punctured froggie dwindled instantly, and died.

I could add to the list of our creatures the anaconda which was found coming aboard by the gangway but that a stoker saw him first, became hysterical, and slew the reptile with a shovel; there were the coral snakes which came inboard over the cables and through the hawse pipes, and the vampire bats which frequented the forecastle. But they are insignificant beside our peccary. I forgot to tell you the Skipper never made a tame creature of her. She refused us. We brought her up from the bunkers where first she was placed, because the stokers flatly refused her society in the dark. She was brought up on deck in bonds, snapping her tushes in a direful way, and when released did most indomitably charge all our ship's company, bristles up, and her automatic teeth louder and more rapid than ever. How we fled! When I turned on my vantage, the manner of my getting there all unknown, to see who was my neighbour, it was my abashed and elderly captain, who can look upon sea weather at its worst with an easy eye, but who then was striving desperately to get his legs (which were in pyjamas) ten feet above the deck, in case the very wild pig below had wings.

After the peccary was released we could not call the ship ours. We crept about as thieves. It was fortunate that she always gave warning of her proximity by making the noise of castanets with her tusks, so that we had time to get elevated before she arrived. But I never really knew how fast she could move till I saw her chase the dog, whom she despised and ignored. One morning his valiant barking at her, from a distance he judged to be adequate, annoyed her, and she shot at him like a projectile. Her slender limbs and diminutive hooves were those of a deer, and they became merely a haze beneath her body, which was a flying passion. The terrified dog had no chance, but just as she closed with him her feet slipped, and so Tinker's life was saved.

Her end was pitiful. One day she got into the saloon. The Doctor and I were there, and saw her trot in at one door, and we trotted out at another door. Now, the saloon was the pride of the Skipper; and when the old man tried to bribe her out of it—he talked to her from the open skylight above—and she insulted him with her mouth, he sent for his men. From behind a shut door of the saloon alley way we heard a fusilade of tusks in the saloon, shrieks from the maddened dog, uproar from the parrots, and the hoarse shouts of the crew. The pig was charging ten ways at once. Stealing a look from the cabin we saw the boatswain appear with a bunch of cotton waste, soaked in kerosene, blazing at the end of a bamboo, and the mate with a knife lashed to another pole. The peccary charged the lot. There broke out the cries of Tophet, and through chaos champed insistently the high note of the tusks. She was noosed and caged; but nothing could be done with the little fury, and when I peeped in at her a few days later she was full length, and dying. She opened one glazing eye at me, and snapped her teeth slowly, game to the end.

March 6.—It was reported at breakfast that we sail to-morrow. The bread was sour, the butter was oil, the sugar was black with flies, the sausages were tinned and very white and dead, and the bacon was all fat. And even the awning could not keep the sun away.

March 7.—We got the hatches on number four hold. It was reported we sail to-morrow.

March 8.—The ship was crowded this night with the boys, for a last jollification. We fired rockets, and swore enduring friendships with anybody, and many sang different songs together. It is reported that we sail to-morrow.

March 9.—It is reported that we sail to-morrow.

March 10.—The "Capella" has come to life. The master is on the bridge, the first mate is on the forecastle head, the second mate is on the poop, and the engineers are below. There are stern and minatory cries, and men who run. At the first slow clanking of the cable we raised wild cheers. The ship's body began to tremble, and there was thunder under her counter. We actually came away from the jetty, where long we had seemed a fixture. We got into mid-stream—stopped; slowly turned tail on Porto Velho. There was old man Jim, diminished on the distant jetty, waving his hat. Porto Velho looked strange again. Away we went. We reached the bend of the river, and turned the corner. There was the last we shall ever see of Porto Velho. Gone!

The forest unfolding in reverse order seemed brighter, and

all would have been quite well, but the fourth engineer came up from his duty, and fell insensible. He was very yellow, and the Doctor had work to do. Here was the first of our company to succumb to the country.

There were but six more days of forest; for the old "Capella," empty and light as a balloon, the collisions with the floating timber causing muffled thunder in her hollow body, came down the swift floods of the Madeira and the Amazon rivers "like a Cunarder, at sixteen knots," as the Skipper said. And there on the sixth day was Para again, and the sea near. Our spirits mounted, released from the dead weight of heat and silence. But I was to lose the Doctor at Para, for he was then to return to Porto Velho, having discharged his duty to the "Capella's" company. The Skipper took his wallet, and we went ashore with him, he to his day-long task of clearing his vessel, and we for a final sad excursion. Much later in the day, suspecting an unnameable evil was gathering to my undoing, I called at the agent's office, and found the Skipper had returned to the ship, that she was sailing that night, and, the regulations of Para being what they were, it being after six in the evening I could not leave till the next morning. My haggard and dismayed array of thoughts broke in confusion and left me gibbering, with not one idea for use. Without saying even good-bye to my old comrade I took to my heels, and left him; and that was the last I saw of the Doctor. (Aha! my staunch support in the long, hot and empty time at the back of things, where were but trees, bad food, and a jest to brace our souls, if ever you should see this—How!—and know, dear lad, I carried the damnable regulations and a whole row of officials, the Union Jack at the main, firing every gun as I bore down on them. I broke through. Only death could have barred me from my ship and the way home.)

Next morning we were at sea. We dropped the pilot early and changed our course to the north, bound for Barbados. Though on the line, the difference in the air at sea, after our long enclosure in the rivers of the forest, was keenly felt. And the ship too had been so level and quiet; but here she was lively again, full of movements and noises. The bows were at their old difference with the sky-line, and the steady wind of the outer was driving over us. Before noon, when I went in to the Chief, my crony was flat and moribund with a temperature at 105°, and he had no interest in this life whatever. I had added the apothecary's duties to those of the Purser, and here found my first job. (Doctor, I gave him lots of grains of quinine, and lots more afterwards; and plenty of calomel when he was at 98 again. Was that all right?)

The sight of the big and hearty Chief, when he was about once more, yellow, insecure, and somewhat shrunken, made us dubious. Yet now were we rolling home. She was breasting down into a creaming smother, the seas were blue, and the world was fresh and wide all the way back. There was one fine night, as we were climbing slowly up the slope of the globe, when we lifted the whole constellation of the Great Bear, the last star of the tail just dipping below the seas, straight over the "Capella's" bows, as she pitched. Then were we assured affairs were rightly ordered, and slept well and contented.

Late one afternoon we sighted Barbados. The sea was dark and the light was golden. The island did not look like land. It was a faint but constant pearl-coloured cloud. The empty sky came down to the dark sea in bright walls which had but a bloom of azure. Overhead it was day, but the sea was fluid night. Above the island was a group of cirrus, turned to the setting sun like an audience of intent faces. Near to starboard was a white ship, fully rigged, standing towards the island with royals set, and even a towering main skysail. Tall as she was, she looked but a multiple cloud which had dropped from the sky, and had settled on the dark sea, and over it was drifting in a faint air, buoyant, but unable to lift. We overhauled that stately ship. She was reflecting the day-fall from the white rounds of her many sails. She was regal, she was paramount in her world, and the sun seemed to be watching her, and shining solely for her illustrious progress. The clarity and the peace of it was in us as we leaned against the rail, watching Barbados grow, and watching that exalted ship. "This is all right," said the Chief.

We were coming to the things we knew and understood. In the island near us were men, quays, and shops. This evening had a familiar and friendly look. Barbados at last! There would be something to eat, too, and we kept talking of that. Do you know what good bread and butter tastes like? Or mealy baked potatoes? Or fruit from which the juice runs when you bite? Or crisp salads? Not you; not if you haven't lived for long on tinned stuffs, bread which smelt like vinegar, and butter to which a spoon had to be used.

To the door of the saloon alley way we saw the steward come, and begin to swing his bell. "Tea ho!" said the mate. "Keep it," said the Chief. "I know it. Sardines and hash. Not for me. We shall get some grub in the morning. Oranges and bananas, boys. I'm tired of oil. My belt is in by three holes."

When the sun once touched the sea it sank visibly, like a weight. Night came at once. We passed a winking light, and soon ahead of us in the dark was grouped a multitude of lower stars. That was Bridgetown. Those stars opened and spread round us, showing nothing of the wall of night in which they were fixed. Well, there it was. We could smell the good land. We should see it in the morning. We had really got there.

The engines stopped. There was a shout from the steamer's bridge and a thunderous rumbling as the cable ran out, and then a remarkable quiet. The old man came sideways down the bridge ladder with a hurricane lamp, and stood with us, striking a light for his cigar. "Here we are, Chief," he said. "What about coals in the morning?" The night was hot, there was no wind, and as we sat yarning on the bunker hatch another cluster of stars moved in swiftly together, came to a stand near us, and a peremptory gun was fired. That was the British mail steamer.

We looked at her with awe. We could see the toffs in evening dress idling in the glow of her electric lights. What a feed they had just finished! But the greatest wonder of her deck was the women in white gowns. We could hear the strange laughter of the women, and listened for it. That was music worth listening to. Our little mob of toughs in turns used the night glasses on those women, and in a dead silence. There were some kiddies, too.

We were looking at the benign lights of the island and trying to make out what they meant. The sense of our repose, and the touch of those warm and velvet airs, and the scent of land, were like the kindness and security of home. "I know this place," drawled Sandy. "I was here once. Before I went into steam I used to come out to the islands, when I was a young 'un. I made two voyages in the 'Chocolate Girl.' She was my first ship. She was a daisy, too. Once we lifted St Vincent twenty-five days out of Liverpool. That was going, if you like. If old Wager—he was the old man of the 'Chocolate Girl'—if he could only get a trip in a ship like this, like an iron street with a factory stack in the middle! But he can't. He's dead. He had the 'Mignonette,' and she went missing among the Bahamas. There's millions of islands in the Bahamas. They're north of this place. You couldn't visit all those islands in a lifetime.

"If you ask me, some of the islands in these seas are very funny. There's something wrong about a few of them. They're not down in the chart, so I've heard. One day you lift one, and you never knew it was there. 'What's that?' says the old man. 'Can't make that place out.' Then he reckons he's found new land, and takes his position. He calls it after his wife, and cables home what he's done. The next thing is a gunboat goes there and beats about and lays over the spot, but she doesn't find no island. The gunboat cables home that the merchant chap was drunk or something, and that he steamed over the spot and got hundreds of fathoms. They're always so clever, in the navy. But I've heard some of these islands are not right. You see one once, and nobody ever sees it again.

"I knew a man, and he was marooned on one of those islands. He sailed with me afterwards on one of the Blue Anchor steamers to Sydney. One time he was on a craft out of Martinique for Cuba. She was a schooner of the islands, and fine vessels they are. You'll see a lot about us in the morning. This man's name was Moffat—Bill Moffat. His schooner had a mulatto for a master, and that nigger was a fool and very superstitious, by all accounts. They ran short of water and it's pretty bad if you fall short of water in these seas. Off the regular routes there's nothing. You might drift for weeks, and see nothing, off the track.

"Then they sighted an island. The mulatto chap pretended he knew all about that island. He said he had been there before. But he was a liar. It was only a little island, like some trees afloat. They came down on it, and anchored in ten fathoms and waited for daylight.

"Next morning some wind freshened off shore, and Moffat takes a nigger and rows to the beach. There was only a light swell breaking on the coral, and landing was easy. Moffat told the nigger to stay by the boat while he took a look round. There was a bit of a coral beach with a pile of high rocks at the ends of it, like pillars each side of a door-step. What was inside the island Moffat couldn't see, because at the back of the beach was a wood. He said he heard a sound like a bird calling, but he reckoned there wasn't a soul in that place. The schooner was riding just off. He turned and was crunching his way up the coral with the idea of looking for a way inside. He got to the trees, and then heard the nigger shout in a fright. The black beggar was pushing out the boat. He got in it too, and began rowing back to the schooner as if somebody was coming after him.

"Moffat yelled, and ran down to the surf, but the nigger kept right on. There was Moffat up to his knees in the water, and in a fine state. The boat reached the schooner—and now, thinks Moffat, there'll be trouble. Do you know what happened though? For a little while nothing happened. Then they began to haul in her cable. She up-anchored and stood out. That's a fact. Bill told me he felt pretty sick when he saw it. He didn't like the look of it. He watched the schooner turn tail, and soon she found more wind and got out of sight past the island, close-hauled. He watched her dance past one of the piles of rock till there was nothing but empty sea behind the rock. Then his eye caught something moving on the rock. Something moved round it out of his sight. He never saw what it was. He wished he had.

"Well, he had a pretty bad time. He couldn't find anyone on the island, in a manner of speaking. But somebody was always going round a corner, or behind a tree. He caught them out of the tail of his eye. He said it was enough to get on a man's nerves the way that thing always just wasn't there, whatever it was. 'Curse the goats,' Bill used to say to himself.

"One day Bill was strolling round figuring out what he could do to that mulatto when he met him again, and then he found a sea cave. He went in. It was a silly thing to do, because the way in was so low that he had to crawl. But the cave was big enough inside for a music-hall. The walls ran up into a vault, and the water came up to the bottom of the walls nearly all round. The water was like a green light. A bright light came up through the water and the reflections were wriggling all over the rocks, making them seem to shake. The water was like thick glass full of light. He could see a long way down, but not to the bottom. While he was looking at it the water heaved up quietly full three feet, and the reflections on the walls faded. Then he saw the hole through which he had crawled was gone. 'Now, Bill Moffat, you're in a regular mess,' he says to himself.

"He dived for the hole. But he never found that way out, and the funny thing was he couldn't come to the top again. Bill saw it was a proper case that time, and no more Sundays in Poplar. He was surprised to find that the deeper he went the thinner the water was. It was thin and clear, like electric light. He could see miles there and down he kept falling till he hit the bottom with a bang. It scared a lot of fishes, and they flew up like birds. He looked up to see them go, and there was the sun overhead, only it was like a bright round of green jelly, all shaking. Bill found it was dead easy to breathe in water that was no thicker than air, so he got up, brushed the sand off, and looked round. A flock of fishes flew about him quite friendly, and as beautiful as Amazon parrots. A big crab walked ahead, and Bill thought he had better follow the crab.

"He came to a path which was marked with shells, and at the end of the path he saw the fore half of a ship up-ended.

While he was looking at it, somebody pushed the curtains from the hatchway, and came out, and looked at him. 'Good lord, it's Davy Jones,' said Bill to himself.

" 'Hullo, Bill,' said Davy. 'Come in. Glad to see you, Bill. What a time you've been.'

"Moffat said that Davy wasn't a decent sight, having barnacles all over his face. But he shook hands. 'You're hand is quite cold, Bill,' said Davy. 'Did you lose your soul coming along? You nearly did that before, Bill Moffat. You nearly did it that Christmas night off Ushant. I thought you were coming then. But not you. But here you are at last all right. Come in! Come in!'

"Bill went inside with Davy. There was sea junk all over the place. 'I find these things very handy, old chap,' said Davy to Bill seeing he was looking at them. 'It's good of you to send them down though I don't like the iron, for it won't stand the climate. See that old hat? It's a Spanish admiral's, I clap it on, backwards, whenever I want to go ashore.'

"So they sat down, and yarned about old times, though Bill told me that Davy seemed to remember people after everybody else had forgotten them, which was confusing. 'Oh, yes,' Davy would say, 'old Johnson. Yes. He used to talk of me in a rare way. He was a dog, was Johnson. I've heard him, many a time. But he's changed since his ship came downstairs. He's a better man. He's not so funny as he was.'

"Then they had a pipe, and after a bit things began to drag. 'Come into the garden, Bill,' said Davy. 'Come and have a look round.'

"All round the garden Bill notices the name-boards of ships nailed up. Some of the names Bill knew, and some he didn't, being Spanish. 'What do you think of my collection?' said Davy. 'Ever seen as fine a one? I lay you never have!'

"Then they came to a door. 'Come in,' said Davy. 'This is my locker. Ever heard of my locker?'

"Bill said it was pretty dark inside. Just light enough to see. But there was only miles and miles of crab-pots, all set out in rows, with a label on each. 'What do you think of that lot, Bill?' asked Davy. 'I shall have to get larger premises soon.' Bill choked a bit, for the place smelt stale and seaweedy. 'What's in the crab-pots, Davy?' said Bill.

" 'Souls!' said Davy. 'But there's a lot of trash, though now and then I get a good one. Here now. See this? This is a fine one, though I mustn't tell you where I got it. And people said he hadn't got one. But I knew better, and there it is.'

"But Bill couldn't see anything in the pots. He could only hear a rustling, as if something was rubbing on the wicker, or a twittering. At last Davy came to a new pot. 'Do you know who's in this one, Bill,' he said. But Bill couldn't guess. 'Well, Bill, it's your soul, and a poorer one I never see. It was hardly worth setting the pot for a soul like that.' Then Davy began to shake the pot, and soon got wild. 'Here, where the deuce has that soul gone,' he said, and put his ear to the bars. Then he put the pot down and made a rush at Bill, to get it back; but Bill jumped backwards, got through the door, ran through the house, grabbed the admiral's cocked hat, and clapped it on backwards. Then he shot out of the water at once, and found himself on the rocks outside the cave, with the cocked hat still on his head. He's kept that hat ever since, and money wouldn't buy it."

When I woke next morning it was like waking to a great occasion. The tropic sun was blazing outside. The day seemed of a superior quality. An old negress shuffled by my cabin door, through which was a peep of the town across the harbour, and she had some necklaces of shells strung on one skinny black arm and carried a basket of oranges on the other. I jumped up, and bought all the oranges. A boat came to our gangway and some of us went ashore. I don't know what a man feels like who is released one fine day from imprisonment into the stream of his fellows, but I should think he is first a little stunned, and afterwards becomes like a child's balloon in a breeze. The people we had met in the Brazils never laughed; and I myself had always felt that there we had been watched and followed unseen, that something was there, watching us, waiting its time, knowing well it could get us before we escaped.

We were at last outside it and free. The anchorage of

Bridgetown seemed anarchic, after our level sombre experience, for the sea was a green light, flashing and volatile, with white schooners driving upon it, negroes shouting and laughing over the bulwarks, or frantically hauling on the sheets. The rushing water was crowded with leaping boats, all gaudily painted; and even the sunshine, moving rapidly on quivering white sails and the white hulls buoyantly swinging, was a kind of shaking laughter. Our negro boatmen sang as they rowed, when they were not swearing at other boatmen. The world had got wine in its head.

We went to the Ice House, and bought English beer. (Oh, the taste of beer!) In the brisk and sunny streets there were English women, cool, dainty, a little haughty, their dresses smelling of new linen, and they were looking in at shop windows. We had got our feet down on home pavements, and the streets had the newness and sparkle of holiday. "Hi, cabby!"

He drove us along coral roads, under cocoanut palms, and there were golden hills (hills once more!) one way, and on the other hand was a beach glowing like white fire, with a sea beyond of a blue that was ultimate, profound, and as tense and as still as rapture. We came to a hotel where there was still napery, with creases on it, on a breakfast table. There was a silver coffee-pot. There was sweet-smelling and crusty bread, butter in ice, and new milk. There was a heaped plate of fruit. There was a crystal jug filled with cold water and sunshine, and it threw a wavering light on the damask.

We had some of everything. We ate for more than an hour, steadily. A man could not have done it alone, and without shame. There was one superior lady tourist, with grey curls on her cheeks and a face like doom, and she sent for the manager, and asked if we were to breakfast there again. She wanted to know. The Chief begged me, as the youngest of the party, to go over and kiss her. But I pointed out that, seeing where we had come from, and what we had suffered, it was the plain duty of any really dear old soul to come over and kiss us on a morning like that.

In the afternoon we were aboard again, waiting for the Skipper to return with the new orders. To what part of the world would the power in Leadenhall Street now consign us? Sandy thought New Orleans; but we could rule that out, for there was no cotton just then. Pensacola was more likely, the Chief said, with a deck cargo of lumber for Hamburg. That guess made the crowd glum. Winter in the Atlantic, she rolling her heart out, and the timber that was level with the engine-room casing groaning and straining at every roll—to dwell on that prospect was to feel a cold draught out of the Valley of Shadows.

Two nigger boys were overside, diving for coins. You threw a coin—Brazil's nickel muck, a handful worth nothing—and it went below oscillating, as though sentiently dodging the contorted and convulsive figure of the boy diving after it. The transparency of the fathoms was that of a denser air. When the sea was still, at the slack of the tides, this tropic anchorage was not like water. You did not look upon it, but into it, being hardly aware of its surface. It was surprising to see our massive iron plates stand upright in it. We were still an ugly black bulk, as we were on the ditch water of Swansea, but our sea wagon had lost its look of squat heaviness. Even our iron ship was transmuted, such was the lift and radiance of Barbados and its sea, into the buoyancy of the unsubstantial stuff of that scene about us, the low hills of greenish gold so delicate under the sky of malachite blue that you doubted whether mortals could walk there. Bridgetown was between those hills and the sea, a cluster of white cubes, with inconsequential touches of scarlet, orange, and emerald. Beneath our keel was a boy who might have been flying there.

On one side of the town was a belt of coral beach. It was a-fire, and the palms above the beach, with their secretive villas, and the green-gold hills beyond, floated on that white glow. The sea below the beach was an incandescent green; it might have been burning through contact with the island. Then the sea spread down to us in areas of opaque violet and blue, till in the neighbourhood of the ship it became transparent and was but a denser atmosphere. You, in the hard and bitter north, on the exposed summit of the world where Polaris glitters in the forehead of a frozen god, hardly know what young and luscious stuff this earth is, where the constant sun and tepid rains and salt air have preserved its bloom and flush of abounding life.

There came the Skipper's boat, he in his shore-going white ducks and Panama hat in the stern sheets, his wallet in his hand. He knew that we all looked at him with assumed indifference, when he stepped among us on deck. That was his time to show he was the ship's master. He feigned that we were not there. He turned to the chief mate: "All ready, Mr Brown?" "All ready, sir." Then the master walked slowly, knowing our eyes were on his back, to his place aft, first going in to speak to the Chief. The Chief came out some minutes after. "Tampa, boys," said he. "Florida for phosphate, then home."

That evening we were on our way, and turned inwards through the line of the Caribbees, passing between the islands of St Lucia and St Vincent, high purple masses of rock, St Lucia's mass ascending into cones. The Skipper had been to most of the West Indian islands, and remembered them, while I listened. We stood at the chart-room door, watching the islands across the evening seas. The sun, just above the sharply dark rim of ocean, touched the sea, and sank. A thin paring of silver moon had the sky to itself. I went into the chart-room; and the old man who, grim and sour as you might think him, mellows into confidential friendliness when he has you to himself, spread his charts of the Spanish Main under the yellow lamp, which was a slow pendulum as she rolled, and he put his spectacles on his lean brown face, talked of unfrequented cays, and of the negro islands, and debated which route we should take.

The fourth morning at breakfast-time, was a burning day, with a sky almost cloudless, and a slow sea which had the surface of its rich blue deeps shot with turquoise lights, while fields of saffron gulf-weed stained it; and we had, close over our port bow, the most beautiful island in the world. It is useless to deny it, and to declare you know a better island. Can't I see Jamaica now? I see it most plain. It descends abruptly from the meridian, pinnacles and escarpments trembling in the upper air with distance and delicate poise, and comes down in rolling forests and steep verdant slopes, where facets of bare rock glitter, to more leisurely open glades and knolls; and then, being not far from the sea, drops in sheer cliffs to where the white combers pulse. It is a jewel which smells like a flower. The "Capella" went close in till Port Antonio under the Blue Mountains was plain, and though I could see the few scattered houses, I could not see the narrow ledges where men could stand in such a steep land. We crawled over the blue floor in which that sea mountain is set, and cruised along, feeling very small, under the various and towering shape. For long I watched it, declaring continually that some day I must return. (And that is the greatest compliment a traveller on his way home can pay to any spot on earth.)

It faded as we drew northwards. Over seas to the north was a long low stratum of permanent cloud, and beneath it was the faint presentiment of Cuba. Still we were in the spell of the very halcyon weather of old tales, with the world our own, though once this day there was a great rain burst, and the "Capella" was lost in falling water, her syren blaring. We neared the Cuban coast by the Isle of Pines, a pallid desert shore, apparently treeless and parched. The next morning we came to the western cape of the island, rounding it in company with a white island schooner, its crew of toughs watching us from her shadeless deck; and changed our course almost due north.

Now we were in the Gulf of Mexico, and soon upset its notoriously uncertain temper, for a "norther" met us and piped till it was a full gale, end-on, and it kicked up a nasty sea which flung about the empty "Capella" like a band-box. There was a night of it. Towards morning it eased up, and I woke to a serene sunrise, and found we were in the pale green water of coral soundings, with the Floridan pilot even then standing in to us, his tug bearing centrally on its bridge a gilded eagle with rampant wings. In a little while we were fast to the quarantine quay at Mullet Island, detained as a yellow fever suspect. The medical officers boarded us, ranged amidships the "Capella's" crowd from the master down, and put in the mouth of each of us a thermometer; and so for a time we stood ridiculously smoking glass cigarettes. One stoker was put aside, for he had a temperature. Then into the cabins, and the saloon, the forecastle, and into the holds, were put gallipots of burning sulphur, and the doors were closed. We became a great and dreadful stench; and I went ashore.

There was a deserted beach of comminuted shells, its glare as bright as snow in sunshine. It was littered with the relics of old wrecks, with sea rubbish, and the carapaces of crabs. Beyond the beach was a calcereous desert, with a scrub of palmetto and evergreen, and patches of flowering coreopsis and blue squills. Hidden by the scrub were shallow lagoons. It is hard to tell the sea from the land in warm and aqueous Florida, for sea and land so invade each other's dominions. Water and land were asleep in the sun. I was alone in the island, and sat in a decaying boat by the shore of a lagoon where nothing moved but the little crabs playing hide and seek in the moist crevices of the boat, and the pelicans which sat round the interminable flat shores. Sometimes the pelicans woke, and yawned, and fanned the heat with great slow wings.

In the early afternoon we were allowed to proceed to Tampa, which we reached in three hours; and there we came once more to the press of the busy and indifferent world. The muddle of roofs and steeples of a great city were about us, and men met us and talked to us, but they had no leisure for interest in the wonders of the strange land from which we had come, and would not have cared if afterwards we were going to Gehenna. We made fast under a new structure of timber and iron which was something between a flour mill and the Tower of Babel, for it was wan and powdered, and full of strange noises; and it had a habit of eating, in a mechanical way, an interminable length of railway trucks, wagon after wagon, one every minute. A great weariness and yearning filled me that night. The strangulating fumes of the sulphur clung to all the cabin, and puffed in clouds from the pillow when I changed sides; for the wagons clanked and banged till daylight. I sat up and beat my breast, and swore I would leave her and go home. The next morning that inexplicable structure beside us began from many mouths to vomit floods of powdered phosphate into us, and the "Capella," in and out, turned pale through an almost impalpable dust. Everybody took bronchitis and cursed Tampa and its phosphate.

I spoke to the Skipper and the Chief about it, and they agreed that nobody would stop with her now, who could leave her; but that yet was I no pal to desert them. What about them? They had yet to see her safe across the most ruthless of seas at a time when its temper would be at its worst; and what about them? Though they admitted that, were they in my case, they would certainly take the train to New York, and catch there the fastest steamer for England. Then come with me to the British Consul like an honest man, said I to the captain, and get me off your articles.

The three of us left her, I for the last time. I turned upon the "Capella," and the boys stood leaning on her taffrail watching me; and I am not going to put down here what I felt, nor what the lads cried to me, nor what I said when I stood beneath her counter, and called up to them. We came to a corner by a warehouse, and I turned to look upon the "Capella" for the last time.

Tampa, the noisy city about us, was rawly new, most of its site but lately a shallow lagoon, and one of its natives, the ship's agent who was entertaining us at lunch, did not fail to impress that enterprise and industry upon us with great earnestness. Tampa was a large, hasty, makeshift standing of depôts, railway sidings, cigar factories, wharves, and huge elevators which could load I forget how many thousands of tons of bulk cargo into a steamer in twelve hours, as though she were an iron bucket under a pump. A town spontaneous, unexpected and complete, with a hurrying population in its sidewalks, pushing to secure foothold in life, and not a book-shop there, and no talk but in its saloons and commercial exchanges. We went into many of those saloons, the Skipper, and the Chief, and the late Purser, shaking hands for the last time in each, and then dropping into another to recall old affairs; and shaking hands finally again, and so to the next bar.

That night I was alone in Tampa, with a torrent of urgent affairs surging past. I could not find the railway station. Standing at a corner, outside a tobacconist's shop, a huge corridor train shaped among the lights of the street, trundled down the centre of the roadway, then edged close to the sidewalk , bumping past a row of shops as casually as a tram for a penny journey, and stopped just where I stood with a hand-bag wondering how I was to get to New York. New York was a thousand miles away. The train was but a mere episode of the open street, and I could not feel it bore out the promise of my railway vouchers. This train, a row of lighted villas in motion, came down the roadway, out of nowhere, while carts and women with market baskets waited for it to pass, stopped outside a tobacconist's shop, and the light of the shop window illuminated a round of a huge wheel which stood higher than my head. The wheel came to rest upon an abandoned newspaper. A negro was passing me, and I stopped him. "Noo Yark? Step aboard right now!" His word was all I had to go upon that this train would take me to the precise point in a continent I did not know. A struggle for existence eddied fiercely round the train, and assuming it was the right train, and I missed it—it was an unbearable thought! The train had to be mounted. It was like climbing a wall; but I would have cast my luggage, scaled more than walls, and dealt conclusively with any obstruction if the way home left me no other choice. The traveller who has been in the wilds and has lived with the barbarous, though he has not allowed his thoughts to look back there, yet he knows something of that eagerness which dumb things feel when he turns about. I took my train on trust, as one does so many things in the United States, found we should really get to New York, in time, and lay listening to the beat of the flying wheels beneath my berth; tried to count their pulse, and fell asleep.

There were some more days and nights, and all the passengers of the earlier stages of the journey had passed away. Then the train slowed through imperceptible grada-

tions, and stopped. I thought a cow was on the line. But the
negro attendant came to me and told me to get out. This was
New York. Outside there was a street in the rain, the stones
were deep with yellow reflections, and some cabmen stood
about in shiny capes. No majestic figure of Liberty met me.
A cab met me, on a rainy night.

It was on one of those huge liners, and the steward told
him they would reach Plymouth in the morning. He was
packing up his things in his cabin. England to-morrow! The
things went into his trunks in the lump, with a compressing
foot after each. It did not matter. All the clothes were in
ruins. The only care he took was with the toucans' brilliant
skins, the bundle of arrows, the biscuit tins full of
butterflies—they would excite the Boy—and the barbaric
Indian ornaments for Miss Muffet and the Curly Nob; how
their eyes would shine. His telegram from Plymouth would
surprise them. They did not know where he was.

But he knew, when they did not, that there was but one
more day to tick off the calendar to complete the exile. He
had turned back that day to the earlier pages of the diary and
found some illuminating entries; "Gone," or "That's another," were written across some spaces which otherwise
were blank. It was curious that those cryptic entries recalled
the hours they stood for more vividly to his mind than those
which had happenings minutely recorded. He threw the
diary into a trunk; the long job was finished.

The sunshine all that day was different from the well
remembered burning weight of the tropics. It was frail and
grateful spring warmth, and the incidence of its rays was
happy and illuminating, as though the light had only just
reached the world, and so things looked just discovered and
interesting. A faint silver haze hung upon a pallid sea, and
the slow smooth mounds of water were full of fugitive
glints and flashes. You hardly knew the sea was there. The
mist was the luminous nimbus of a new world, a world not
yet fully formed, for it had no visible bounds. Night came,
and a nearly full moon, and the only reality was the
stupendous bulk of the liner. She might have been in the

clouds, herself a dark cloud near the moon, with but rumours of light in the aerial deeps beneath. It seemed another of the dreams. Would he wake up presently to the reality of the forest, with the sun blazing on the enamel of its hard foliage?

He wanted some assurance of time and space. He would stay on deck till the first sign came of England. So he leaned motionless for hours on the rail of the boat-deck, gazing ahead, where the outlook remained as unshapen as it had since he left home. Far on the port bow appeared the headlight of a steamer.

He watched that light. This, then, was no dream sea. Others were there. But was it a headlight? . . . No!

The Bishop's! England now!

The steward came again, peeping through his curtain, and said, "Plymouth, sir!" and turned on the glow lamp, for it was not yet dawn. There was an early breakfast laid in the saloon; but he went on deck. The liner had hardly way on her; the water was but uncoiling noiselessly alongside. There were shapes of hills near, with villas painted on them, but so bluish and immaterial was all that it might have rippled like the flat water, being but a flimsy background which could be easily shaken. The hills drew nearer imperceptibly, grew higher. A touch of real day gave a hill-top body; and there was a confident shout from somebody unseen in plain English. The vision grounded and got substance. Not only home, but spring in Devon.

From the train window the countryside in the tones and flush of the renascence absorbed him. He went from side to side of the carriage. What was most extraordinary was the sparsity and lowness of the trees and bushes, the fineness of the growth. The outlines of the trees could be seen, and they crouched so near to the ground and were so very meagre. The colours were faint enough to be but tinted mists. The biggest of the trees were manageable, looked like toys. The orderly hedges, the clean roads, the geometrical patterns of the fields, gave him assurance once more of order and security. Here was law again, and the permanence of affairs long decided upon. He closed his eyes, sinking into the cushions of the carriage as though the arms under him were proved friendly and could be trusted. . . .

The slowing of the train woke him. They were running into Paddington. He got his feet fair and solid on London before the train stopped, and looked into the crowd waiting there. A flushed youngster ran towards him out of a group, then stopped shyly. He caught The Boy, and held him up. . . . Here again was the centre of the world.

THE END